OUR PRECARIOUS HABITAT

OUR PRECARIOUS HABITAT

MELVIN A. BENARDE

W · W · NORTON & CO · INC · New York

301.3
B456 σ

To my father and mother,
Isidor and Belle

Nothing in life is to be feared, it is only to be understood.

MARIE CURIE

CONTENTS

ILLUSTRATIONS

10 ☉ Our Precarious Habitat

TABLES

FOREWORD

Life for all of us is a continuous series of risks in a constantly changing world, where all too often we ourselves generate the forces that are potentially dangerous to us. We must, it seems, continually alter the world around us. We develop synthetic products and we alter the air we breathe, the water we drink, and the food we eat. We build cities, factories, and machines that generate waste, stress, and injury; and we create radioactive devices that can sow the seeds of further harm. As life becomes more congested and technology more advanced, these new factors may in turn become the agents of new diseases. Man's power to manipulate and exploit his world has obscured his appreciation of the damage he inflicts on the environment. We are, for example, only beginning to explore the implications of water pollution for the health of the community. Similarly, we actually know little about the effects on community health of air pollutants, radiations, noise, insecticides, and a host of other environmental pressures.

To cope with the increasing number of actual and potential environmental health problems at the community level requires a well-informed citizenry. My purpose in writing this book will have been achieved if the presentation enables the interested reader to evaluate these problems from a basis of knowledge and understanding, rather than of emotional fervor founded on ignorance, superstition, and prejudice. After considerable reflection, I have come to realize that the scientific community has almost entirely ignored the need of the general public to know how science and technology in fact affect its life. This condition has gone on far too long and is one of the contributing reasons for the large readership of books and magazine articles of the "purple prose" variety.

As a working scientist, I have stood on the sidelines far too long watching this happen. Additionally, six years ago, when I began to instruct non-biologists in environmental health problems, I searched in vain for a book that would be of use to students entering this area for the first time. A suitable volume was unavailable. From colleagues around the country I learned of the growing need for a good book in this area, as an increasing number of formal courses in environmental health or environmental sciences were instituted. The material gathered together herein can serve the needs of either a one- or a two-semester course. Although this is a dynamic, multidisciplinary area in which new findings occur almost daily, experience has shown that this material can provide a sound basis for more advanced training. It is hoped that the interested non-student—the general reader—will also find it helpful in understanding what is happening to his world.

ACKNOWLEDGEMENT

The ideas presented in this book were tested and retested in discussions with many colleagues, who were forced to suffer my continued need to talk, to discuss, to question, and, most necessary, to argue controversial ideas.

The brunt of this testing fell upon one person, whose office—unfortunately for him, but fortunately for me—was always open. Dr. W. Brewster Snow of Rutgers University has that rare quality of being able to suffer a fool gladly; he suffered often. But he could give as good as he got, which meant that I had to back up everything I wrote or chuck it. Consequently, he forced me to refine and sharpen my thinking and writing. If this book is received as a significant contribution, he deserves a large measure of credit.

My gratitude is extended to Dr. Frank Jankowski of the Department of Nuclear Engineering, Rutgers University, for his close reading and detailed comments on Chapter 14, Ionizing Radiation; to Dr. John Lawler of the firm of consulting engineers Quirk, Lawler and Matusky, for his critical comments, on Chapters 7 and 8, Sanitary Sewage, and Water Polution and Its Control. To Mrs. Bernice Marcus, principal of Public School 128, Brooklyn, New York, who waded through each chapter checking for readability, giving each the benefit of her knowledge of the English language.

My gratitude is also extended to Mrs. Marilyn Tobias, who single-handedly prepared the manuscript and did such a remarkably good job without previous experience.

Finally, I must acknowledge the help of my family: my wife, Anita; my son, Scott; and the girls, Andi and Dana, who were short-changed many weekends and holidays, and who were so often told to "be quiet while Daddy works." Perhaps, in time, they'll think it was worth it.

OUR PRECARIOUS HABITAT

THE ENVIRONMENT AS A SYSTEM

Much has been written about air pollution, water pollution, poisons in our food, noise levels, flood control, overpopulation, the concretizing of our countryside, and the rest of man's alterations of his environment. Little has been said, however, about the fact that the health and welfare of man—both as an individual and as a society—are rooted not in air, water, food and so on, but in a complex system made up of *all* the facets of his habitat, including man himself, interacting with and on each other. No study of our physical environment makes sense if it focuses on one without the others.

The stresses created by our industrial society impinge upon us all. But does it really follow that many stresses are, or need be, harmful? Much of the popular writing on this subject would have us believe that these stresses are indeed harmful and that much of the population is thus on the brink of illness or death. No one would argue that air pollution, radioactive fallout, or chemical insecticides washed into a water supply, to take a few examples, are beneficial; but I would suggest that the physiological effects of these environmental pollutants are not so well established that the popular purveyors of gloom and doom can write about them with such lack of impunity. We must learn to be chary of such dramatic alarms as: "Man is exposing himself to hundreds of new chemicals in the air he breathes, the food he eats, and the water he drinks. As chronic bronchitis, lung cancer, and emphysema grow more prevalent, man seems to be choking to death on his own technology." Such statements abound with pitfalls for the unwary; they do little to help us understand the very dangers they seek to expose. They are as oversimple as is the statement that since the life expectancy of Western man is rising steadily and the world population is "exploding," the pollution of his environment obviously is beneficial to health. The failure of both approaches is the failure to realize that our environment is a vast complex incapable of being grasped by understanding any one of its parts.

It is impossible to understand and deal with air pollution, for example, without considering its relationship to waste disposal, electric power generation, public transportation, human and animal health, or the chemistry of agriculture, to name just a few parts of an intricate interrelationship. In 1969, the town of Westport, Connecticut, scored what its more enlightened citizens considered a notable victory for conservation and progressive thinking. Banding into committees and threatening action in the state legislature, they successfully defeated an entrenched electric power company which planned to build an atomic power plant on a scenic island in Long Island off Westport's shores. The citizens' committee that led the battle consisted of the educational elite of a highly educated and progressive community. They did not rely entirely on emotional pleas for the preservation of beauty and recreational areas. They were sophisticated enough to call in ecologists who warned of the effects on sea-life of warming the waters of the Sound. Their victory was considered a triumph for conservation. But how real was it? Since the island in question was one of the very few sites near the urban power consumers and on a body of water large enough to supply the cooling needed by atomic power plants, the electric company's defeat forces it to return to coal-burning on an ever-increasing scale. The effect this will have on air pollution in an already polluted area is foreseeable.

Another example of the results of man's failure to think of his environment as an interacting *system* is the Aswan High Dam on the Nile. It is a dramatic example of man's constant tinkering with an environment which he understands only slightly. Although a few pertinent facts have emerged, the full impact will undoubtedly remain unknown for years.

The diplomats and engineers responsible for the dam saw it as the rescuer of Egypt's agriculture, the supplier of needed power—in short, the savior of her starving poor. They were unaware of its impact on the sardine industry in the eastern Mediterranean Sea. Late in 1966, at a meeting sponsored by UNESCO in Split, Yugoslavia, scientists from thirteen concerned countries divulged the facts: the Aswan High Dam had sharply reduced the sardine population; the annual catch was down by 50 percent. By the time the dam is fully operative, the catch should be reduced still further, and with that will come the elimination of the sardine industry—a staple of the Mediterranean economy.

It is well to note how a dam on the upper reaches of the Nile can alter sardine fishing from Alexandria to Lebanon; comparable indirect consequences must be anticipated from any tampering with the environment. Before the dam was built, each year, with the flooding of the Nile, millions of tons of nitrates and phosphates were carried by the silt into the relatively mineral deficient Mediterranean. This yearly dose of fertilizer permitted the growth of luxuriant blooms of phytoplankton (microscopic aquatic plants).* The phytoplankton provided zooplankton (microscopic aquatic animals) with a ready source of nutrition that allowed them to flourish in great numbers. And on the abundant zooplankton the sardines quickly fattened and filled the nets of the local fishermen. This cycle had been in existence longer than recorded history. With the completion of the dam the Nile will no longer carry

---

* This would be considered pollution in the streams and rivers of the U.S., where algal blooms are unwanted.

minerals and fresh water to the Mediterranean; the phytoplankton and zooplankton will migrate to more hospitable areas, or die— and with them will go the sardines.

Other effects of the dam on man and his health have not yet been proved, but the evidence thus far indicates that the additional dislocations will be far-reaching. For example, the dam is expected to initiate a precipitous increase in the incidence of bilharziasis, by extending the range of infected snails into new but hospitable habitats. Thus, before its completion, this great engineering achievement, another monument to man's technical skill, will have disrupted two ecological relationships, and both will prove inimical to man's best interests.

Surely there must be a better way than uninformed tinkering. A beginning has been made, but biologists will have to unravel a great many more of the complex interrelationships before "total planning" for a healthy community becomes possible. Whether it is called an ecologic community or an ecosystem, this interrelated complex governs the life of man and his biological and physical associations. Disease and disorder may be viewed, therefore, as a lack of adequate adjustment by man to factors in the environment. The significant feature is that the social, physical, and biological components function as an integrated system, and any tampering with any part of the system will affect each of the other parts and alter the whole.

An excellent and oft-recited description of the unity of our habitat that still has lessons for us today is the statement of Hippocrates on "Airs, Waters and Places," written some twenty-five hundred years ago. He said:

> Whoever wishes to investigate medicine properly should proceed thus: in the first place to consider the seasons of the year and what effects each of them produces. Then the winds, the hot and the cold, especially such as are common to all countries, and then such as are peculiar to each locality. In the same manner, when one comes into a city to which he is a stranger, he should consider the situation, how it lies as to the winds and the rising of the sun; for its influence is not the

same whether it lies to the north or the south, to the rising or to the setting sun. One should consider most attentively the waters which the inhabitants use, whether they be marshy and soft, or hard and running from elevated and rocky situations, and then if saltish and unfit for cooking; and the ground whether it be naked and deficient in water, or wooded and well watered, and whether it lies in a hollow, confined situation, or is elevated and cold; and the mode in which the inhabitants live and what are their pursuits, whether they are fond of drinking and eating to excess, and given to indolence, or are fond of exercise and labor, and not given to excess in eating and drinking. . . . if one knows all these things, or at least the greater part of them, he cannot miss knowing when he comes into a strange city, either the diseases peculiar to the place, or the particular nature of common diseases, or commit mistakes, as is likely to be the case provided one had not previously considered these matters.

Hippocrates did not have all the answers, but surely he pointed to the questions. The deeper the analysis of the "web of life" is pushed, the more meaningless becomes the word *independence*.

CHAPTER

2

ECOLOGY OF HEALTH AND DISEASE

Not a day passes without a report by investigators in the U.S., or elsewhere around the world, concerning the effect of some aspect of the environment on human health. One in particular that is being studied in several countries for its possible contribution to chronic disease is water. A spate of reports have appeared that tend to correlate water softness with coronary heart disease. Thus far it is only a correlation; a cause-effect relationship remains to be established. Magnetism, and its effect on human physiological processes, long considered in the realm of quackery, is currently a respectable subject of investigation at several universities in the U.S. In the Netherlands, scientists are investigating the differing effects of the same drug therapy when administered at different hours of the day; there are indications that man's physiological processes are affected by the presence or absence of daylight, as are those of lower forms of life. At the University of Pennsylvania, scientists are studying arthritics who claim to be able to predict twenty-four to forty-eight hours in advance, impending changes in the weather. The researchers seek to discover how the body receives and uses weather signals.

An ecological view of life may lead to an acceptance of some theory such as holism,* the idea that man is but one unit, a part of a comprehensive system of "dynamic interdependencies" which, in fact, is not merely the sum of its parts. Several formidable examples may serve to illustrate this concept.

An ecological upset that vividly portrayed the "dynamic interdependencies" and man's role as only one thread in the total tapestry of life was witnessed by the ornithologist Robert Cushman Murphy, who described it several years ago. This disruption occurred along the coast of Peru in 1925.

Each year around Christmas, the dry desert regions along the northern coast are watered by rains brought by currents of warm air. These rains are so regular and so welcome in this otherwise arid land that they have come to be called *El Niño,* "the Christ child." These rains sustain life through the many months of drought.

Although El Niño's arrival usually means periods of plenty (crops of some of the finest cotton in the world are grown in the northern coastal areas of Peru), it can also mean disaster. Two to three times a century, El Niño makes its way too far south and does not quickly return to its usual area. This change in position disrupts the ecological balance on land and sea so drastically that even man does not escape the consequences.

In 1925, the warm current ranged far south, killing as it came the marine life adapted to the normally cold-water coast. Unable to outrace the warm current, fish in fantastic numbers perished and were cast up on the beaches. To the vast seabird population that frequented the coast, the death of the fish meant starvation. The bodies of countless dead and dying birds literally concealed the beaches and blocked the harbors. The putrefaction

* Holism is the term given by General Jan Christiaan Smuts to the concept of whole-making or the holistic tendency fundamental in nature, that links and binds both the living and non-living elements of the universe into a unified process.

was so great that hydrogen sulfide, a product of the microbial degradation of protein, was produced in quantities sufficient to blacken the paint on ships in the harbors. The pollution of the sea with the dead birds, which implies an overabundance of nitrate nitrogen, gave rise to blooms of a microscopic marine protozoan that actually turned the water blood-red.

On land, where rain fell for five months, the barren soil eroded, destroying the huts of the inhabitants. Without their supply of fish, the people began to starve. In the standing pools of water, mosquitos began to breed in large numbers and malaria flourished. Contamination of the water supply with human fecal matter, as a result of seepage into wells, precipitated an outbreak of typhoid fever. The rat population, cut off from its normal food supply, began to die of plague, and, shortly thereafter, so did the natives.

This havoc resulted from a slight elevation of the temperature of the seawater. And it clearly shows the links that bind man, animals, and plants so closely together with the physical environment. Also, it underlines the necessity to know in advance what effects on water, on its flora and fauna, and on other forms of life dependent upon it may be expected from nuclear wastes or toxic chemicals disposed at sea. And the question arises: If the decision not to dispose at sea is made, what then will be the disposition of the waste?

Another example of the intimate weaving of the biological with the physical environment emerged as a result of the investigations concerning prevention and control of African or Gambian sleeping sickness.

In Central and East Africa, the agent associated with the clinical symptoms of sleeping sickness is a microscopic protozoan, *Trypanosoma gambiense.* This parasite was early found to be transmitted to the human population by the bite (injection) of the tsetse fly, *Glossina palpalis,* when taking a blood meal.

The natural habitat of *G.palpalis* is restricted to the dense tropical forests that border lakes and rivers. Its usual source of nourishment is the marshbuck, or Situtunga antelope, which is, in turn, the main dietary staple of leopards. Thus, there is an ecological relationship between the leopard population and the incidence of human sleeping sickness. In those years when leopards abound, the marshbuck is kept low, and as a consequence, the tsetse flies obtain few animal blood meals to sustain them between human blood meals.

Intensive, detective-like investigations aimed at controlling sleeping sickness uncovered a unique chain of events in the Rhodesias. Control now depends in large measure upon preventing the tsetse fly, in this instance a different species, *G. morsitans,* from reaching adulthood. To accomplish this, the natives in the area are prevented from burning off the grass in the treeless savannah regions.

It was found—after years of arduous searching—that the grass fires destroyed the ants which fed on the tsetse fly pupa (the developmental stage between larva and adult). The heavy mats of grass aided in increasing soil moisture, which in turn encouraged the growth of the ant population, which kept the tsetse fly population in check, which ultimately meant fewer transmissions of protozoan parasite and fewer cases of sleeping sickness.

From French Polynesia in the east, through New Caledonia, to the Philippines, Thailand, and China, eosinophilic meningitis is a widespread and well-known ailment that manifests itself in agonizing headaches. In January 1967, the final clue uncovering the ecological chain of events leading to the disease appeared to have been discovered.

The headache is caused by a microscopic flatworm that resides in the heart and blood vessels of rats, doing them no harm. These worms are regularly passed out in feces and are present in garden soil and other areas frequented by rats. In turn, the planarian worms are ingested by snails and slugs during their nocturnal maraudings in garden soil.

South Sea Islanders and Thais who eat raw or partially cooked snails and slugs are especially susceptible to the headache of eosinophilic meningitis. When the snails are eaten by the natives, the thread-like worms are liberated in the stomach and begin eating their way to the brain, where they initiate an infection that gives rise to the excruciating headache.

The infection can also be gotten by eating fish and shrimp that have previously eaten worm-infested snails and slugs, or from eating improperly washed strawberries, salad greens, or tomatoes. Once the infection occurs, no medication can alter its course; relief can be effected only by spinal taps.

Charles Elton, an ecologist, described an illuminating example of the many interrelations within a community which also showed that the balance of nature is not as neat an arrangement as some would have us believe.[1] He stated that:

> In a year of mouse abundance, many animals change their feeding habits to feast royally on mice. Bears and wolverines do this. In 1905 Cabot says that the grazing was so much spoilt by the mice that the caribou left this part of Labrador in a body to seek food elsewhere. In consequence of the absence of caribou, the Indians in the interior were compelled to subsist mainly upon fish, being also greatly handicapped for lack of deer skins from which to manufacture their clothes. In one area the annual crop of crowberries failed in some places, owing to the young shoots having been devoured by mice. According to Hutton, the shortage of empetrum fruit, the usual and almost the only berry food of the Eskimos, gave rise to a pandemic of a pustular skin disease, due apparently to the deficiency of some food factor contained in the crowberries.

An example closer to home may be useful. Lead encephalopathy—lead poisoning—takes its toll of thousands of children in Philadelphia, New York, and Chicago each year. The cases of lead poisoning begin their annual rise in the spring, reaching peak proportions in July and August. Apparently, after ingestion of a quantity of chips of lead-based paint, the higher temperature, combined with the active (ultraviolet) rays of the sun stimulate increased intestinal absorption of the lead. Thus the number of cases appears dependent upon season of the year.

The idea that physical factors exerted an influence on health is as old as man himself. Primitive peoples everywhere have reference in their language and traditions to the ill effects of certain winds, the changing of the seasons, the phases of the moon, and the influence of the sun and stars. While it is currently acknowledged that some such effects exist, much remains in the realm of speculation.

Until the 1860's physicians believed that health and disease were influenced by the external environment. During the 1860's however, Pasteur in France and Koch in Germany, were laboring on their investigations of human microbial diseases. The idea that a completely invisible living agent might be the cause of many highly fatal diseases of men and animals was considered utterly preposterous to most people. How could so small an entity kill a man?

Although it was in 1857 that Pasteur published a paper describing the bacterial fermentation of grape sugar to wine—an historic event because it ascribed to germs, what was heretofore regarded as a purely chemical reaction—it was the year 1877 that was truly memorable: then, for the first time, a microbe was shown capable of causing an important human disease. "The Golden Age of Bacteriology" was thereby swiftly ushered in. For the next seventy years, microorganisms were believed to be responsible for all man's ills; the germ theory of disease had ascended to center stage, relegating the environment to the wings.

With the germ theory of disease, which states each disease is provoked by a specific microbe, with characteristic pathological effects, scientists acquired insight into an important and widespread mechanism of death and disease. Many leaders in medicine and public health were convinced that the germ theory explained fully the spectrum of disease and firmly believed that vaccines and antitoxins were the principal means for the protection of the health of the public. Unfortunately, too many still do.

Between 1930 and 1950 several new concepts were introduced into medicine, with far-reaching implications for public health. These were: *homeostasis, deprivation,* and *stress.* Essentially, they implied that illness or disease could occur as a result of exposure to sudden or marked changes in the environment which subjected an individual to pressures in excess of his ability to tolerate them. Infectious living agents had no place in this scheme.

Beri-beri, pellagra, rickets, iron-deficiency anemia, and hypothyroidism are several dramatic examples of deprivational disorders. However, a young child denied the care and affection of its mother can be seriously affected for the remainder of his life. This too, is an example of deprivation and stress.

Stress is a concept which is easier to appreciate than define; it may be considered as any force to which the body responds in order to maintain its economy and/or protect itself against injury. During a lifetime, stressful situations are encountered regularly: entrance to school, adolescence, acceptance into or rejection by college or university, selection of a mate, middle life, working conditions, living conditions, income, availability of food. Each can impose a hazard upon people, and individuals respond in a variety of ways. The increasing number of hospital beds used for mental patients or for patients whose illnesses have a psychosomatic component attests to the severity of many of the stressful stimuli and the inability to deal with them without becoming ill.

In June, 1967, the *New England Journal of Medicine* carried a report by four physicians from Johns Hopkins Hospital. They concluded that family strife could stunt the growth of a child who was emotionally disturbed by a constant contact with the marital discord of his parents. They noted that "an adverse environment acting during the early critical years of childhood can be responsible for the growth retardation." They went on to say that when the children they had studied were placed in a convalescent hospital they demonstrated remarkable growth acceleration. In fact, one boy grew seventeen inches after being abandoned by his parents. When the children were released and sent home, they stopped growing again.

Today, illness and disease are increasingly being studied not from the view of a single causative factor, but rather as the result of a multitude of causes. That is, it is now believed by a growing number of investigators that prevention and control may be given increased impetus by breaking one or several of the links in the chain of causation. This chain or web of causation implies that a series of events rather than a single event is necessary for illness to occur. It also suggests that a choice of "sites" is available for interdiction; that if one is not feasible or practicable, another may be. In this scheme, control and/or prevention is much more attainable.

For example, today the attempt to control typhoid fever is not directed solely to a search for a bacterium. Instead, there is concern about such factors as raw milk, inadequate sewage disposal and unprotected water supply systems, poor personal hygiene, low educational levels, inadequate community financial resources, lack of industrialization and the historical development of the country.

It is not sufficient to isolate a microbe and simply plan its eradication. It has been found that in many instances people can harbor a microbe without showing clinical symptoms of illness. Some people are more resistant to the invasion of microbes than others. For example, all people who have tuberculosis are infected with *Mycobacterium tuberculosis,* the organism associated with TB. However, not all people from whom this organism can be recovered have tuberculosis. This is not contradictory. It implies a spectrum of resistance or susceptibility in the population. The microbe is a necessary but not sufficient cause of the disease. Something in addition to the microorganism is needed for the disease to occur. If all the factors predisposing to illness were known, prevention, control, and even eradication might be possible.

Considering the concept of multiple causation, programs to control or prevent lung cancer should consider the contribution of air pollutants, cigarette smoke (and cigarette advertising), entrenched habits, radioactive particles, the tobacco plant, environmental stress, and insecurity. Perhaps other considerations are more important, but what they may be has as yet not been ascertained.

Study of the environment as it relates to human health presents great obstacles. Scientists may not yet be ready or prepared for such an enormous task. For the most part, their research investigations are usually based on maintaining all but one factor constant while testing the effect or effects of a single variable on cats, dogs, fish, fowl, or humans. Only in special cases, have two variables been investigated. The fact that health depends on the interreactions of a multitude of variables which can be understood only as a whole system, rather than as separate parts, is a staggering realization to the researcher.

In a democratic society additional difficulties are imposed. For example, the association of cigarette smoking with lung cancer has received significant support from a multitude of different types of competent investigations. The evidence, albeit circumstantial, and the relationship appear highly valid, yet large segments of the population demand absolute direct proof before accepting preventive legislation. The only way to obtain this type of evidence would be to gather together several thousand children about age ten, divided them into two comparable groups of equal size, lock them in a stockade and observe them for several years, then start one group smoking while preventing the others from doing so. Since the effects of smoking are generally seen in the fifth or sixth decade of life, these two groups would be required to be under lock and key for at least forty years, under the scrutiny of scientists recording their every activity. Then and only then would absolute direct evidence of a cause-effect relationship be forthcoming. As this experiment is not possible, one can only wonder about the motives of those who clamor for "real" proof.

Currently, the U.S. and most of the countries of Western Europe are experiencing a major epidemic of two infectious diseases, syphilis and gonorrhea. Gonorrhea was well known in Biblical times, but the bacterium associated with it was not isolated until 1879. The corkscrew-shaped bacterium that causes syphilis, a disease apparently unknown in Europe before the return of Columbus and his crews in 1493, was described in 1905. Both diseases are readily rendered impotent by the antibiotic penicillin. Yet we are experiencing a greater number of new cases of both venereal diseases than ever before. Knowledge of the microorganism is simply insufficient to control or prevent its incursions. Today, a total environmental or ecological offensive is needed. It is necessary to consider the psychology of promiscuity, prostitution, social mores, homosexuality, drug addiction, penicillin, the microbe, educational levels, and family life. Factors such as these are currently being used in the attempt to control the precipitous increase in cases in the fifteen-to-twenty-five age group, those with the highest incidence rates.

The day of the individual scientist working alone on an infinitesimal part of the whole may be passing. In its place may have to come an integrated team effort to arrive at an understanding of the cause-effect relationship between man and the world around him. So many different forces or stresses impinge upon us simultaneously during each hour of the day that to understand the contribution of each, or the combined action of several acting in concert, will require experimental models not yet devised. Thus, statements purporting to incriminate some environmental factor as responsible for human illness, based on single variable studies, are of doubtful validity.

The investigation into man's interrelationships with his environment entails studying the whole man and studying him as a functioning unit. This will prove difficult, but the challenge is being taken up. New departments of community medicine and community health have been formed and are being formed in medical schools and schools of public health. These are dedicated to the idea that today's physician cannot merely treat the sick patient but must consider him as a member of society as well. It is therefore incumbent upon the physician to restore the patient to health and to prepare him to return to his place in the community. This calls for a greater knowledge of the many environmental problems that impinge upon an individual and can influence the pathogenesis, aggravation, and continuance of disease.

Some years ago, Adolf Gustave Vigeland created a statue depicting man's constant struggle with the forces of nature; it is plain that he believed man had not yet overcome—nor would he in the near future—the many forces that impinge upon and affect him. His statue, *Man Struggling with His Environment,* stands today in the city park of Oslo, Norway. It speaks for itself, this chapter, and the book.

FIGURE 1. *Man Struggling with His Environment* by Adolf Gustave Vigeland

BACTERIAL FOOD POISONING

August, 1959, will long be remembered by thousands of people in Indiana. To the 1,216 men, women, and children who became violently ill after eating poisoned food at two picnics that month, the memory will be especially vivid.

On August 15, seventeen hundred employees of a large pharmaceutical plant and their families gathered for a picnic lunch. Food was served beginning at about 11:30 A.M. By 1 P.M., the first cases of food poisoning (gastroenteritis) began to occur. By 4 P.M.,over eight hundred people had become ill. The Indiana Department of Health had recorded one thousand victims by 9 P.M.

Since "forewarned should be forearmed," planners of a picnic to be given by an electrical parts manufacturing firm scheduled on Saturday, August 22, had been cautioned by the previous week's experience, but apparently it was not a learning experience. August 22 was a particularly warm day; 1,813 people turned out for the festivities. Food was served at 4:30 P.M. By 7 P.M. that night, symptoms of severe gastroenteritis were evident in 25 to 30 people. An additional 100 were ill by 10:30 P.M. In all, 216 cases were reported.

Indiana had its August, but other communities in the United States and around the world are not immune. Food poisoning is experienced regularly throughout the United States and around the world. The incidence of one form of gastroenteritis has risen from seven hundred cases reported in 1946 to over ten thousand in 1962. As the incidence of food-borne disease is poorly reported in most countries, the number of illnesses reported doubtless represents only a fraction of those actually occurring.

Food poisoning of bacterial origin is primarily a result of improper food sanitation. Although food sanitation may mean many things to many people, L. V. Burton's pithy appraisal that "sanitation is nothing more than a race between men and the lower forms of life to determine who gets the food supply first" admirably epitomizes the subject. Bacterial food poisoning and food sanitation are often facets of the same problem; the absence of one may give rise to the other. There is no general method of food protection analogous to pasteurization of milk or chlorination of water supplies. Suitable protection must be attained by the use of accepted procedures of cleanliness and handling. The number of illnesses which may be transmitted by food is large indeed, but the incidence or attack rate of individual food-borne illnesses varies considerably throughout the world.

The range of disease spread or conveyed by foods can conveniently be placed in three major groups: those containing a toxin as an end-product of bacterial metabolism; those containing significant numbers of bacteria that on ingestion set off an irritation; and those containing a more complex form of parasite that can initiate a more involved type of disease. The following list of food-borne infections, though not exhaustive, indicates the wide range of biological forms involved. We will be concerned with only a number of these.

    I. *Bacterial Toxins*
       Botulism
       Staphylococcal intoxication

II. *Bacterial, Viral, and Rickettsial Infections*
   Typhoid and paratyphoid fevers
   Salmonella food poisoning
   Streptococcal sore throat, scarlet fever, and streptococcal
      food poisoning
   Bacillary dysentery (shigellosis)
   Diphtheria
   Anthrax
   Brucellosis
   Tuberculosis
   Tularemia
III. *Parasitic* (*Protozoal and Zooparasitic*)
   Amoebiasis (Amoebic dysentery)
   Taeniasis (beef tapeworm infestation)
   Trichinosis (pork roundworm infestation)
   Ascariasis
   Hydatidosis

At this point bacterial food poisoning must be distinguished from food spoilage. Although it is erroneously believed that one is synonymous with the other, they are, in fact, quite dissimilar conditions. In order to understand the difference, it may be helpful to recall that bacteria are unicellular plants that exist in three main forms: as rod-shaped cells, with and without flagella, and as spherical cells called *cocci*. Figure 2 is a typical rod-shaped bacterium with flagella arranged completely around the body. A curved rod (vibrio)—Figure 3-a—is typical of the organism associated with cholera, a water- and food-borne disease. Figure 3-b shows the chain-like aggregation of streptococci, 3-c the grape-like clusters of staphylococci, and 3-d pairs of diplococci, of which the gonococci are representative. The third group, spiral forms, are seen in Figure 3-e. They are not involved in any known food-borne disease. Figure 3-f shows clostridial forms of the type involved in food spoilage and food poisoning. These cells have a spore stage, shown in Figure 3-g, that is instrumental in protecting them against destruction by heat. This characteristic, as we shall see, is particularly significant in food processing and sanitation. It would make a very neat package if I could now say that the cocci

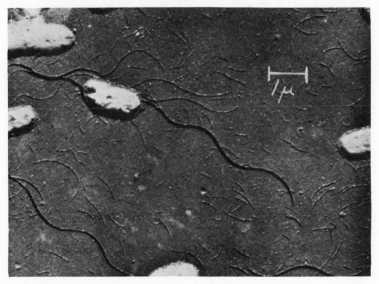

FIGURE 2. A typical rod-shaped salmonella bacterium

or grape-like forms are primarily responsible for food poisoning and the rod-shaped forms for food spoilage. Unfortunately, this is not exactly the case. Although cocci do cause a form of food poisoning and rods do produce food spoilage, two rod-shaped organisms are responsible for food-borne disease.

The question must now be asked, "When is food fit to eat?" Perhaps you would reply that food is fit to eat when you can look at it, smell it, and judge it to be fit to eat. If this is a true evaluation, then a food is not fit to eat when your eyes and your nose say, "this is not fit to eat." Some people, mainly Europeans, like their game meat "high." Most Americans would call such meat spoiled, and not fit to eat. "High" or "gamey" meat usually has a strong odor and taste, both produced by bacterial action. Titmuck, fish buried to allow bacterial fermentation to occur, is eaten by Eskimos as a delicacy. Eskimo dogs, however, refuse to eat this semiliquid, foul-smelling delight. Most Americans would call it putrid. Yet it is putrefaction that gives Limburger cheese its gourmet qualities! These examples of spoilage represent the growth

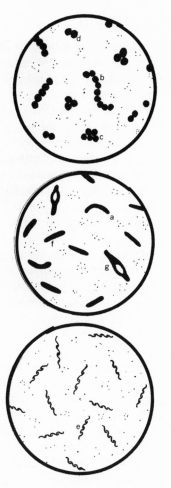

FIGURE 3. (a) curved rod (vibrio); (b) typical streptococci chain; (c) grape-like clusters of staphylococci; (d) pair of diplococci; (e) typical spiral forms; (f) clostridial rods with rounded ends; (g) spore stage

and metabolic activity of microorganisms, but food poisoning is not involved. Food poisoning, which is also due to the activity of microbes, is produced by only a few types of bacteria, which impart no off-odors or tastes to foods. You would never know that the food in question contains either a toxin or an infectious agent.

Every housewife is familiar with the common signs of food spoilage. Many would consider fruit spoiled and unfit to eat when partially or wholly covered with mold. Aesthetically such fruit may be unattractive, but it is not poisoned. That is, it does not evoke gastroenteritis if eaten. Many people pare away molded areas of fruit to enjoy the winey flavor imparted by the microbial conversion of fruit sugars to alcohol. Cottage cheese and hamburger are two readily perishable products. To some people, they become unfit to eat after two days of refrigeration. Others accept these items after a week or more. The point is that spoilage is a relative thing, associated with offense to the senses, but is not inherently dangerous.

Most foods are subject to some degree of deterioration. Considering the ease of spoilage, foods can be categorized as *non-perishable, semi-perishable,* and *perishable.* The degree of perishability simply refers to the ease with which microbes are able to use a food as a source of nourishment. Examples of relatively non-perishable foods are dry grains, sugar, flour, and beans. Without sufficient moisture, microbes find it difficult to spoil foods. Potatoes and apples are examples of semi-perishable foods containing more available moisture, while meats, fish, poultry, eggs, and milk—the high-protein foods with large amounts of moisture—are the highly perishable foods. Because these foods are desirable sources of nutriment to both humans and microbes, it is easy to see why L. V. Burton's statement that food sanitation is nothing more than a race between man and animals to see who gets the food supply first is appropriate.

Foods undergoing bacterial spoilage are usually contaminated with large numbers of rod-shaped organisms called pseudomonads. Pseudomonads of one species (type) or another spoil cottage cheese, poultry, meats, and fish. Pseudomonads have not been found to elaborate toxins capable of initiating human illness. Additionally, ingestion of pseudomonads has not resulted in gastrointestinal upsets. On the other hand, certain clostridial organisms can spoil low-acid canned foods. But the presence of a *specific* clostridium is required to produce the food poisoning known as botulism.

One of the most striking changes in public health over the past twenty-five years has been the enormous increase in the incidence of bacterial food poisoning. Figure 4 shows the steady in-

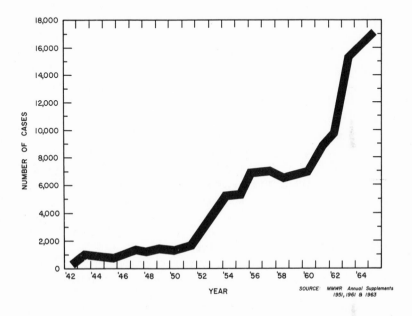

FIGURE 4. Yearly increase in salmonellosis, 1942–1965

crease of one type of food poisoning.

Strangely enough, our knowledge of the multiple factors responsible for bacterial food poisoning has also increased. A recent publication issued by the U.S. Department of Health, Education, and Welfare states that "despite the progress which has been achieved, food-borne illness continues to be a major public health problem," and it also notes that "the total amount of food-borne illness in the United States is not known, since reporting is neither complete nor accurate." Estimates of the number of cases that occur yearly range from 200,000 to 300,000. Apparently, only a fraction of the actual number that occur are reported to local, state, or federal agencies.

The magnitude of the food poisoning cases due to improper handling by individuals in the community, as opposed to persons engaged in commercial preparation, is seen in Table 1. It represents reported illnesses of persons eating in large groups at private homes, schools, picnics, and church gatherings. A similar chart for the contribution of public dining places is unavailable. The lack of such information should not be construed as implying greater safety in restaurants than in private homes, although this has been suggested. A newspaper article recently stated that it is safer to eat in restaurants than in homes or at private functions because health departments receive fewer reports of food poisoning from restaurants than from picnics, private parties, and private homes! Eighty million meals are believed to be served each day in public places in the United States. The difficulty of tracing a case of gastroenteritis to a restaurant is formidable indeed. It may well be that restaurants are less safe than private homes, even though fewer cases of food poisoning are reported per meal served. The determination of this, however, must await a more efficient system of detection and reporting.

A second major contribution to explosive outbreaks of especially severe and often fatal food poisoning is inadequately processed canned and packaged low-acid food, from both home and factory. Botulism is undoubtedly the most severe and most dramatic of all types of food poisoning and is being seen more and more as new packaged foods appear.

At this point, two questions are appropriate: (1) Why do we have bacterial food poisoning, and (2) Why is it increasing in magnitude?

Curiously enough, the answer to the first question has been known for some time. It has been reasonably well advertised but flagrantly ignored. Disease transmitted by food usually originates with an infected person who inadvertently inoculates the food during handling. Careless or inadequate food-handling practices later foster abundant growth of the organism in a highly nutritious medium. The elapsed time between preparation and serving to

TABLE 1.

*Types and incidence of food-borne illness
at large private gatherings*

	STAPHYLOCOCCAL FOOD POISONING		SALMONELLOSIS		STREPTOCOCCAL INFECTIONS		SHIGELLOSIS		GASTROENTERITIS, ETIOLOGY UNKNOWN	
	No. of outbreaks	No. of persons affected	No. of outbreaks	No. of persons affected	No. of outbreaks	No. of persons affected	No. of outbreaks	No. of persons affected	No. of outbreaks	No. of persons affected
Poultry	10	340	6	464	1	30	1	50	18	1,188
Other Meat	21	519	2	21	0	—	1	3	41	1,496
Custard-Filled Dessert	10	167	2	23	0	—	0	—	12	186
Salad	2	36	3	105	2	900	1	192	7	456
Other	10	231	7	135	1	100	1	12	12	106
Not Determined	5	367	10	859	0	—	7	497	42	2,503
Total	58	1,660	30	1,607	4	1,030	11	754	132	5,935

an unsuspecting, happy, and hungry population allows sufficient toxin to be produced by the multiplying bacterial population to permit large numbers of those present an adequate sampling. The potent toxin requires the ingestion of only a morsel of food to evoke the characteristic set of symptoms now so well known. A review of many food-poisoning experiences allows categorizing on the basis of laxity in food sanitation.

TABLE 2.

Ascribed causes and incidence of food poisoning

Ascribed Cause	% of Outbreaks
Inadequate refrigeration	41
Disease carriers	18
Infected sores (fingers, arm)	17
General insanitation	12
Cases of disease (sick people)	9
Chemicals in foods	4

Food handlers cannot afford to ignore these findings. The category of general insanitation must not be glossed over. We shall treat it at length shortly.

To answer our second question we must look to our changing environment. A radical change has been brought about in the very manner of our daily lives by the rapid substitution of a technological, industrially oriented society for an agricultural one. Intricately involved in this changeover are, surprisingly enough, factors that abet food poisoning.

An affluent industrial society encourages women to join the labor force in the factory alongside men. In order to purchase the available goods and services the income of both husband and wife is often necessary. The homemaker of the past is now a salesperson, or clerical or factory worker, or contributing in some other capacity. Whatever the job, she is no longer able to spend long hours at home preparing meals. Domestic help, once abundantly available, has also succumbed to the siren call of industry. For those women who do not have to work, free time for pleasurable pursuits is more compelling than kitchen drudgery. As if to punctuate the problem, the smaller homes and apartments of the urban areas have forced grandparents to live away from children. All this mitigates against home cooking. As a consequence, one now routinely brings home ready-to-eat, precooked, prepackaged foods. We also eat out more often. And to cater to our newly educated tastes, large quantities of specialty foods are brought from places around the world where food sanitation practices are quite often less than adequate. New types of food items are sold in unique types of packaging whose potential for disease transmission is unknown until an illness occurs.

While studying the effects of cooking temperatures on antibiotic residues in breaded and fried crab and oyster cakes, we noted that heat penetration was slow but sufficient to kill bacterial pathogens. We speculated on the degree of heat penetration into precooked frozen crab cakes. To assuage our curiosity, a small-scale study using the following experimental procedure was undertaken:

> Several varieties of frozen crab cakes were obtained from retail stores in our area. Since many housewives often save additional minutes in preparing precooked frozen items by placing them in cold ovens, and bringing to suggested temperature, the samples were split, one half being placed in an oven preheated according to label instructions and the second half in a cold oven. It was noted that different companies recommended different cooking times at the specified temperature. Temperature readings were obtained by inserting 24-gauge copperconstantin thermocouple wires into the approximate center of the cakes and the terminal ends connected to a Brown portable potentiometer (Model 126W3).

The results obtained, while interesting to us, were of particular concern to frozen food packers, many of whom subsequently changed their label directions. Before the heat penetration determinations were made, the surface and internal temperatures of the frozen cakes were obtained. Readings of 32° to 35° F were obtained at the surfaces and 19° to 23° F internally. The suggested cooking time on the wrapper was eight minutes in an oven set at 300° F. After eight minutes in the "cold" oven, the cakes had reached 142° F, approximately the minimum temperature considered necessary to prevent food poisoning. The cakes in the preheated oven reached 175° F. Although this might indicate safety, I wrote that it "might not provide adequate heat treatment in view of the protective effects of many of the colloidal materials contained in crab cake mix." Another experiment was carried out using larger cakes and wrapper directions that called for twenty minutes of cooking after the oven arrived at 400° F. We found that "after twenty minutes in the cold oven, 126° F was recorded at the center of the cakes, while 150° F was attained in the preheated oven. Our findings indicated that present wrapper directions for home heating of precooked frozen crab cakes leave much to be desired in providing an adequate heat treatment from a public health standpoint, especially if heating is done in an unpreheated oven."

In 1965 the National Academy of Sciences issued a special report recommending that emphasis be given to research in new foods and packaging, as they produce wholly new conditions for microbial growth.

I noted earlier that the great majority of food-poisoning experiences fall into three main groups. By far the most common is that due to staphylococci enterotoxin. Not all strains of "staph" elaborate enterotoxin, nor do the toxin-producing strains produce enterotoxin in all foods. Staphylococci are commonly found in the nose and throat, and on the skin in pimples, boils, carbuncles, and whitlows.

Such items as ham, chicken, and egg salad, custard-filled cakes, meat pies, boiled ham, and salad meats are the most notorious sources of food poisoning. They offer a most nutritious, high-protein diet to the staphylococci, and they are usually prepared in large amounts that are difficult to cool rapidly. Put this same organism on a slice of tomato and no growth or toxin production will occur. When refrigeration is unavailable, inadequate, or simply not used, the microbe, gaining entry from a sore finger or droplet from the nose, finds conditions suitable for growth—warmth and nourishment—and toxin production begins. As the hours pass, the unrefrigerated food becomes a potential bomb. At mealtime nothing is suspected. The food has not changed in appearance, odor, or taste.

Two to six hours after eating the explosion occurs. The first symptoms are usually nausea and vomiting (the body tries to rid itself of the poison as rapidly as possible), abdominal cramps, and diarrhea. In severe cases, blood and mucus may appear in the patient's stool and vomitus as a consequence of violent retching.

Just such a set of events occurred in Indiana in August, 1959. The explosive outbreak of August 15 was ascribed to boiled ham that had become contaminated during preparation. The episode on the following Saturday was due to toxin in potato salad and ham. This was pinned down by swift laboratory analysis. Both outbreaks could have been prevented by proper refrigeration.

Botulism, the most striking form of food poisoning, results from ingestion of an enterotoxin elaborated by *Clostridium botulinum* and *para-botulinum*. This sublimely potent toxin is the most deadly natural poison known to man.* Since the clostridia are normal inhabitants of the intestinal tract of animals, they are universally found in agricultural areas in close proximity to crops. It has now been established [1] that these bacteria are also natural inhabitants of marine environments, probably as a result of soil runoff. Consequently, food fish harbor them as part of their natural flora. Unlike the staphylococci, which are introduced as a result of poor personal hygiene on the part of food handlers, clostridia are already present and not adequately removed from the produce when it is washed before canning or packaging. Most cases of botulism can be traced either to ingestion of underprocessed home- or factory-canned low or nonacid foods, or to packaging in containers providing suitable conditions for toxin production.

* Less than 1×10^{-10} grams can kill a mouse.

Recall Figure 3-g, in which a spore was shown. Spores are generally considered to be the most heat-resistant forms of life on our planet. It is just this characteristic that food processors must guard against, especially home canners and purveyors of specialty items that receive only light heat treatments. Foods such as string-beans, corn, beets, asparagus, mushrooms, tuna, chicken pie, and smoked fish, known to be naturally contaminated with spores of *C. botulinum,* must be processed for at least thirty-five minutes at 240° F (115° C) to guarantee safety. Spores of several food-spoilage (but not food-poisoning) clostridia are more heat-resistant than spores of the botulism organism. When heat processing is adequate to destroy the food spoilage forms, food poisoning will not occur. Commercial canned food processors have developed heat treatments for each food and can size, based on the heat resistance of a test organism known to be more heat-resistant than most of the spoilage organisms. Interestingly enough, a form of built-in protection also exists. The food "spoilers" produce unbearably putrid end-products as a result of anaerobic metabolism in canned foods. Consequently, if processing has been inadequate, the insufferable odors present as a result of the activity of these organisms will prevent the food from being eaten, thus affording protection against consuming the botulism toxin present along with the malodorous products.

In most cases of botulism no warning odors are present. The foods are eaten usually at home during the dinner meal, which accounts for the extensive family involvement. The first symptoms appear about twelve to thirty-six hours later. In some cases on record the incriminated food had been eaten more than four days before, but this is unusual. An astounding case was reported by Dr. Dack of the University of Chicago [2]: that of a patient who was active for eight days before hospitalization, even attending the funerals of other victims and testifying at the coroner's inquest! Typically, however, the toxin seeks the central nervous system. Thus, in addition to nausea, vomiting, and diarrhea, the characteristic symptoms are double vision * and difficulty in swallowing. This is followed by slurred speech. In fatal cases the pharyngeal

* Indicating involvement of the third cranial nerve.

muscles are paralyzed and death results from respiratory failure. Over 70 percent of cases end in death, primarily because treatment with antitoxin is started too late. For antitoxin to be useful, it should be given before symptoms appear. Unless there is reason to suspect botulism, this is seldom done. In addition, symptoms of botulism are often confused with a half-dozen other nervous-system illnesses, and treatment is often delayed until information is obtained that the patient ate certain foods that are commonly associated with botulism.

As noted above, food poisoning could occur in either of two ways: eating food containing toxin, or eating food containing large numbers of certain bacteria. Salmonellosis is that form of food poisoning produced by the rod-shaped bacteria *Salmonella typhimuriam* rather than by a preformed enterotoxin. Salmonellosis epitomizes poor personal hygiene in food handlers. It represents the contamination of food by human fecal matter. Of all food-borne illnesses, this is the most inexcusable, particularly because of the high level of sanitation attainable in our society. It is estimated that in 1968, two million people, 1 percent of the population, suffered attacks of salmonellosis. Thus, the magnitude of under-reporting can be inferred.

Salmonella organisms, the rod-shaped cells shown in Figure 2, are natural inhabitants of the bowel (colon) of man and animals. Thus, they are passed out with feces and can be introduced into food from soiled hands. Additional sources of human infection are animal products such as poultry, eggs, and milk; egg products such as noodles and cake mixes; and meat items such as meat pies, brawn, pressed beef, and sausages that have contacted animal excreta. In March, 1966, chocolate candy bars were recalled from stores because of salmonella contamination. Usually, the source of the spread of the infectious organism is the human excreter, either those with frank cases of the illness, those convalescing from the illness, or asymptomatic healthy carriers. Healthy carriers are our greatest problem. They don't know they are shedding salmonella organisms and outwardly appear perfectly healthy. Because of the difficulty in detecting carriers who have no symptoms, preventive measures are largely ineffective.

As with the toxin types of food poisoning, the appearance, smell, and taste of food contaminated with salmonellae are unaltered. Similarly, the foods and the conditions of their preparation offer excellent media for bacterial growth. Ten to twenty hours after eating, the first symptoms of gastroenteritis appear. The onset is sudden. Headache, shaking, chills, abdominal pain, elevated temperature, and foul-smelling diarrhea usually appear. Prostration, muscular weakness, and dehydration can be severe, leaving the patient totally debilitated. The severity of the illness depends on the number of organisms ingested and on individual sensitivity. Infants and adults over fifty tend to have severe symptoms, and considerably more fatalities occur in these two groups.

Food poisoning is not the only illness caused by salmonellae. Unlike other salmonella infections, the only known reservoirs of infection of typhoid fever are human carriers. Typhoid fever, also due to the ingestion of food or water containing fecal matter from people ill with the disease, is a very different illness from food poisoning. Classical symptoms of typhoid fever include high fever, abdominal tenderness, enlarged spleen, slow pulse, a rose-colored skin rash, headache, cough, and nosebleeds *—quite a different set of symptoms from those seen in salmonella food poisoning. To the more than five hundred men and women who were hospitalized with typhoid fever in Aberdeen, Scotland, in the summer of 1965, canned corned beef will always recall their narrow escape from death. On May 19, 1965, ambulances brought to the City Hospital in Aberdeen four people ill with high fevers. By midnight the following day the Health Department had identified the suspected microbe, *Salmonella typhi,* from stool and blood cultures. *S. typhi* is the agent of typhoid fever.

Desultory outbreaks of typhoid occur from time to time, but in countries with modern sanitation facilities they are usually of little consequence. However, in Aberdeen, as the days passed, it became all too clear that this was no ordinary episode. By May 30, the number of confirmed cases jumped to 136 and the first death was recorded. The following day a newspaper carried the following account: "The trim streets of Aberdeen were nearly

* Of course, not all symptoms occur with each case.

deserted tonight and in some places the air was heavy with the odor of disinfectant as the city fought to stamp out a typhoid epidemic."

By June 27 the epidemic had run its course and Queen Elizabeth sent a message indicating that she would visit the city. Over five hundred had been hospitalized and five had died. Aberdeen, a major tourist attraction, had also suffered disastrous losses in trade. Thus, the news was welcomed as a sign that the Queen thought Aberdeen was safe enough for her and for her subjects, safe from the havoc wrought by a can of corned beef.

During the period of the outbreak, a great deal of confusion and misunderstanding regarding the nature of the disease's communicability elicited behavior in many segments of the population reminiscent of that of the Middle Ages rather than the twentieth century. For example, the streets of Aberdeen were sprayed with disinfectant, as though the typhoid bacterium had blanketed the environment and could be picked up and carried about on the soles of shoes. Workers in cities far to the south of Aberdeen went so far as to refuse to unload trucks that passed thru Aberdeen. Students were told to avoid public transportation, as though the bacillus could be transmitted from person to person much like influenza, a respiratory-tract infection spread by droplet nuclei from a cough or sneeze.

To make matters still worse, prophecies of impending national disaster were foretold. That these tragicomic behavior patterns should have occurred in the sixty-sixth year of the twentieth century is cause for concern over our educational processes. I say *our,* for I am quite certain that similar behavior would result in the U.S. should a major outbreak of typhoid occur.

The cycle of events leading to the epidemic began in a meat-canning plant in Argentina. After a canned food is heated (to reduce * the bacterial population and cook the food), it is placed in

* Canned food, although subjected to temperatures as high as 240°F for thirty-five minutes, is not meant to be completely sterilized. Sterilization, the complete absence of life, would produce a product unfit to eat. Consequently, the heat treatment is designed to reduce the microbial population to harmless levels.

cold water to lower its temperature rapidly, which prevents over-cooking. Heating causes the seams to expand and offers an entrance to bacteria. The cooling water in this case was drawn from a stream that was polluted with fecal matter containing typhoid bacteria. Chlorination, which was not practiced, could easily have sterilized the water and prevented the episode. Bacteria were thus reintroduced after cooking. By the time the corned beef arrived in Scotland and was used, a significant increase in bacteria had occurred. One of the busier supermarkets on the city's main street opened one of the six-pound tins and sliced the beef on its slicing machine. As other meats were also sliced on that machine, they in turn were inoculated with the typhoid organisms. Several of the employees became infected while handling meat, and they became sources of further spread. But for the expert protective measures instituted by Dr. Ian MacQueen at the onset of the illness, additional thousands could have become ill.

Asymptomatic carriers are people who harbor typhoid organisms in the gall bladder, where the bacteria multiply slowly. The organisms leave the gall bladder in bile and are passed out of the body in feces. These people do not appear ill and on medical examination show no signs or symptoms of typhoid; they are healthy (chronic) carriers who continue for years to shed infectious organisms. These people can be the focus of explosive epidemics if allowed to work in any aspect of food handling. In New York City, for example, 264 healthy carriers are constantly under surveillance to prevent their employment in the food industry.

Late in May, 1967, a sizable typhoid outbreak occurred at the Beta Theta Pi fraternity house at Stanford University in Palo Alto, California. Apparently, healthy carriers working in the kitchen were responsible for passing the infection to some eighteen fraternity members. Positive stool cultures were obtained from the cook and two waiters.

The problem of the carrier is particularly troublesome since the bacteria are lodged in the confines of the gall bladder, defying all current forms of medication. Surgical removal of the gall bladder (cholecystectomy) is the only positive means of preventive treatment, but most known carriers will not submit to it.

TABLE 3.

*Mechanisms of food poisoning by the
three leading infectious microbial agents*

Staphylococcus

Found in salads (egg, chicken, ham, etc.), custards, sliced meats.

The bacteria inoculated into these foods by food handlers, then multiply
when conditions are favorable, producing thermostable toxin.

The toxin is ingested with food and acts directly on the intestines and
the central nervous system.

In two to seven hours, vomiting, diarrhea, cramping, and prostration
occur.

Clostridium botulinum

Found in low-acid canned foods (stringbeans, corn, beets, tuna, smoked
fish).

These bacteria are naturally present in soil and marine environments;
they gain entrance to containers when food is canned or packaged.

The organisms multiply only when conditions are favorable.

The organisms produce heat-labile toxin as a byproduct of its
metabolism.

The toxin, ingested with food, acts on the central nervous system and on
peripheral nerves.

As early as two hours or as late as four days after ingestion, vomiting,
diarrhea, and diplopia occur, usually followed by inability to talk
and swallow.

The disease is frequently fatal as a result of respiratory collapse.

Salmonella gastroenteritis

Found in food and water contaminated by food handlers with fecal
matter containing bacteria.

The organisms are ingested with food and multiply in Peyer's patches
of the small intestine.

The presence of the organisms irritates mucosal lining.

In twelve to twenty-four hours, pain, diarrhea, vomiting, and fever
generally occur.

In the United States, 369 cases of typhoid were reported in 1966. About 3 percent were fatal. Babies and invalids are the most vulnerable.

Table 3 shows the mechanisms of the three major types of food poisoning. In each instance the mechanism yields the means whereby prevention can be instituted. That such preventive measures have been known and widely disseminated for many years testifies to the lack of concern on the part of individuals. Bacterial food poisoning has no place in highly industrialized, affluent societies. That it not only persists but continues to increase constitutes community failure to protect itself.

During the ten-year period 1950–1960, thousands of outbreaks of food poisoning occurred in both the United States and England. A comparison of the type of foods incriminated indicated close similarities between the two countries. Table 4 indicates the frequency with which particular types of food were associated with an outbreak.

TABLE 4.

Frequency with which particular food types
are associated with outbreaks of food poisoning

% Frequency	Associated with
4	meat
8	bakery items (custard-filled cakes)
6	fish
6	egg and egg products
3	milk and milk products
2	vegetables
1	other foods

This type of information should indicate where additional preventive measures would reap large benefits in terms of fewer outbreaks.

Thus far I have not mentioned the word *ptomaine* or ptomaine poisoning, and for good reason. There really is no such thing. Ptomaine poisoning is an old concept that is hardly dying. Although it has been established beyond question for many years that ptomaines are not involved in bacterial food poisoning, the term persists. *Ptomaine* comes from the Greek *ptoma,* meaning *dead body* or *cadaver;* ptomaines as a class are foul-smelling chemical compounds. For those with training in chemistry, it may be useful to note that ptomaines are aliphatic diamines formed from the decomposition of proteins by bacteria. Actually, the

FIGURE 5. Decarboxylation reaction

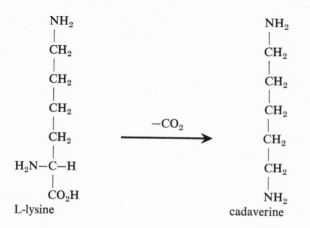

ptomaine putrescine is formed by the decarboxylation of the amino acid *ornithine,* and the ptomaine *cadaverine* is formed by the removal of CO_2 from lysine. Figure 5 shows the decarboxylation reaction. Neither of these ptomaines is harmful when taken by mouth. That is, they do not produce symptoms of gastroenteritis. If, however, a large amount were introduced directly into the bloodstream with a hypodermic syringe, illness would occur, but, again, no food poisoning symptoms. Perhaps the less said about ptomaines the better.

Investigations of the causes of bacterial food poisoning invariably turn up evidence of failture to employ basic sanitary food-handling practices in preparing and preserving food. As noted earlier, bacterial food poisoning has no place in a modern, affluent society. It is an entirely preventable disease. Prevention requires attention to two broad areas: personal hygiene and temperature control. For example:

1. Hands must be washed with soap before preparing, handling, or serving food following use of toilet facilities. Unwashed hands, particularly those soiled with human or animal waste, can introduce food-poisoning organisms to food.

2. The nose and mouth should be covered with a handkerchief or other effective barrier when a person handling food is sneezing or coughing. After handkerchiefs containing exhaled mucus and sputum are handled, hands should be washed with soap.

3. Fingers should be kept out of glasses and dishes, and off bowls, spoons, fork tines, and knife blades.

4. In commercial food establishments, food handlers should be checked regularly for evidence of open sores, boils, sore throats, colds, and intestinal disorders. An employee who reports to work with any of these signs should not be allowed to handle food.

5. Salads made of meat, poultry, seafood, potatoes, and eggs must be held below 45° F until served. This applies as well to custards and cream-filled cakes. All these items should be eaten on the day prepared.

6. Stuffings, poultry, and stuffed meats should be heated to

reach at least 165° F deep in the center of the product.

7. If a food that can be heated must be stored for two to three hours, it should be maintained above 145° F while stored.

8. If there is any suspicion that a canned food—particularly a homecooked, low-acid food—is undercooked, poorly sealed, or leaking, the contents should be heated to boiling before being eaten.

Although there is no substitute for proper training in food handling, adherence to these eight rules should prove helpful in preventing outbreaks of bacterial food poisoning.

4

CHEMICALS IN FOODS

Thanksgiving was less than two weeks away. The cranberry growers around the U.S. had harvested a bumper crop, the largest of any in the past ten years, and large stocks of cranberry products were on grocers' shelves throughout the country. No one would be without cranberry sauce—or so it was thought.

On November 9, 1959, Arthur Flemming, the then secretary of the Department of Health, Education, and Welfare, held his usual Monday press conference; but this was to be no routine conference. The next day, newspapers, radio, and TV were retelling with high drama versions of the distressing affair: "The Federal Government warned the public today that some cranberries grown in Washington State and Oregon had been contaminated by a weed-killer—Aminotriazole—that induces cancerous growths in the thyroid of rats. * . . . If housewives were

* Aminotriazole, a weedicide with a long history of use in cornfields, blocks formation of chlorophyll (the green pigment of plants),

unable to determine where berries were grown, the government advises them not to buy either in canned or fresh form despite the approach of Thanksgiving. . ⸺. It has not been proved that the weed-killer produces cancer in human beings." Across the country, the commotion started in Washington that Monday caused grocers to remove cranberry products from their shelves and restaurants to drop cranberry sauce from their menus.

That episode, along with the earlier warnings of potential cancer hazard from the black dye used in jellybeans and the chemical diethylstilbestrol used in chickens to produce caponettes, is still reverberating today.

In March, 1960, George P. Larrick, commissioner of the Food and Drug Administration, stated that "the general public, confused by the cranberry, caponette, and black jellybean episodes, and by misleading information from various sources, is understandably uncertain over just what the so-called chemicals-in-foods-problem is all about."

Two questions continue to be asked, and rightly so: (1) Is our food supply safe? (2) Is it necessary to add chemicals to food? The answer to both of these questions must be an unqualified yes, but not without extensive evidence and reason.

Between 1900 and 1960, our country more than doubled its population. Between 1960 and 2000, just thirty-one years from now, we are expected to more than double again. Figure 6 indicates the projected estimates based on current birth and death rates. In 1920, the arable land under cultivation fed 106 million people. In 1969, an additional 99 million people will be fed on less arable land, and by 2000 there will be more than two mouths to feed where there was only one thirty-one years before. The simple fact is that not only must more food be produced on less and less available land, but, perhaps even more important, what is produced must be protected until it can be harvested, bought, and eaten. Crop and livestock pests exact an appalling tribute despite

thus preventing carbohydrate formation and thus causing the death of the weed. Feeding rats ten to one hundred times the amount of amino-triazole found on cranberries for seventy to one hundred weeks caused the formation of thyroid carcinomas in the animals.

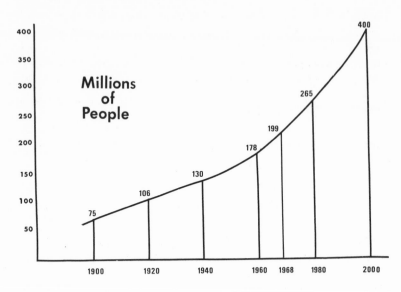

FIGURE 6. The population of the U.S., and projected estimates

all our efforts to thwart them. Each year the equivalent of eighty-five to ninety million acres of crops is debased by all manner of pests. Added to this are the losses suffered in storage, processing. and transportation, equivalent to another thirty million acres of crops. Agricultural economists estimate that 20 to 25 percent of our annual production is lost to predation: either ruined "on the vine" or spoiled after harvest. To prevent additional losses the farmer uses the only effective means thus far available to him—chemical pesticides.* In order to curtail or prevent losses in livestock, milk production, meat, and hides, by the ravages of microbes, ticks, lice, flies, and worms, chemical control is vital.

In addition to protecting the food supply at its source, chemicals aid in coping with the development and changes wrought by an industrial society. The complexity of modern life and changes

* See Chapter 5, Insecticides, for a discussion of natural pest-control methods presently being investigated.

in our eating habits require that in addition to the fresh * or freshly cooked items available in season locally, new methods be found to provide for year-round requirements, in and out of season. In 1920, a few hundred food items were available to consumers. By 1941, some fifteen hundred items could be counted on grocers' shelves. It was quite clear people wanted variety in their diets; they were not content with the drab, unvaried fare served up day after day. In 1960, we could choose our foods from over six thousand items, and in 1968, over seventy-five hundred were available. Variety the year round is now readily available to the consumer.

A problem dealing with the lack of variety in diet presented itself during World War II. In the early years of the war, Britain was besieged. The problem of feeding a nation that relied so heavily on imports became a matter of acute anxiety. A study was undertaken to determine the nutritional requirements of an adequate diet. It was soon learned that all the nourishment for such a diet could be obtained from a combination of green vegetables, bread, and milk. Using men and women in scrupulous tests, it was found that such simple but tedious fare could easily support vigorous activity. This diet would have drastically reduced the need for imported food. To the consternation of many, it was not adopted because it was considered to be far too monotonous and dull for the maintenance of a highly advanced country for any sustained period. A British scientist, Magnus Pike, commented: "A diet may be perfectly balanced nutritionally, but if it is not

---

* The concept of *freshness* implies a time factor: the interval between harvesting and eating. To a person with a pea, melon, or tomato patch, food eaten directly off the vine is fresh. To a person buying from a typical supermarket that imports from a distance, *fresh* should connote an interval of perhaps several days between picking, packing, shipping, retailing, and eating.

The length of time elapsed between harvesting and freezing a ten-ounce package of green peas, for example, is relatively short. That frozen item arrives at the supermarket several days after harvesting, but resembles closely the product picked days before. *Freshness* then might properly describe the condition of the food at the moment of eating, irrespective of when it left the vine.

sufficiently attractive a workman may not eat enough of it to do his work. If a chemist can enhance the attractiveness of such a diet harmlessly, he is, in fact, contributing to nutritional well-being."

The entrance of large numbers of women into the labor force, coupled with their desire to spend less time preparing meals, has given great impetus to the precooked, prepackaged, ready-to-eat foods. To accomplish this, many types of chemicals are needed.

New discoveries from nutritional investigations during the past forty years have measurably changed our food supply. I think it safe to say that most of us are aware of the importance to general health of vitamin, minerals, proteins, fats, and carbohydrates. Many of these nutrient chemicals can be manufactured so that foods can be "fortified" or "enriched." Potassium iodide, for example, added to common table salt, has all but eliminated simple goiter. Enrichment of bread with chemicals such as the B-vitamins (thiamin, niacin, and riboflavin) has just about eliminated pellegra from the U.S. The minerals, vitamins, and other nutrients so common in many foods today—the list would read like an inventory of a chemist's laboratory—has undoubtedly upgraded the general health of our population.

Finally, use of chemicals in foods, combined with other forms of preservation, permits the stockpiling of food to cope with emergencies. Food technologists are in fact modern day Josephs evening out the fat and the lean years.

All foods are subject to microbial attack. Some foods keep better than others: cereal grains (wheat, barley, rye), nuts, and seeds, for example, require little additional intervention for their preservation. Such items as potatoes, carrots, flour, dried fruits, and butter, because of their relatively low moisture content, have a fairly long storage life. Foods of high moisture content, such as meats, fish, and poultry, have poor keeping characteristics and thus require effective means of preservation if they are to survive microbial onslaughts. Of the many methods of food preservation —heating, freezing, dehydration, smoking, pickling—chemical methods are assuming increased importance. Certain chemicals are used to color foods; others add flavor; some impart firmness, while others soften; still others thicken, moisten, dry, or acidify, while others retard or hasten chemical reactions. Recall that what are called "foods" are in reality plant and animal tissues composed of proteins, carbohydrates, fats, minerals, water, and a host of other organic and inorganic substances, all of which are chemicals that can enter into many chemical reactions. The browning of sliced apples, peaches, and potatoes is an example of the chemical change that occurs when the oxygen in the air contacts specific enzymes released by the cut tissue. To prevent or retard these chemical reactions, such chemicals as sodium bisulphite or ascorbic acid (Vitamin C) are added to processed foods.

Although baking can destroy the spores of molds and most bacteria that are naturally present in flour and other ingredients, baked goods are constantly exposed to spores present in the air and on baking utensils. The mixture of chemical ingredients we call cake, bread, and pastry is as tempting to bacteria as they are to man. Despite sanitary precautions, molds develop when temperature and moisture conditions favor their growth. Flour contains the spores of a hardy bacterium, *Bacillus mesentericus,* which are able to survive the heat of baking. During storage the bacteria become active and multiply, producing a "ropy" condition which renders the bread inedible. Small quantities of sorbic acid or sodium propionate or other weak organic acids retard the growth of molds and bacteria in baked goods.

Wheat flour, in it natural, freshly milled state, has a yellowish tint due to the presence of small quantities of carotenoid and other natural pigments.* When this flour is stored it slowly becomes whiter and undergoes an aging process that ultimately yields a dough of enhanced breadmaking quality. Until fifty years

---

* *Carotenoid* means "resembling carotene," a natural pigment found in carrots and other yellow vegetables.

The carotenoids are precursors of Vitamin A that can be converted to Vitamin A in the human body. Thus one must distinguish between the actual Vitamin A content and the Vitamin A activity of food. The carotenes are thus provitamins. Not all carotenes are effective in this respect, however, and lycopene, the red carotenoid pigment found in tomatoes and other vegetables, is devoid of any Vitamin A effect. The same is true of xanthophyll, a yellow carotenoid found in wheat.

ago it was necessary for the miller to age flour so that the baker could produce the type of loaf the public would buy. It was then found that certain chemicals incorporated into flour in small amounts would alter the natural yellow tint and improve the baking quality in short order. This also reduced the storage costs and the losses that inevitably occurred via microbial spoilage and rodent and insect infestation over the long storage periods. Some of the chemicals used, such as benzoyl peroxide and the oxides of nitrogen, exert only a whitening activity without influencing the baking properties. Others, such as chlorine dioxide and niitrogen trichloride, exert both bleaching and baking properties. In fact, nitrogen trichloride was known commercially as Agene.*

The maturing of flour is of much greater practical significance than bleaching and is done chiefly because consumers prefer bread with a creamy texture.

The flour milled from some wheats requires little chemical treatment (oxidation), while that milled from other species requires a good deal more to yield a dough with satisfactory rheological properties for mechanized baking and to produce bread of consistently good quality. The maturing and bleaching agents aid in smoothing out the wide variations encountered in wheat and thus enable the miller to produce a uniform product from day to day and year to year.

Bread improvers used by the industry contain such substances as potassium bromate, calcium peroxide, mono-, di- or tricalcium phosphates, or ammonium chloride. They serve as food for the yeast cells, which helps assure vigorous and even fermentation (gas production, for the most part) of the dough to produce loaves of uniform quality.

Fatty or oily foods that have become rancid have character-

---

* In 1946 Sir Edward Mellanby reported that when puppies were fed a diet consisting largely of flour heavily treated with Agene, they developed running fits, or canine hysteria. Although agene has not been found harmful to humans, its use was discontinued.

In 1950, the mechanism of canine hysteria was discovered. Apparently, Agene (nitrogen trichloride) reacted with methionine, an amino acid naturally present in flour protein, to form methionine sulphoximine, a compound toxic in puppies.

istic odors. To prevent or retard rancidity, which may be due either to bacterial attack on the food or to the reaction between naturally occurring chemicals in the food with air or minerals, chemical antioxidants such as butylated hydroxyanisole (BHA), butylated hydroxytoluene (BHT), or propyl gallate are added in small amounts.

Foods are among the most difficult materials to package successfully. Such considerations as protection from microbial invasion, penetration by atmospheric oxygen, loss of volatile substances through evaporation, and choice of a container which will not itself adversely affect the food are important if the item is to come to the consumer in an edible state the year round. Chemicals help make this possible.

In the past five years aerosol dispensers of food have come onto the scene and added a new dimension to both diversity and chemistry. In 1964 some 110 million cans of aerosol dispensed whipped topping and cheese were sold. By 1972, it is estimated that 625 million cans will be sold. I suspect a major problem will be how to get rid of all those cans.

In order to propel the food from the pressurized can, a gas— Freon C-318, octafluorocyclobutane—has been approved by the Food and Drug Administration as harmless and thus suitable for human consumption. But can a chemical with so obviously ominous a name, barely pronounceable, really be safe for human consumption? The fact is that the recital of unfamiliar technical names and scientific terms or the mere statement that a large number of strange-sounding substances are used in foods is singularly uninformative to consumers who are not chemists. These chemicals are offensive mainly because they are unfamiliar and create the specter of the unknown. While it would be less frightening if everyone knew what these chemicals are, the extent to which they are used, and the reasons for their use, unless we all become chemists one wonders how useful this would really be.

Synthetic or man-made chemicals may be incorporated in a good item during the growing or during the storage and processing of food. For convenience these are described as "additives." It is generally understood that an additive is any substance used in food directly or indirectly that affects its characteristics and usually becomes a component of the food. When introduced to preserve or improve the quality of a product they are known as *intentional* additives because they are purposely added to serve a specific need. Such materials as artificial coloring, synthetic flavors, sweeteners, vitamins, microbial inhibitors, antioxidants, emulsifiers, and minerals are all intentional additives. All are added to the food product in carefully controlled amounts during preparation. Common table salt, sodium chloride, is one of the oldest intentional additives known; octafluorocyclobutane, Freon C-318, is one of the newest; and cyclopentanoperhydrophenanthrene,* used to enhance the nutritive quality of milk or bread, is simply the chemist's name for Vitamin D!

When primitive man first learned to preserve a portion of his food supply by the smoke of his fire, he was utilizing chemicals unknowingly. It was (and still is) the production of formaldehyde, phenol and related compounds coupled with the drying action of heat, that retarded microbial spoilage. Chemicals in the wood smoke also impart unique organoleptic properties.

Chemicals in foods are not new; what is new is the means of adding the chemical in pure form with correct measurement, which results in a uniform product every time.

Diethylstilbestrol, a white, odorless, crystalline powder, is a man-made chemical exhibiting female sex hormone (estrogenic) activity. It was used for a time to produce caponettes. A capon is a male bird that has been castrated to fatten it. This is usually done surgically. Accomplishing the same thing by chemical means produces a caponette. Although the Food and Drug Administration authorized chemical use in 1947, tests on laboratory animals later showed the chemical to be toxic for them and thus hazardous for human consumption. It was withdrawn and is no longer in use.

In addition to intentional additives, other chemicals may be present in food at the time of consumption. These are usually called

---

* Cyclopentanoperhydrophenanthrene is actually the skeletal framework for a group of compounds such as steroids, hormones, natural pigments and vitamins. Each of these differs by specific additions of carbon and hydrogen atoms to the basic skeleton.

incidental or unintentional additives and get into the food in a variety of ways. A chemical insecticide or weedicide such as aminotriazole may be applied to a crop prior to harvesting and can be carried over into the processed food as a result of insufficient washing. A steer may eat a plant in the field that has a chemical residue on it. The chemical could survive the metabolic gyrations intact and appear in the meat of the steer. Packaging material such as a wrapper may contain a chemical that may migrate into an oil-based food as a result of its being oil-soluble. Butter and lard are good examples of this. Or the ink on a wrapper or carton may migrate for the same reason. Radioactive particles, the result of fallout from testing fission or fusion weapons, are another example of an unintentional additive. These particles can settle on foods such as vegetable crops. In essence, these are all chance contaminants, and as a consequence of inadequate washing they may be ingested with food.

There is a second category of intentional additives which could more properly be termed *malicious*. In this category are those chemicals added by dealers who want to peddle spoiled or nearly spoiled food. In this group are included those processors who label a food as "the fresh natural product" when in fact it is a mixture prepared by them.

Several years ago a fish dealer in Philadelphia wanted to vend a batch of spoiled fish. In order to do so, it was necessary to mask the "off" odor and color to make the fish fresh. Accordingly, he liberally dosed the fish with sodium nitrate. Sodium nitrate, or Chile saltpeter, is one of the most abundant naturally occurring nitrates. When used properly, it is a rather innocuous substance. During the late Middle Ages it was discovered that the color of meat became fixed when nitrate was added. It has been used ever since. It is also well known that nitrates in sufficient quantity can affect a rapid drop in blood pressure through vasodilation—enlargement of the blood vessels.

In this instance, the fish was freely dosed with the nitrate and shipped out to markets along the Atlantic Coast. Within a short time 150 people became ill with nitrate poisoning; many were hospitalized and a three-year-old child died.

In another instance, hundreds of people in North Africa became blind when cooking oil was diluted with a cheap organic chemical. The chemical destroyed the optic nerve.

Fortunately, marginal operators responsible for such incidents are rare, and, as is discussed later in this chapter, the foods we eat are subject to a great deal of inspection, supervision, and control.

At this point, it seems proper to raise three questions: (1) Is there a difference between naturally occurring chemicals and the synthetic or man-made variety? (2) Are chemicals inherently poisonous? (3) How is the safety of a chemical evaluated?

There is a notion that anything produced from the soil is proper and safe to eat, while changes produced or chemicals added by man are harmful. Actually, there is no fundamental difference between a hamburger, a fish patty, emulsifiers, vitamins, mold inhibitors, or non-nutritive sweeteners; they are all chemicals. Foods, as I noted earlier, are much more complex arrangements of chemical structures than food additives, whose exact chemical formula are known. Nobody can write the chemical formula or structure of a T-bone steak, crepe suzettes, or a western omelette. Obviously, some chemicals and some additives may be injurious, and these must not be used, but chemicals as a whole cannot be condemned out of hand without adequate evidence.

On the other hand, some of the deadliest substances known are produced by natural processes. Ergot, produced when rye and other grains are infected with a certain mold, has been a notorious killer. The beautiful mushroom *Amanita phalloides* contains a chemical that is about as mortal as any can be, with the possible exception of the toxin produced by the bacterium *Clostridium botulinus,* the deadliest poison known.

Even parts of common vegetables such as the potato may contain poisonous substances. In May, 1967, the Food Protection Committee of the National Research Council published a booklet, *Toxicants Occurring Naturally in Foods.* Some of the substances listed in the booklet are capable of producing goiter, tumors, and cancer when consumed. Many plant alkaloids that sicken range animals are well known, as is the poppy, which contains opium.

That a substance is naturally occurring is no guarantee of its safety.

I mentioned cyclopentanoperhydropenanthrene as the chemical designation for Vitamin D and Vitamin D-like compounds. When prepared in the laboratory (as it can be by any good senior university student) or extracted from fish oil, no difference can be found when both are fed to animals or people. No differences can be found between them when judged by standard analytical procedures. When Swiss cheese is chemically analyzed, one of the naturally occurring products found is sodium propionate. This is the same chemical used in bread baking to inhibit mold.

Coumarin is a naturally occurring chemical that imparts a unique bouquet to sweet clover, tonka bean, and certain common grasses. It can also be synthesized in the laboratory from acetic anhydride, salicylaldehyde, and sodium acetate. In either case it has proved to be harmful to laboratory test animals and was removed from the list of approved additives after having been used for some years as a vanilla substitute.

Many people who eat fish, tomatoes, or acidic fruits erupt with hives. Their bodies are responding adversely to natural chemicals. Although called *allergy* and at times considered fashionable, this reaction is nevertheless an injury evoked by a natural product. Unfortunately, "natural" or "naturally occurring" is no guarantee of safety; similarly, "synthetic" or man-made is not prima facie evidence of hazard.

No matter whether a chemical is natural, synthetic, intentional, or incidental, the question invariably asked is: Is it poisonous? Before a reliable answer can be given, it is necessary to know what a poison is. If we consider the ancient adage, "One man's poison is another man's porridge," it becomes clear that a poison—a chemical—has variable consequences depending upon the individual involved. This should perhaps suggest that the answer to the question, "Is it poisonous?" is not readily answered by yes or no. Recall the spoiled fish sprinkled with sodium nitrate; when this substance is used in properly prescribed amounts, no problems arise. When greater than prescribed doses are administered, some adults become mildly ill, others so ill as to require hospitalization, while others may not even be uncomfortable. On the other hand, babies often die. Thus, any definition of a poison must consider who is to use it and how much is to be given. In addition, such factors as age, sex, nutritional condition, and general state of health exert much influence on the type and degree of response. Accordingly, everything and nothing can be poisonous depending upon a constellation of factors. Good examples of this concept are aspirin and penicillin, which have a long history of successful use to alleviate pain and infection, respectively. However, overdoses of aspirin are responsible for hundreds of deaths among men and women each year. Aspirin consumption is also the leading cause of accidental poisoning among children aged one to five. Although penicillin, the first broad-spectrum antibiotic, has performed well since its introduction some twenty years ago, increased numbers of severe allergic reactions to its presence in the body (analphylatic shock) are reported each year.

Common table salt is essential to life; yet an "overdose" would probably kill a man if taken over a short time. Many metals such as copper, manganese, zinc, and cobalt are essential to health in trace amounts but become poisonous in larger quantities. Both Vitamins A and D, when taken in doses larger than prescribed, are known to cause severe damage to the human system. Thus, to answer the original question, a poison can be any substance that may cause death or illness when taken in sufficient quantity. This was well known to the Romans, who coined the expression, *"Dosis sola facit veneum"*—"what makes a poison is dose."

A further distinction that must be made is that between *hazard* and *toxicity*. While these terms appear to be used synonymously and interchangeably, in reality they connote totally different ideas. Toxicity is the capacity of a substance to produce injury. Hazard, on the other hand, is the probability that injury will result from the use of the substance, if continued in the manner and amount proposed. Whereas toxicity implies a known fact, hazard is a presumption based upon the statistical likelihood deriving from a number of events or experience that has previously occurred. In short, it is speculative.

Although we are yet quite unaware of the cause of cancer, the fear of it is widespread in our society. Since this is an understandable reaction to the unknown, it is not surprising that there is noisy clamor to prohibit the use in food of any substance however remote the possibility that it is a carcinogen. The reaction of many people when told that a chemical is hazardous—that it has produced cancer in laboratory rats or running fits in puppies—is to shy away from it.

Although this may seem a reasonable reaction, the situation is not as simple or straightforward as it may appear. Such basic nutrients as glucose (dextrose) and sodium chloride have produced cancer in laboratory animals when injected in 20-percent and 15-percent solutions, respectively; yet both are needed for survival.

Rene Dubos recently noted that "according to a recent report, even hens' eggs contain a carcinogenic substance. Chickens and mice fed a diet made up of wheat bran and eggs grew faster and became sexually more mature earlier, but developed cancer of the ovary." He went on to say that "it is unreasonable to insist on zero concentrations of a given substance in food merely because administration of massive doses of it has increased the incidence of tumors in the experimental animals. . . . It is far from simple to evaluate whether the consequences of complete prohibition of a food additive are beneficial to society on balance."

To protect the public from potentially hazardous chemicals, Public Law 85929 was enacted. Also known as the Food Additives Amendment of 1958, it contains the Delaney Clause, which states that "no additive shall be deemed safe if it is found, after tests which are appropriate for the evaluation of safety of food additives, to induce cancer in man or animal." Clearly, any theory or injunction that proscribes the use in food of any chemical producing cancer in animals must be called into question. Too many fundamental nutrients can be shown to be carcinogenic by devising the proper laboratory experiment.

The current concept of protection of the health of the public via food consumption requires that certain additives such as pesticides or other suspected carcinogens be present in zero quantity. What is the meaning of zero tolerance? As analytical techniques become more accurate and precise, what was not measurable today may well be measurable tomorrow. Thus, zero one day can be a positive finite number another. In reality, nothing has changed except the ability to detect and measure smaller quantities. The concentration of an additive in a food has not changed. As a consequence, the concept of zero changing from month to month loses its original meaning and, in fact, has no meaning. As the methods for the detection of additives in biological systems become more sensitive, the investigator needs to become more critical in his interpretation of the significance of these trace levels.

Magnus Pike, writing on "Food Facts and Fallacies" in the *Royal Society of Health Journal* for April, 1967, said:

It is now recognized that to demand what the United States authorities describe as "zero tolerance" is a philosophical impossibility. For a number of years, however, there was a legal demand for officially approved foods to contain zero amounts of certain chemical compounds. Chemical analysis, however, is science not magic. Analytical determinations demand that at the end one drop of reagent shall cause the color to change, to take a simple example. This one drop can represent 1 part per million and allow the analyst to say that this amount is or is not present. Should he develop a method ten times as sensitive, he can say that one-tenth part of a substance under investigation is or is not there. But he can say nothing about less, and no analyst can ever say that the amount of allegedly toxic agent is zero. In order to avoid cross-examination by a lawyer prosecuting on behalf of the public authorities, the best a food manufacturer could do was make sure that his product has not been analyzed at all!

Dr. Pike went on to illustrate the absurdity of this position by noting that

the difficulty of distinguishing wisdom from fallacy when presented with the problem of where to draw the line has been grotesquely high-lighted by an argument about fish flour. This is a product composed of fat-extracted, dried and powdered fish. Incorporated in an impoverished diet, it could contribute protein. The United States Food and Drugs Authority hesitated to approve it as fit for human consumption, not because anybody has ever been harmed by eating it, but because since it contains the viscera of fish and their contents as well as fish muscle, it was classified as "filthy." By a historical anomaly . . . oysters, clams, cockles and mussels, all of which are offered as human food with their digestive parts in them, are accepted as wholesome." [1]

It appears that in a society altered by huge population increases, by women in large numbers going into the labor force and having little time for kitchen chores, and with the great bulk of the population insisting upon a widely diverse selection of foods all the year round, chemicals are a necessary part of our lives. This does not sanction or even suggest that any and all chemicals have a place in foods. It does suggest that as reasonable people we understand the need for their use and we also understand that certain chemicals, after proper testing and proper surveillance, can increase, improve, and preserve our food supply.

In view of the foregoing, it may be helpful to review the criteria used in establishing acceptable daily intakes of any chemical, intentional or incidental.

The Food Protection Committee* of the National Academy of Sciences–National Research Council, a private, non-profit organization of scientists dedicatd to the furtherance of science and its use for the general welfare, has undertaken to study the procedures

* The Food Protection Committee operates under the Food and Nutrition Board, but is independently financed by grants from food, chemical, and packaging companies, commercial laboratories, and individuals.

The Food and Nutrition Board was established in 1940 under the Division of Biology and Agriculture of the NAS-NRC. It serves as an advisory body in the field of food and nutrition, promotes research, and helps interpret nutritional science in the interests of the public welfare. The members of the Board are appointed from among leaders in the food and nutrition sciences on the basis of experience and judgment.

for investigating and evaluating the safety of chemicals used in foods.

Studies of the biological effects on experimental animals of chemicals that may be introduced into the environment have as one of their major objectives the prediction of possible hazard to man. One of the foremost difficulties that arise as a consequence of these animal studies is the interpretation and prediction of safe levels in man. Generally, the aim of toxicity experiments is to obtain acceptable estimates of maximum daily intakes that would be safe for all segments of the population.

To judge the safety of an additive, several factors must be considered. First, the most suitable animal species must be chosen, as no one species can be said to be *the* satisfactory substitute for man. Another factor is information as to the expected amounts and patterns of consumption of the food containing the additive; this is particularly germane and highly variable. An important practical objective is to select animals with short lifespans. This is not a difficult criterion to satisfy, as the only species that are available in large numbers and convenient to house are all rodents: the rat, mouse, hamster, and guinea pig. Both the rat and mouse have been shown to be susceptible to the carcinogenic action of a large variety of chemicals; in fact, most of the current data on the carcinogenic action of chemicals are rodent data.

Because of the difficulties of extrapolating from rodent to man, a non-rodent is often used as a second test type. Although the dog, monkey, and pig have relatively long lives, they are often used.

Toxicity is usually determined on both a short-term and a long-term basis. An estimate of the acute toxicity of a chemical may be obtained relatively rapidly—within a few days to a few weeks—by determining how much of the chemical in a single dose is necessary to kill 50 percent of the test animals—the LD_{50}. The purpose of the acute toxicity test is to obtain a first approximation of the inherent toxic character of the compound. If the proposed level of use of the substance approximates the lethal dose, the tests can be readily concluded and the chemical quickly disapproved.

Experiments to provide an estimation of the effects analogous to lifetime ingestion can be carried out over a period of ninety days. These subacute toxicity tests can serve as guides for selecting feeding levels for the chronic toxicity studies.

Long-term feeding (chronic toxicity) studies are carried out on the premise that the effects of lifetime ingestion of an additive by man cannot be predicted from experiments less rigorous than the total lifespan of a short-lived animal (two to three years).

In a chronic toxicity study using rodents, the chemical is generally fed to three or four groups, each at a different concentration. A control group receiving the same diet minus the additive is always included to avoid confusion of nonspecific effects. Feeding is started as soon as possible after weaning and is continued for at least two years. During the two years of the tests a host of qualitative and quantitative observations are made; these include total food consumption, growth, weight, mortality, chemical analysis of blood and urine, behavior, and reproductive capacity. Parallel tests are usually carried out on dogs to obtain a mammalian response.

The decision as to whether a proposed chemical is safe can be arrived at only after evaluation of several factors: the maximum dietary level which produced no untoward response in both test species; experience with other chemicals of similar structure; and estimation of the potential human consumption of all foods containing the additive.

Dr. Frederick J. Stare put it quite well when he said: "Goodness is still in our foods. The poisons are in the pens and tongues of those who, by peddling misinformation, half-truths, statements out of context, and downright falsehoods gain temporary notoriety, inflate their own egos, and make a profit, or hope to."

It may be more to the point to suggest that we eat too much; that the real food problem is that foods are too abundant, too available, and too inviting for the sedentary life most of us lead.

5

INSECTICIDES

A million men, women and children, fatigued from working round the clock, are plucking the leaf worm and its cocoon and eggs from the cotton leaves in a struggle to save Egypt's cotton crop. At least a quarter of the national crop is believed to have been destroyed already. The final figure is likely to be much higher. A sense of crisis pulses across the cotton-growing lands flanking the River Nile. This week is likely to be crucial in the effort to save the vital crop on which the country's hard-pressed economy so closely depends.

This dispatch from Cairo, in 1966, dramatized the fact that insects have not yet succumbed to man's attempt to protect his crops from their depredations.* The leaf worm and the boll weevil

---

* On June 26, 1967, Cairo radio announced that the cotton-leaf worm was ravaging the cotton crop. This time, little if any insecticide was available. Thousands of children were ordered into the fields to pick the worms by hand from the cotton plants.

are so resistant to chemical insecticides that the only sure method of destroying them is by hand-picking.

Insects pose a real threat to our food, fiber, health, and comfort, and must be contained. Unfortunately, nature does not go out of her way to favor man. We live as one of the many species inhabiting this planet and must struggle as best we can with nature's laws.

Fortunately for us, however, we are endowed with the intelligence to regulate our environment to our advantage. Our handling of this enormous problem may suggest how intelligent we really are. Of course, the insects start with a great advantage; they have evolved over some 250 million years, compared to our one million years. This seniority has led to some remarkable survival characteristics that have attuned them almost perfectly to their ecological niche. Their ability to adapt to a hostile environment was seen in the resistance they displayed to chemical agents they had never before encountered. How resourceful we humans will be remains to be seen.

Insects and other arthropods* are all around us: they live in our houses, puncture our skin, and consume our food and clothing. There is scarcely a place on the planet that is not home to at least one insect. They have been found in deep underground caves, and termites have been trapped at altitudes of twenty thousand

---

* When we speak of insects and arthropods, we refer to specific forms. True insects differ in several major characteristics from other arthropods. True insects have three body parts: head, thorax, and abdomen; three pairs of legs; usually two pair of wings; and one pair of antennae. Ticks and mites, on the other hand, have a sac-like body with no segmentation, four pairs of legs, and no antennae. They are not true insects. All arthropods (*arthros*=joint-legged) are classified as follows:

PHYLUM ARTHROPODA

Class Crustacea:	crabs, shrimps, barnacles
Insects:	ants, bees, flies, mosquitoes, beetles, wasps, lice, roaches, aphids, moths, fleas, termites, and locusts (to note a few)
Arachnida:	spiders, scorpions, ticks, mites
Chilopoda:	centipedes, millipedes

feet. Some forty varieties live in the Antarctic region; mosquitoes and other biting insects penetrate the polar regions as far as the warm-blooded animals on which they feed. Insects are abundant in desert areas and in rushing waters. Different species are adapted for life in the air, on land, in soil, and in fresh water, brackish water (1-percent salt), or salt water (3-percent salt). Wherever they live, they seem to be indestructible. Man has never eradicated a single insect species from the earth. In fact, a number exhibit increased resistance to chemical agents designed specifically for their destruction. Insects have been frozen solid at $-35°C$ and have still lived. Others inhabit hot springs where temperatures reach $50°C$ (120 to 125°F). Petroleum flies spend part of their lives in pools of crude oil around well heads. Many insects can endure long periods without water; they possess fuel reserves and can get the water they require by metabolizing carbohydrates to carbon dioxide and water.

Insects have an enormous size range—probably greater than any other major animal group. The smallest, approximately 250 microns, are smaller than some single-celled protozoa; the largest are larger than mice. The Atlas moth of India measures twelve inches from wing tip to wing tip.

Why are insects so successful? Their success as a group seems to be due to at least six major assets:

1. *Adaptability*: As previously noted, they can live within a wide range of environmental conditions. They can eat anything—corks, mummies, tobacco, cotton, paper, etc.

2. *External skeleton**: Their cylindrical shape offers the strongest possible construction for a given amount of material. Being wax-coated, it is resistant to drying from inside and outside.

3. *Small size*: As a consequence of their usually small size, their food and water needs are comparatively quite small.

4. *Ability to fly*: Wings allow wide distribution and thus greater choice of food and environment and escape from predators.

* The exoskeleton or cuticle contains a polysaccharide, chitin, which is made up of a series of glucosamine units, joined by beta-linkages, which imparts structural integrity.

5. *Metamorphosis*: This is the gradual change in form or structure that occurs during its developmental period. Three types of insects are recognized: Some, such as flies, mosquitos, and moths, undergo complete metamorphosis, consisting of four stages—egg, larva, pupa, and adult. In those insects that undergo incomplete metamorphosis, with egg, nymph, and adult, several nymphal stages can occur in which the insect simply grows larger. Cockroaches, grasshoppers, and body lice are examples of this type. The third type exhibits no metamorphic development. The young possess all the features of the adult; they simply increase in size. The silverfish, a primitive type of insect, is an example of this type of development. These various types of metamorphosis confer enormous survival value, as each stage is often spent in a different environment. Thus, the insect is not dependent upon a single food supply, nor one set of environmental conditions. (While these types of metamorphosis serve the insects, they also permit a variety of methods for controlling insect populations.)

6. Specialized system of reproduction: After mating the female can often delay fertilization until the proper food supply and environmental conditions are located. When mating occurs, the sperm from the male is stored in a special sac; when conditions are favorable, the sperm are released for fertilization. This mechanism has extraordinary survival value.

Thus it can be seen that after 250 million years insects have evolved their own bag of tricks to frustrate our attempts at preventing them from taking our food supply or making us ill.

Although the number of insect species is between 670,000 and 1,250,000, the number of insect pests is relatively small; less than 900 types attack humans, animals, and plants. Of the 900, by far the largest number are agricultural pests. It has been estimated that the yearly loss in food crops in the U. S. approximates three billion dollars. Until the advent of chemical pesticides, it was evident that the battle for the food supply between man and insects was being won by the insects. Crops, like humans, are susceptible to disease and injury, which either destroy them completely or reduce their food-yielding capacity. In 1963, the corn borer was responsible for reducing the available corn supply by 120,-648,000 bushels. Because plants cannot as yet be vaccinated against disease, (this may be a possibility by 1978) the next best thing to do is to spray them with chemicals to keep them healthy and edible or productive. Figures 7 and 8 show the depredations

FIGURE 7. Khapra beetle larvae feeding on powdered milk. Note caking.

of foods by insects. Figure 7 shows Khapra beetle larvae in powdered milk, while Figure 8 shows them in lima beans.

Trees and plants are susceptible to over fifteen hundred diseases. Together, the loss in food crops and trees is placed at ten to fifteen billion dollars annually. In addition, carpet beetles, silver-

FIGURE 8. Khapra beetles feeding on lima beans

fish, and moths destroy another two hundred million dollars worth of property. The losses from termite destruction are far higher. Before chemical insecticides were introduced, millions of people in the world died each year from a host of insect-borne diseases. Table 5 lists examples of plant and human diseases transmitted by insects and ticks. Before the availability of chemical insecticides, malaria alone killed millions each year. For example, the case rate in 1955 was estimated to be 250 million. By 1962, it had dropped to 140 million, and by 1967 there were less than 100 million cases. Figure 9 indicates the dramatic effectiveness of DDT against typhus, a disease of rats transmitted to man by the bite of the rat flea. It is clearly seen how the application of this chemi-

TABLE 5.

*Examples of diseases transmitted
by insects and ticks*

DISEASE	TRANSMITTING ARTHROPOD	TYPE OF DISEASE AGENT
Dutch elm	Bark beetle	Fungus
Cucumber wilt	Cucumber Beetle	Bacterium
Curly top of sugar beet	Beet leaf hopper	Virus
Yellow fever	Mosquito	Virus
Bubonic plague	Flea	Bacterium
Malaria	Mosquito	Protozoan
Typhus	Louse and flea	Rickettsia
Tularemia	Fly and tick	Bacterium
Encephalitis	Mosquito	Virus
Filariasis	Mosquito	Nematode worm
Rocky Mountain spotted fever	Tick	Rickettsia
Texas cattle fever	Tick	Protozoan
Chagas disease (South American sleeping sickness)	Giant bedbug	Protozoan
Dog tapeworm	Louse and flea	Worm

cal precipitously reduced the number of cases of typhus. Similar charts could be presented for relapsing fever, yellow fever, smallpox, cholera, and bubonic plague.

Figure 10 shows the direct application of DDT to a child in a village in Afghanistan, in order to prevent typhus and malaria. Figure 11 shows the use of DDT on the walls of a home in Mexico. This type of treatment leaves a residue on the wall that remains effective for up to three months. Mosquitos that seek a blood meal indoors alight on the DDT-treated walls and pick up the chemical on their legs. In the process of cleaning their legs with their mouth parts, they swallow the insecticide, which acts as a stomach poison.

It has been suggested that the prosperity of a country is inversely proportional to the time and effort required to produce

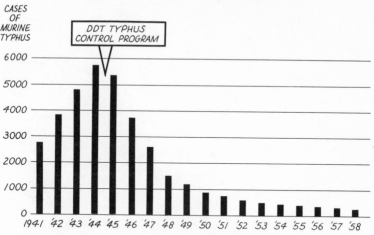

FIGURE 9. Effect of DDT on the incidence of typhus

the necessities of life. In 1913, for example, it took about 135 to 140 man-hours to produce one hundred bushels of corn. Today, one hundred bushels can be obtained in 15 hours. Approximately 8 percent of our labor force produces our food needs, leaving 92 percent to work elsewhere. Time-consuming manual methods of weed control, requiring the labor of many people, have been eliminated through the application of chemical weed-killers by tractor-drawn sprayers. It is also important to bear in mind that by the year 2000, just thirty-one years from now, the population of this country will be between 350 and 450 million, which will mean two mouths to feed for every one in 1960. It must be done on less and less arable land each year. It has been well established that chemical insecticides and herbicides not only increase yield per acre, but also increase grade or quality.

Barnyard grass, a weed that bears a striking similarity to rice, is easily killed by most herbicides; but so is the rice. The presence of one barnyard grass plant per square foot will reduce the yield of rice by one thousand pounds per acre. A new chemical, Propa-

FIGURE 10. Direct application of DDT in a village in Afghanistan

nil, applied within eight days after barnyard grass germinates, essentially eliminates it. In the three years since its introduction the national rice yield has increased from three thousand pounds per acre to over four thousand.

If we are to eat, remain relatively disease free, and prosper, the insects' freedom must be interdicted. At this point in our technological development, chemical pesticides are the only significant means of interdiction at our disposal.

Five classes of chemical pesticides are generally recognized:

1. *Naturally Occurring (Plant) Products:* For years, extracts, dusts, and smoke from the dried heads of the chrysanthemum have been used as insecticides. Pyrethrin I and II are the active agents in these formulations. Rotenone and nicotine are examples of other natural products.

2. *Inorganics:* These are preparations containing such metals as lead, copper, zinc, arsenic, and mercury as the insecticidal ingredient. In the early 1870's Paris green, an arsenical (copper aceto-arsenite), was used to control the codling moth in apple and pear orchards. Bordeaux mixture, a compound containing copper, was first used in 1882, as a fruit spray. Currently, inorganic, metal-based insecticides are not widely used, having been superseded by the organic compounds. However, in cases where resistance to organics has arisen, the inorganics may again be of value.

3. *Chlorinated Organics:* The best known and most widely used of the synthetic organic insecticides is DDT (dichlorodiphenyltrichloroethane). Although it was first prepared in 1879, its insecticidal value was not discovered until 1937. The modern era of chemical control began with the commercial introduction of DDT in 1946; it had first been used on a large scale in World War II to combat typhus in military and civilian populations. Some other members of this group of insecticides are benzene hexachloride (BHC), methoxychlor, dieldrin, chlordane, and heptachlor. All are barely sparingly soluble in water and several are more potent than DDT.

4. *Organophosphorus Compounds:* This new group of in-

secticides was originated during World War II by Gerhard Schrader, a German chemist, who was searching for more potent agents of chemical warfare. Such compounds as parathion, malathion, and diazinon are highly toxic to insects. All of these are poorly soluble in water but readily so in aromatic hydrocarbons and vegetable oils. They are highly effective in extremely small quantities against a wide variety of insects.

5. *Petroleum Oil Fractions*: These oils are generally used alone or in combination with one of the other classes of insecticides. They have proven most useful as mosquito larvicides. The oils are applied as a thin film on the surface of water of mosquito-breeding sites. The larvae coming to the surface to feed or breathe contact the oil film, which penetrates the breathing tube (trachea) and kills by suffocation or poisoning.

This brings us to the fact that insecticides do not all act in the same way, and for good reason: insects do not all feed in the same way, no do they attack the same parts of plants, and their habits are markedly different. For these reasons, insecticides must be developed to perform a specific function. Thus, the five groups of insecticides are also categorized by the way they get into the insect's body cavity. Stomach poisons must be swallowed or absorbed through the gut; this restricts their use to insects whose mouth parts are suitable for biting, sucking, or lapping food. Contact poisons enter through the cuticle or skin, and thus must be fat-soluble, while fumigants enter the respiratory system through the spiracles, the external openings of the trachea. Although insecticides have been categorized as to what types of substances they contain and how they enter the insect's body, neither of these categories should be confused with the mechanism by which the insecticide kills or stuns. For example, pyrethrin penetrates through the cuticle, but it causes paralysis by blocking nerve impulses in the insect's central nervous system. Rotenone appears to cause paralysis of the breathing mechanism. Paris green, a stomach poison, is considered a general protoplasmic poison which disrupts several enzyme systems. Lindane, a chlorinated organic, is a fumigant, entering via the spiracles, while DDT is classed as a contact insecticide; both appear to affect the peripheral nervous system and muscle tissue of insects. The organophosphorus compounds are powerful contact insecticides that inhibit the action of cholinesterase, thereby preventing the normal mechanism of nerve-impulse transmission.

In 1962, 194 million acres of land were treated with three-quarters of a billion to one billion pounds of a host of insecticides. Nearly one acre in ten has been treated with an average of about four pounds per acre. By 1966, the outlay for insecticides and herbicides in the U.S. had reached one billion dollars.

There is no doubt that the question of the use and accumulation of pesticides is dangerous to health is an important one. I think it is necessary to accept one important fact: safety is a negative condition, that is, it is the absence of hazard. Actually, no amount of research or study will ever provide absolute assurance of safety. It is possible, however, to assure practical certainty of safety. People vary over wide ranges with respect to their sensitivity to chemicals. Some people are hypersensitive to aspirin, others to penicillin. This does not prevent the beneficial use of these drugs by millions of others who are not sensitive.

Care should be exercised in using pesticides. Their chemical and physiological characteristics must be studied and understood so that they can be employed in the smallest quantity that will achieve the desired effect. It is estimated that the annual death rate from all types of pesticides is about 150 persons per year. This is primarily due to acute poisoning. Unfortunately, one-half to three-quarters of these deaths are in young children who, playing in kitchens or garages where pesticides may be stored, manage to open and eat these chemicals. An occupational hazard appears to exist for spray pilots, greenhouse workers, and those working directly in the production of insecticides. On the other hand, chronic or long-term, low-level contact is decidedly more complicated. For example, it has been well publicized that DDT has an affinity for fatty tissue and that hardly anyone is free of DDT. This has been cited as evidence that we are being "poisoned" by the accumulation of pesticides in the environment. That fact is that the U.S. Public Health Service has made it quite clear that "there is no well described case of fatal uncomplicated DDT poisoning"

FIGURE 11. Application of DDT to the walls of a hut in a Mexican village. Residual concentrations on walls remain effective against malarial mosquitoes for up to three months.

resulting from proper use. Cases do exist of people who died after swallowing DDT solutions, but I must consider that akin to placing one's head inside an oven and turning on the gas. Figure 12 indicates the death rate per 100,000 people for a half-dozen non-infectious diseases, and their relationship to DDT. The slope of the curves suggests that leukemia was on the rise long before DDT was introduced and continued to rise at the same rate after its introduction. Thus, one would not tend to implicate DDT as a factor in leukemia. Hodgkin's disease and agranulocytosis show a similar lack of correlation. For purpura and aplastic anemia there is too little data collected before 1948 to yield meaningful interpretation.

As with air pollution and pollution by ionizing radiation,

DEATH RATE PER 100,000 POPULATION

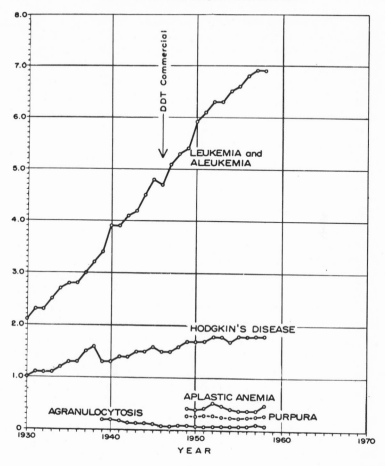

SOURCE: *Vital Statistics of the United States*

FIGURE 12. Effect of the commercial introduction of DDT on several non-infectious illnesses

many believe that the accumulation of pesticides in the environment causes actual and potential harm in the form of residues ingested in food and water, or inhaled with each breath; others maintain that the effects of long-term low-level exposure are unknown. At this stage of our knowledge, both views must be considered. Consequently, the most reasonable course balances benefit against risk. By determining the amount of pollutant (whatever it may be) that a given population can be expected to contact, an estimation of the risk of injury may be calculated. By estimating dividends accruing to the community from the use of pesticides, ionizing radiation, or the processes that release polluting effluents to the atmosphere, benefit can be calculated. When both are "known," perhaps an acceptable accord between benefit and risk can be established.

A more concrete problem that can be readily corrected is the inefficient and wasteful application of pesticides. The recent White House Conference on Environmental Pollution [1] pointed out that only 10 to 20 percent of insecticides applied as dusts and 25 to 50 percent applied as sprays is deposited on plant surfaces where it can be effective against pests. Under the best conditions, the report noted, present methods waste 50 to 75 percent of the insecticide, which drifts away to become an undesirable environmental contaminant. Much research is needed to curtail or prevent this inadvertent contamination. A second requirement is the development of pesticides with molecular structures capable of degradation by microorganisms. Too many commercially available pesticides persist in soil and water because bacteria and fungi are incapable of using them as a source of nutrition; the chemical structure of the pesticide does not offer the bacteria a "handle." Chemists must make chemicals that the microbes can digest.

All these considerations have given impetus to the development of methods of biological control which are based on the fixed behavior of insect pests and on the fact that certain insect species are natural enemies of others, upon which they feed. In either case, chemicals are not used and, consequently, environmental contamination does not occur.

Many insects locate their food supplies, their mating partners, and favorable sites to lay eggs by built-in automatic responses to chemicals emanating from these sources. The three types of chemical stimuli are known as food attractants, sex attractants, and oviposition lures.

Food attractants are probably responsible for the fact that certain insect species feed only on a specific plant or animal host. For example, the boll weevil feeds almost exclusively on the cotton plant. It has recently been found that volatile substances released into the atmosphere by the cotton plant enable the weevil to find the plant, its food supply. Attempts are currently being made to isolate and identify these substances. Their use to lead insects to capture and death would be a major step forward. Once the insect is led to the food supply by the food lure, other chemical components of the food source may induce or stimulate the insect to begin feeding. Recently, a synthetic feeding lure, methyl eugenol, which attracts only male flies, was used in combination with an insecticide to eradicate the oriental fruit fly from the island of Rota in the Pacific.

Sex attractants, the second type of stimulant, are chemicals emitted by one of the sexes, usually the female, to attract the males for mating. Males may be lured upwind over distances as far apart as two miles. These attractants are extremely potent—they require only trace amounts and are wholly species-specific. Male bees, for example, do not respond to female butterflies. Thus far, the chemical structure of the sex attractants of the gypsy moth and the silkworm have been determined. This is useful in attracting these insects in order to determine the degree of their infestation in some area.

In the case of the gypsy moth, a synthetic homolog, gyplure, has been synthesized and found to be almost as efficient as the natural product. A sex lure has been isolated from the male cockroach (*Periplaneta americana*) that is so powerful that females respond to it in concentrations as low as 10^{-14} micrograms—approximately thirty molecules of the substance!

A third type of attractant, oviposition lures, induce the female to lay eggs (oviposit) on materials that serve as food for the larvae.

Another recent approach to insect control is based on the use of chemosterilants—chemicals capable of producing sexual sterility in insects. Ideally, a chemosterilant should have no effect on the insect other than to prevent the hatching of eggs, that is, it should cause the insect to produce infertile eggs. Use of chemosterilants eliminated the screwworm fly (*Cochliomyia hominovorax*) from Texas, Florida, and Curacao. In this program male screwworm flies were sterilized by gamma irradiation from a cobalt-60 source. The sterile-male technique* has three important advantages over the conventional application of chemical pesticides. In the first place, it is highly selective, involving only a specific insect while leaving all other forms, (insects, worms, birds, plants, etc.) undisturbed. In addition, the target species cannot acquire immunity to sterile mating, as it too often does to chemicals. Finally, chemical agents often become less efficient as the population against which it is being used declines. As a consequence, the few survivors can begin to rebuild their decimated ranks. On the other hand, the sterile-male procedure becomes even more efficient as the population dwindles.

The adult female screwworm fly lays a mass of two hundred to three hundred eggs in the wounds of cattle, sheep, goats, or horses. Any wound, accidental or surgical, a tick bite, or the navel of a new born animal can be an egg-laying site. From twelve to twenty-four hours later, maggots (larvae) hatch and begin to feed on the flesh of the wound. The feeding causes an additional bloody discharge that attracts more flies for egg-laying. Death of the animal is inevitable unless it is found and treated. Even though treatment can save the animal, the hide will have holes and blemishes that reduces its value, and the irritation caused to cattle in particular serves to reduce milk production. Before the elimination of screwworm flies from this area in 1959, the economic loss to industry in the southwestern part of the U.S. amounted to about twenty-five million dollars annually.

With the sterilization procedure, thousands to millions of fly eggs are collected on screens or in troughs. The eggs are placed on an artificial food until the larvae emerge. The larvae are reared through pupation. The pupae, in plastic containers, are placed in a gamma cell to be exposed to radiation from a cobalt-60 source. The radiation is sufficient to sterilize them without greatly reducing

* Although this is called the sterile-male technique, in actual fact both sexes are sterilized and released, because the cost of separating the sexes in mass-reared species is prohibitive.

their activity. After sterilization the pupae are placed in paper bags, in which they develop into adult flies. These bags of flies are placed into dispersing tubes aboard an airplane. The dispersing tube can handle one bag every two to three seconds and thus is capable of dispersing millions of flies over a wide area. Air streaming through the dispersing tube whips the bag out of the tube. As it leaves the tube, the bag is slashed by a hinged knife; the bag sticks on a hook for a moment and the flies are scattered.

This technique, a modification of that used to eradicate the screwworm fly in 1959, is now being used in an attempt to eradicate another insect pest.

The Mediterranean fruit fly lays its eggs in the peel of fruit, and the maggots (larvae) penetrate to the meat. Even where the eggs do not develop, the hole caused by the fly's sting leads to decay. Some countries prohibit imports from areas infected by the fly.

In 1955, the Mediterranean fruit fly (*Ceratitis capitata*) appeared in Costa Rica. It spread from there to El Salvador, Guatemala, Honduras, Nicaragua, and Panama, despite all attempts to contain it. It is feared that unless it is brought under control, the annual loss in fruit crop could exceed eighty million dollars. On July 1, 1965, a three-year project was launched to demonstrate the feasibility of eradicating the fruit fly with the help of radiation and the sterile-male method.

In April, 1966, the Agro-Technical Division of the Government of Israel's Citrus Board announced that it would be sending millions of sterile male flies to the island of Capri in an attempt to eradicate the Mediterranean fruit fly. It was expected that by the fall of 1967, some one hundred million flies would have been sterilized at the nuclear reactor in Nahal Sorek, Israel, then flown to Capri, and released. It is anticipated that a successful eradication campaign will be accomplished, as Capri is an island and not subject to continuous reinfestation from infected neighboring countries.

Knowledge of chemical attractants suggest ways in which an insect's responses may be used against it. Used in traps, the attractants can be employed to detect and estimate insect populations; to delineate areas of infestation; to ascertain when insecticide applications should begin and end; and to detect accidental introduction of foreign pests via international transportation, such as recently occurred in El Salvador. San Salvador, the capital of El Salvador, had been free of yellow fever since 1959. In 1965, *Aedes aegypti,* the mosquito carrying the virus of yellow fever, was detected in the city. The mosquito's eggs were apparently reintroduced in used tires imported from abroad. Rainwater trapped in the hollow tires were the breeding pools for the mosquito. *Aedes aegypti* is a fast-breeding type of mosquito, and in several months it had infested all of San Salvador plus about twenty-five localities ringing it.

Attractants could be used to lure harmful insects to limited and selected areas where they would be deprived of their natural food supply or subjected to the action of insecticides or chemosterilants. Feeding stimulants might be incorporated into insecticides or chemosterilant preparations to induce insects to feed on these harmful substances. Oviposition lures might be used to induce egg-laying in non-nutrient materials where the developing young would starve. It has also been suggested that spraying a sex attractant over a wide area might confuse the males in their attempt to find the females.

Unfortunately, most of these techniques will remain laboratory curiosities until many questions are answered. This requires trained investigators, time, and money. But answers will come.

Another potentially useful phase of biological control is natural control, by which one species is used to exterminate, reduce, or maintain constant the population of another species. The observation that species do not increase indefinitely in numbers and distribution is based on the checks one species imposes on another. The Arabs of Yemen, for example, have for hundreds of years used predaceous ants to protect date palms from other harmful ants. Each year the date growers of Yemen bring down from the mountains colonies of the beneficial ants and place them in palm trees, where they eat the ants that feed on the palms.

The study of natural control of pest populations is that part of ecology which attempts to understand how potential population increase is limited and more or less stabilized by environmental factors. Natural control can be defined as the maintenance of a certain population density of an organism—within certain definable upper and lower limits—over a period of time by the actions of abiotic or biotic environmental factors. The upper and lower limits will change appreciably only if the actions of the regulatory factors are changed, or if certain ones are eliminated or new ones added. Natural control is, therefore, an essentially permanent condition, as opposed to chemical control, which reduces populations only temporarily unless indefinitely repeated. Darwin's term "struggle for existence" is what we now call natural control. Biological control, a phase of natural control, is the action of parasites, predators, or pathogens in maintaining another organism's population density at a lower level than would otherwise occur.

The fact that an organism achieves and maintains pest status makes it obvious that climatic and other ecological factors are favorable to its prosperity. Thus, it reasonably follows that to curtail or depress its density, a modification in environment or ecological relationship is needed. Natural enemies are such a means.

Snails, fish, amphibians, birds, and mammals have been used from time to time to control economic pests. Insects that prey on other insects (entomophagous species) and microbes that initiate infection and disease have also been used. In 1965, as an experiment, the state of Florida imported several sea cows (manatees) to check the growth of aquatic plants that had made navigation all but impossible in their inland waterways. Both chemical and physical treatments had proven useless. By 1966, the manatees were reported to have done such a good job of weed control that several more were imported.

Currently, the greatest activity in natural control efforts centers on microbial agents. In particular, bacterial infections appear to offer the most hope for a commercially feasible product.

A bacterium, *Bacillus thuringiensis,* originally isolated from a diseased flour moth in Thuringen, Germany, in 1911, appears to be pathogenic to 110 species of moths and 8 species of flies. It is currently recommended for the widespread control of the cabbage looper, the alfalfa caterpillar, and the tobacco hornworm. This bacterium produces a diamond-shaped proteinaceous crystal that destroys the gut lining of many insects. It was selected for commercial use because of its ability to grow readily in large numbers on artificial sources of food. The preparations are made to be used as either a dust or a spray which the insect must ingest, and which acts as a stomach poison that eventually produces paralysis and death. Although this product has not been widely accepted because of the equivocal results obtained, new formulations are being readied that are expected to produce more uniform results.

The most outstanding example of pest control by a microbial pathogen is milky disease of the Japanese beetle (*Popillia japonicum*), which generally infests and destroys vegetables and fruit. The beetle grub (larva) ingests *Bacillus popilliae*,[2] and the bacterium multiplies in the insect's gut. The blood of the infected grub becomes milky-white, and it loses its activity and dies.

In the commercial preparation, spores of *Bacillus popilliae* are mixed with powder to be broadcast over soil. The larvae of beetles or other susceptible insects ingest the spores and are destroyed within two weeks by milky disease. Applied to turf in the eastern part of the U.S., the preparation has provided excellent control of the Japanese beetle. The spores of *Bacillus popilliae* persist for long periods in soil and achieve long-term control of the beetles.

Natural methods of control have intrigued the public for many years. Some mistakenly believe this type of control can entirely supersede chemical insecticides and thereby put an end to such concerns as insect resistance, chemical residues in food, and harm to wildlife. But it is in the natural order of life that nature provides for the survival of both beneficial and destructive insects. The destructive insect is actually a creation of man, who provides the environmental conditions necessary for an insect to become a pest. There is also no guarantee that a predator introduced to check a pest population will not itself become a pest; and as had been so dramatically demonstrated in Australia, a pest can develop immunity to a microbe. The myxoma virus was introduced into Australia from England to eradicate the rabbit population, which had become a severe economic threat. In the first year of the virus' dissemination, rabbits fell ill and died in great numbers. By the third year it became evident that the rabbit population had developed an immunity to the disease, myxomatosis, and was rebuilding is decimated ranks.

In June, 1967, the World Health Organization and the Pan-American Health Organization met in Washington, D. C., to review the state of insect insecticides.

It was noted that although the sterile-male technique had proved so successful with the screwworm fly and the Mediterranean fruit fly, it had little success with mosquitoes. Apparently, gamma-irradiated sterile male mosquitoes did not compete as well for the female as did their non-sterile counterparts. Consequently, enough fertile unions occur to maintain significant population levels. However, a new technique was reported that may yet eradicate certain species of mosquito on a local level. Field trials of the new technique were successfully held in Rangoon, Burma. Each day scientists released five thousand male mosquitoes obtained from Fresno, California. Although they were the same species as the Rangoon mosquito, *Culex pipiens fatigans,* there were sufficient genetic differences between the two to prevent normal conception; fertilization produced no living progeny. In twelve weeks, the Rangoon species was eliminated from the area.

Dr. Rajindar Pal of the World Health Organization suggested that this species difference would probably be found for other forms and could result in the control of insect carriers of many important diseases.

At this meeting, Dr. George B. Craig of Notre Dame University proposed yet another approach for controlling insect pests. His method, thus far still a laboratory experiment, calls for the breeding of insect strains that have an abnormally increased genetic tendency to produce male offspring. Certain mosquitoes are known to produce ninety-five males for each one hundred fertilized eggs. Because of the precipitous shortage of females, these insects breed themselves into extinction within a few generations.

Although natural control offers many advantages, we cannot look for an early end to the use of chemicals; our knowledge of the pests is not yet great enough.

CHAPTER

6

ZOONOSES:
DISEASES OF ANIMALS
TRANSMISSIBLE TO MAN

Yetlington is a tiny farming village in the north of England and not the most likely place for history to be made. But Bob Brewis lived in Yetlington, and he made history in December, 1966, when foot-and-mouth disease ravaged the area.

Although foot-and-mouth disease is one of the most contagious infections of cattle, sheep, goats, and pigs, world attention would not have focused so sharply on Yetlington had not Brewis become involved.

During the height of the epizootic,* Bob became ill. He reportedly told his physician that he felt groggy and thought he was getting the flu. On examination, the blisters characteristic of foot-and-mouth disease were found in his mouth. Laboratory examination of the blister fluid confirmed the presence of the virus. Bob Brewis had foot-and-mouth disease, the first case ever reported in

* An epizootic is a disease of epidemic proportions among animals.

a human. To make matters worse, *he* had to be quarantined to prevent *his* infecting the remaining healthy animals in Yetlington.

Animals and man have lived in close association for thousands of years. Man has used animals for food, clothing, and shelter, and has taken animals into his home to warn him of danger, control rodents, and serve as a companion for his family. The friendship of men with animals, especially dogs and horses, has been immortalized in the songs and stories of many lands. The breeding and selling of domestic animals and the commercial processing of animal products are fundamental to the economy of many countries.

In these close associations between men and animals, man has exposed himself to their diseases. When animals are brought into living quarters, exposure becomes even more thorough. Members of the household play with, hug, kiss, and occasionally share food and bed with domestic animals. As increased leisure time permits more people to camp out, more contact with wild animals is made, and as we push our communities further into sylvan areas, additional new contacts are made. By living in such close proximity, it is not surprising that man contracts illnesses from the many animals around him. The animal world must be considered a constant reservoir of various infections that can be transmitted to man either directly, or through the agency of biting insects, or by the consumption of food derived from infected animals.

To veterinarians and other public health scientists, diseases of animals transmissible to man are called zoonoses: some one hundred are known. (The reverse is also true: man can transmit certain infections to animals.) Table 6 lists some of the more common zoonoses.

Not only has man's welfare been endangered by epidemics of animal diseases, but colonization of many areas has been restricted by his inability to control certain zoonoses. A dramatic example of this can be seen in Central Africa, where African sleeping sickness (Gambian fever) has prevented the use of hundreds of thousands of acres of arable land; this is the tsetse-fly belt.

TABLE 6.

Some major zoonoses

viral	bacterial
rabies	arthrax (wool sorter's disease)
encephalitis	brucellosis (undulant fever)
cat-scratch fever	leptospirosis
ornithosis-psitticosis	tularemia (rabbit fever)
	tuberculosis
	diphtheria
	salmonellosis

rickettsial	fungal
Q-fever	ringworm
spotted fever	tinea corporis—body
typhus	tinea capitis—scalp
	tinea pedis—foot
	histoplasmosis
	coccidioidomycosis (San Joaquin fever)

protozoal

scabies (the itch)
toxoplasmosis
American leishmaniasis (Chiclero ulcer, espundia)
trypanosomiasis (Chagas' disease)

helminthic

hydatidosis
taeniasis (beef tapeworm)
trichinosis (pork tapeworm)

During World War II, the pressing need for South American rubber galvanized efforts to clean out the heretofore uninhabitable yellow fever mosquito areas, in order that additional rubber trees be planted and cultivated. Cost was not a consideration. In other circumstances, the cost might well have been considered prohibitive, and the effort would not have been made.

This interaction is not without its benefits. The fact that certain illnesses are shared commonly by animals and man makes it possible to use animals in experimental biochemical research and for the production of vaccines used to immunize both animals and man against a host of communicable diseases.

Even as our society moves inexorably from an agricultural to a technological environment, the health of animals and the health and well-being of man remain closely linked. This may be seen in the numbers of domestic animals that play an intricate part in our lives. Bear in mind that these are probably low estimates. Table 7 indicates the number and type of household pets in the U.S.

TABLE 7.

Household pets in the U.S.

Dogs	
Cats	
Parakeets	
Canaries	
Finches	75,000,000
Turtles	
Monkeys	
Skunks	

Table 8 indicates the number of domestic animals, including an estimate of dogs and cats, both pet and stray.

TABLE 8.

Domestic animals in the U.S.

Cattle	100,000,000
Hogs	57,000,000
Sheep	31,500,000
Goats	4,020,000
Horses	
Mules	3,100,000
Dogs	24,135,000
Cats	22,100,000

It is obvious that there are far more domestic animals than people. If to these are added the great number and variety of wild animals, such as oppossum, rats, foxes, raccoons, wolves, deer, rabbits, and bats, it becomes clear that animals far exceed people and that animals must play a significant role in our lives.*

Zoonoses do not occur with equal frequency around the country. Of the hundred known to be transmissible to man, forty-nine are known to occur in the southern states, forty-six in Texas alone. Although brucellosis (undulant fever) occurs chiefly in Illinois, Iowa, Nebraska, and Kansas, where raw milk and dairy products abound and large numbers of carcasses are handled, it is a problem not only in rural areas; 41 percent of the cases reported in 1957 occurred in urban areas. On the other hand, tularemia (it is sometimes called rabbit fever but can occur in many rodents) is found primarily in the rural areas of Missouri, Arkansas, and the Gulf Coast states, where squirrels, rabbits, and other rodents are hunted and trapped. The virus of rabies, once thought to be transmitted solely by the bite of rabid dogs, is now known to be disseminated by bats, foxes, skunks, and raccoons. These four species are concentrated from the East Coast westward to the Central states.

Of particular importance for those concerned with the prevention and control of zoonoses is the observation that many exhibit marked seasonal fluctuations. For example, the several types of arthropod-borne encephalitis (St. Louis encephalitis, Western equine encephalitis, eastern equine encephalitis) principally occur from July to October, whereas the incidence of brucellosis climbs sharply between April and August. Leptospirosis appears to begin its rise in May, peak in July, and fade as fall approaches. This pattern is unique in the U.S.; the disease has a different pattern in Vietnam, for example, where the conditions promoting its survival and passage are singularly distinctive.

For convenience, animal diseases transmissible to man are divided into two major categories: those occupationally induced and those transmitted to the general public in a variety of ways. Of

---

* See Chapter 9, Solid-Waste Disposal, for a discussion of the problem of water pollution via animal excrement.

course, microbes don't read books and consequently are not aware of what is expected of them: thus there are overlaps in which a disease agent normally of occupational origin infects an individual having nothing to do with that industry or occupation.

Leptospirosis is a disease that overlaps both categories. For the most part, it occurs in sewage-plant operators, miners, and agricultural laborers raising such crops as rice and sugarcane by irrigation. Children, on the other hand, become infected when swimming in stagnant or slow-moving ponds, usually in farm areas. The infecting bacterium is passed into water via cattle, rodent, or dog urine. The microbe, a corkscrew-shaped organism, enters the human body either through breaks in the skin or by penetrating the mucous membranes lining the nose and eyes. Nine cases occurred in one family as a consequence of infection by the family dog. Figure 13 shows the six major sources of infection by

SOURCES OF LEPTOSPIROSIS INFECTION

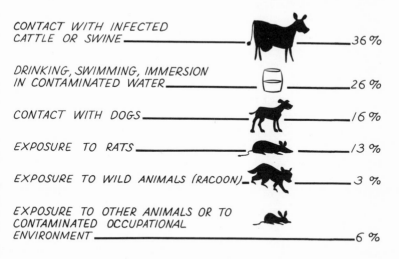

CONTACT WITH INFECTED
CATTLE OR SWINE _____ 36%

DRINKING, SWIMMING, IMMERSION
IN CONTAMINATED WATER _____ 26%

CONTACT WITH DOGS _____ 16%

EXPOSURE TO RATS _____ 13%

EXPOSURE TO WILD ANIMALS (RACOON) _____ 3%

EXPOSURE TO OTHER ANIMALS OR TO
CONTAMINATED OCCUPATIONAL
ENVIRONMENT _____ 6%

SOURCE: *Vital Statistics of the United States*

FIGURE 13. Major sources of infection by leptospires

leptospires. The precipitous rise of leptospirosis in May and June corresponds to the period of use of the "old swimming hole" in which animals have passed urine. A high incidence of leptospirosis has occurred in U.S. troops in Vietnam. Soldiers spend a good deal of time wading waist deep in stagnant rivers and streams polluted by infected cattle and rodent urine. Although the disease has a low mortality rate, it is of sufficient severity to require hospitalization, thus making soldiers who are infected inactive for ten days to two weeks.

Toxoplasmosis, a highly infectious protozoal disease of infants, is also a more common cause of abortion and stillbirth than generally appreciated. In the newborn, toxoplasmosis can be extremely grave, killing some of its victims and blinding, crippling, or producing deafness or mental retardation in others.

Apparently, this exotic-sounding illness is widely distributed in our population on a subclinical level; that is, blood samples from 20 to 50 percent of adult Americans and almost 100 percent of residents of Central America over age forty exhibit antibodies even though clinical symptoms are not evident.

The protozoan parasite that infects man, *Toxoplasma gondii,* obtains its name from the gondi, a rat-like rodent found in North Africa. Since being isolated from the gondi, the parasite has been found in rabbits, rats, mice, swine, dogs, cats, chickens, and birds, all the way from the Arctic to the Antarctic.

Clinical cases of toxoplasmosis have been reported from Japan, New Zealand, Tahiti, the U.S.A., Sweden, and Holland. Women appear to be the chief transmitters of the parasite to newborn infants. Recent studies have demonstrated that the infectious organism passes via the placenta to the fetus. Although it is believed that the mother picks up the parasite from close association with some animal reservoir, the mechanism has not been definitely established. Because the symptoms are variable, the condition can be easily missed on examination. The lack of a good diagnostic test has been a serious impediment to treatment.

Early in June, 1967, Dr. Jack S. Remington of the Stanford University School of Medicine described a new and highly promising test to the meeting of the Pan-American Health Organization. The test is based on the detection of a specific antibody that does not pass to the fetus from the mother's circulation. The presence of the antibody shows that the newborn baby has contracted toxoplasmosis while still in the womb. Accordingly, this identification allows immediate institution of therapeutic measures to prevent or control further harm.

Although epidemiologists believe that millions of people around the world have had contact with *Toxoplasma gondii,* relatively few cases have actually been reported. Until November, 1968, no epidemics of toxoplasmosis had ever been recorded. In that month, five students at New York's Cornell Medical College became ill with fever, muscular aches and pains, rash, and severe pain around the eyes. On investigation, it was learned that two weeks earlier, all five had eaten hamburgers at the dormitory lunch counter and that in the rush to serve all the people who wanted a snack before going to hear a famous surgeon from South Africa, the beef was undercooked and was little more than raw. Dr. B. H. Kean, the physician who attended these students, believes this outbreak to be the first evidence of transmission via beef. If this is proven, the question of how *T. gondii* got into the beef will remain to raise the spectre of another food-borne disease that must be guarded against.

Trichinosis is commonly considered to be of little importance as a community or public-health problem. Most people believe that it is only the rare individual who suffers from trichinosis during sudden outbreaks and requires immediate hospitalization. Unfortunately, this is not the case. Most recent estimates of the national prevalence of trichinosis range from 16 to 36 percent of the population, with an average of 20 percent. This would imply that approximately forty million people—men, women, and children—have unsuspected, subclinical infections. Hence, trichinosis must be regarded as a widespread rather than a limited condition, with a potential of infecting all people who eat insufficiently cooked pork and pork products (see Chapter 9, Solid Waste Disposal). In this condition, larval roundworms encyst in muscle tissue, frequently causing nothing more than sporadic but elusive symptoms often mistaken for a half-dozen non-specific abdominal and chest pains. The larval worms travel through the blood vessels, entering the muscles of the diaphragm, ribs, tongue, and eyes. In the muscles, they continue to increase in size to a maximum of approximately one-eighth of an inch. At these sites they curl up and are walled off by the host as a response to their presence. In severe cases the pain can be intense, and death is not uncommon.

Strangely enough, with all the publicity given trichinosis over the past twenty years, people still eat rare pork. Pork is one meat that must not be eaten rare. Up to 10 percent of the pork sausage in large city markets has been found to be infested with trichinella worms. One of the reasons so few frank cases are seen each year is that many people harbor only a few larval worms in their systems. However, each year three hundred to four hundred new cases are reported, despite the fact that most states do not require that trichinosis be reported.

In 1961, two Canadian scientists reported a high prevalence of trichinosis among the Eskimos of Cape Dorset, who eat rare or raw bear and walrus meat, both of which are known to harbor the parasite.

Authorities agree that trichinosis is a serious public health problem. No specific treatment is available, but the means of prevention is absolutely clear: pork must be cooked at a minimum of 140° F for at least thirty minutes per pound to insure the complete destruction of any parasitic worms that may be present.

Encephalitis is an inflammation of the brain. Several types of arthropod-born encephalitides are of current interest. In the summer of 1964, Houston, Texas, experienced a severe epidemic of St. Louis encephalitis.* Some five hundred adults and children were stricken with the disease. Mental retardation, paralysis, and brain damage with accompanying deformities are some of the conditions that resulted. Areas of New Jersey and Pennsylvania had similar but milder outbreaks that summer. Florida had had a major outbreak two years before. All four were arthropod-borne;

* As the virus of this disease was first isolated in St. Louis in 1933, it bears this name even though it has not appeared in St. Louis for many years.

that is, the virus gained entrance to the human host by the bite of mosquitos. On puncture, the virus particles contained in mosquito saliva are transferred. Actually, man becomes infected accidentally (see Figure 14). Wild birds of many types are natural

MAN AND HORSE
ACCIDENTAL HOSTS OF ENCEPHALITIS

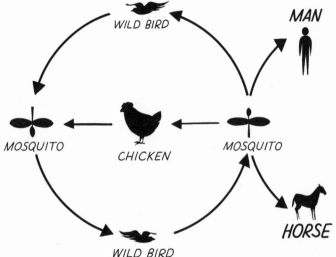

FIGURE 14. Cycle of transmission of St. Louis encephalitis

reservoirs of the virus, which does not appear to produce any symptoms in them. Female mosquitos in the vicinity obtain a blood meal from these birds, at which time they pick up the virus. If a man or a horse should wander into the mosquito-bird environment, or if man allows or encourages bird flocks and mosquitos to flourish in his environment, as is the case in many cities today, the mosquitos will preferentially obtain their blood meals from men or horses. As the bite is made and blood is drawn up, saliva and virus are delivered into the wound: the saliva contains an enzyme that prevents the blood from clotting too rapidly, thus allowing the mosquito to imbibe at his leisure. Regular, planned control of bird and mosquito populations is essential to prevent the spread of this zoonosis to man.

Another disease whose incidence is on the rise today is rabies. Although rabies has been well known throughout recorded history, it is only within the past twenty-five years that reservoirs of rabies other than the dog have become apparent. Rabies as a community health problem was considered well controlled as long as dogs were the only reservoir of infection. Now that it has been established that wild animals such as the fox, raccoon, and bat are additional natural reservoirs, a serious public health situation has developed.

A few years ago it was believed that the vampire bat was solely responsible for human and cattle rabies in Mexico and South America. More recently, insect-eating and fruit bats have been found to harbor rabies virus. As a consequence of this widespread natural infection, control becomes almost impossible. In 1953, a young boy was attacked by a rabid yellow bat in Tampa, Florida. A woman was similarly attacked in Pennsylvania. Attacks by bats have now been reported from a dozen states. Apparently, the bats are passing the infection among themselves in their rookeries in caves. Every so often a rabid bat becomes maddened by the effects of rabies on the nervous-system, and attacks people.

In 1963, some four thousand cases of rabies from all sources were reported in the U.S. Many midwestern states report increasing rabies among campers who are bitten while sleeping. Approximately five hundred thousand cases were reported to the World Health Organization from sixty-three countries in 1963.

Ever since Louis Pasteur successfully used rabies vaccine on Joseph Meister on July 6, 1885, it has popularly been thought that the treatment for rabies should be avoided if at all possible. This aversion has been engendered by two factors: (1) some people are hypersensitive to the proteinaceous material of the vaccine, and (2) the treatment involves fourteen injections. Although fears of the procedure are unwarranted, they persist. The fact is that allergic reactions to brain-tissue vaccine used to occur in perhaps one in two thousand individuals, but the duck-embryo vaccine used over the past five years has all but eliminated such reactions. The inoculations themselves, although still fourteen in number, are made with short needles just under the skin of the arm, leg, or abdomen and are no more unpleasant than a flu shot.

Recently, a vaccine to be used before being bitten was made available for experimental field trials. The vaccine will be given to people in high-risk jobs, such as mailmen and policemen. If successful, it could mean the end of the prophylactic series now given after an individual is bitten.

For the past five years, there has been increasing discussion of the possibility of eradicating * such diseases as rabies, malaria, and yellow fever, among others. Although such a prospect is attractive, when some of the practical realities are fully considered the eradication of rabies, for example, seems highly unlikely. While local outbreaks of rabies usually can be controlled in the U.S. by elimination of stray dogs, coupled with vaccination of all registered dogs, we can dismiss as impossible the widespread eradication of rabies because of the bat reservoir, which is far too inaccessible.

Rabies can infect almost any warm-blooded animal. The virus leaves the animal only in its saliva, so that biting is the normal route of transmission and puncture wounds of the skin the usual portal of entry. So long as canines were the sole source of infection, eradication had possibilities. When, however, it was learned that bats, skunks, squirrels, and a wide assortment of wild animals harbor the virus and can transmit it to man, hope of eradication vanished.

In addition to the biological problems, religious considerations are involved. In Arab and Asian countries, dogs are considered unclean. Accordingly, few Moslems are willing to handle them for the routine vaccination procedures. In those countries of Southeast Asia where Buddhism is the dominant religion, stray dogs are considered an integral part of the cycle of life and must not be killed. Thus, cultural practices foster the presence of disease

---

*Eradication is an all-or-nothing concept. It is similar to sterilization in that neither can be done partially.

and impede prevention and control measures (see Chapter 2, Ecology of Health and Disease).

Brucellosis, or undulant fever, as it is often called (suggesting the cyclic, wave-like rise and fall of fever during a seizure) is a chronic illness of long duration with periods of fever and pain between periods of apparent health. Most cases have come from drinking raw milk from infected cows or goats. Packinghouse and slaughterhouse workers and veterinarians become ill after handling infected carcasses and hides.

Recently, an Iowa packing plant reported 128 cases of brucellosis that appeared to be due to inhalation of airborne brucella, the bacterium responsible for the infection. Apparently, an aerosol of the organisms was generated and dispersed in a wide area and of sufficiently small particle size to penetrate into the alveoli of the lungs (see Chapter 10).

Transmission of brucellosis to humans can be prevented if all milk is pasteurized or, barring that, is from inspected, disease-free herds. Control of brucellosis, like tuberculosis, is under the federal government, through its Brucellosis Eradication Program. Since 1954, when only 24 percent of cattle were under control, to 1959, when 55 percent were controlled, the incidence of brucellosis in man dropped from over eighteen hundred new cases in 1954 to less than five hundred in 1959. Today, there are even fewer cases each year.

Of particular concern to public health scientists are the variety of diseases associated with household pets. One of the newest problem areas concerns a well-known disease, salmonellosis, a typhoid-like illness. Turtles are among the many animals that normally harbor the salmonella bacterium in their intestines. These organisms are regularly passed out in fecal matter and contaminate whatever it contacts.

The state department of health in Minnesota recently reported that pet turtles infected twenty-two children under six years of age. This meant that the children had swallowed turtle feces. When it was discovered that a two-year-old had placed some of the brightly colored pebbles from the aquarium in her mouth, the source of infection became readily apparent.

Two years ago, stuffed chicks and ducklings were imported into the U.S. from Germany and Japan as toys for children. These live birds are natural carriers of salmonella bacteria. A severe case of salmonellosis occurred in a child as a result of touching the ducks to her mouth. Salmonellosis as a general widespread illness is rising precipitously all over the country. This marked incidence was shown in Figure 2, in Chapter 3.

One of the most interesting examples of the interrelatedness of human and animal health is the relationship of influenza virus to both man and animal. It is well known that a wide range of viruses of Group A influenza occur not only in man and pigs but in birds and horses as well. Recent studies have shown that human influenza A_2 (Asian) can cause natural, inapparent infections in horses and swine. It has also been found that swine may act as a reservoir of the human strain. In fact, swine influenza and human influenza are considered to be the same infection; the great pandemic of 1918 was responsible for the epizootic in swine that followed shortly thereafter. Recently, laboratory findings suggested a rather disturbing possibility concerning the human and avian (bird) influenza viruses. It has been discovered that an avian and a human strain could be hybridized. It is thus conceivable that a strain could emerge with the virulence of fowl plague (not normally pathogenic for humans) and the host specificity of a human strain. Fowl plague has a mortality rate of nearly 100 percent within a few hours of onset. While this unique combination of traits may be unlikely in nature, the possibility of the emergence of entirely new strains as a result of interbreeding remains a threat that cannot be disregarded, even though at the moment such hybridization is little more than a laboratory artifact.

Animals and humans are in reality so kindred that knowledge of a certain disease in one can be applied to the other. This area of research is known as comparative medicine. Cardiovascular, degenerative, nervous, and rheumatic diseases occur in animals as well as man. Because domestic animals are slaughtered for food or other useful products, they seldom live on to old age. In recent years, several universities have established research centers in which animals are studied as they live out their full potential of years.

Atherosclerosis occurs in primates (including man), swine, chickens, turkeys, and pigeons. Cerebrovascular symptoms appear to be common in aging pigs. Viral leukemia of chickens and mice is well established and may also occur in dogs, cats, and cattle. Since this virus can infect a large number of animal species, all researchers are pondering the question, Can man be infected from the animals around him? As yet, the viral etiology of human cancer is controversial. Much more research is needed before it can be pinned down.

The existence of degenerative diseases among animals raises the possibility that animal research studies could be as helpful in understanding and controlling chronic degenerative human ailments as they were in understanding communicable diseases. One of the most beneficial aspects of the animal relationship is the far shorter life-span of most animals, which conveniently compresses into a few years events that are spread over a half-century in man.

As we continue to obtain information about our environment, it becomes increasingly evident that man's health is intimately associated with that of the many animals occupying his habitat. Thus, to really comprehend many community health problems, knowledge of both animal and human disease must be encompassed.

SANITARY SEWAGE

"Thou shalt have a place also without the camp, wither thou shalt go forth abroad: and thou shalt have a paddle upon thy weapon; and it shall be, when thou wilt ease thyself abroad, thou shalt dig therewith and shalt turn back and cover that which cometh from thee" (Deuteronomy 23:12–13).

Although the Israelites did not have the benefits of waste disposal by water carriage,* they seemed well aware that human excreta could be a vehicle of disease transmission. It was not until several thousand years later, however, in the filthy, sewage-laden

* The water-carriage system of waste removal is simply a supply of water under pressure to remove excretal waste from dwellings. Its introduction in the 1840's involved engineering problems of considerable magnitude. However, it only shifted the problem to a point away from the dwellings. At some point on the outskirts of the city the combined discharges of the whole community had to be cared for. The introduction of sewage-treatment plants was a logical extension of the waste-removal system.

industrial cities of London, Boston, and New York, that social pressures forced the introduction of the water-carriage system of waste disposal.

As a consequence of a rainfall in the city of London, Jonathan Swift wrote the following lines; they could apply to any community circa 1740: "Now from all parts of the swelling kennels flow and bear their trophies with them as they go; filth of all hues and odors seems to tell what street they sailed from by the sight and smell, sweepings from the butchers' stalls, dung, guts and blood, drowned puppies, stinking sprats, all drowned in mud; dead cats and turnip-top come tumbling down the flood."

Descriptions of conditions in the cities of eighteenth- and nineteenth-century Europe show that the filth was appalling. One traveler wrote: "In the tenements of Glasgow dung was left lying in the courtyards as there were no lavatories in houses. This lack of lavatories led to the habit of house dwellers filling chamber pots with excreta and after some days, when completely full, and with a shout of, beware slops, emptying the contents out of the window into the street below." This practice quickly led to the pollution of wells and to the infestation of cities with rats; both gave rise to diseases of epidemic proportions which regularly took a great toll in human lives.

It was not until the latter part of the nineteenth century that disease transmission via human waste was actually demonstrated. The fact is that modern society as we know it today could not have emerged without the benefits of clean water and the removal of sewage literally from its doorsteps.

While the object of sewage disposal is to get rid of sewage, a more important objective if community health is to be maintained is to collect, treat, and dispose of domestic waste (often called sanitary waste) in a manner calculated to protect health, preserve natural resources, and prevent nuisance conditions.

With the present aggregation of millions of people in large city centers, there is an unprecedented volume of human waste to be treated. In addition, the pathogenic bacteria in this waste must be killed. In any community there are always a number of persons who are either manifestly ill, ill with inapparent infections, or healthy carriers shedding infectious organisms to a degree sufficient to maintain levels of bacteria or viruses in sewage that are potentially dangerous to the community at large. Thus, disposal of sewage implies two entirely different propositions: (1) the removal of energy-laden organic matter from liquid waste and its conversion to an innocuous form in order to prevent or control pollution of lakes, streams, and rivers, and (2) the prevention of water-borne disease.

The term *sewage* usually connotes the liquid wastes from homes, schools, commercial buildings, hotels, hospitals. and industrial plants. In addition to human excretal material, it generally contains industrial wastes such as those from meat-packing operations, breweries, milk and food plants, and chemical processing plants. Domestic sewage is generally limited to household wastes from residential areas and contains wastes from water closets and wash water from baths and kitchens. Curiously enough, in the United States, domestic sewage varies little in composition and strength from community to community across the country. Although we like to think we are a heterogeneous people, in actual fact we have become remarkably similar. This is due in part to the nationwide storage and transportation facilities that permit extensive distribution of similar food products and to the quite similar eating habits and patterns of living of our population. Figure 15 shows the hourly volume of sewage flow resulting from this national pattern of behavior.

Sewage or liquid waste has the appearance of spent dishwater. It usually contains paper, organic material from feces and urine, soap, and such exotic items as dead animals, fruit skins, old shoes, collar buttons, and anything else that finds its way into the sanitary sewer.

A useful measure of the strength of sewage is the proportion of suspended solids it contains. The suspended solids of interest to the chemist are not the dead animals, shoes, or fruit skins, but organic particles of carbohydrates, fats, and proteins. Generally, sewage consists of 99.9 percent water and .02 to .04 percent solids. Although the amount of suspended solids, when evaluated on a percentage basis, is small, the total daily amount from a large

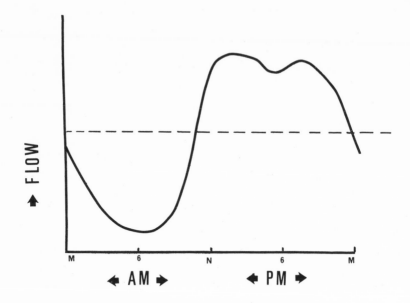

FIGURE 15. Nationwide pattern of sewage flow

SOURCE: *Microbiology for Sanitary Engineers*
(New York: McGraw-Hill, 1962)

city can be considerable. For example, in the sewage of a city the size of Washington, D.C., solids amount to approximately 150 tons per day. Of this, 40 to 50 percent is protein, another 40 to 50 percent consists of carbohydrates (sugars, starches, and cellulose), and the remaining 5 to 10 percent is fat. Discharging 150 tons per day of carbohydrates, fats, and proteins would provide more sumptuous meals for the microbes in lakes, streams, and rivers in and around Washington than they could properly digest (metabolize). The result would undoubtedly be pollution of a magnitude as yet unknown in that area. Although such a discharge is only in the realm of conjecture, it does indicate the degree of treatment necessary.

Before embarking on a discussion of sewage treatment, it

may be helpful to delineate the path taken by sewage as it flows from home to treatment plant to final outfall in a water course. Treatment of sewage from homes with septic tanks, cesspools, or seepage pits will be discussed separately below.

Let us suppose that while you are washing your hand a ring slips off your finger, and before it can be retrieved, it has gone down the drain. Figure 16 is a diagrammatic summary of the

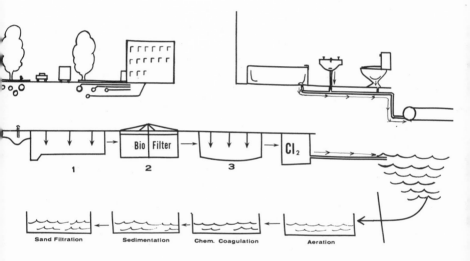

FIGURE 16. Diagrammatic representation of the route taken by domestic waste from an urban dwelling to its final outfall in a river

path the ring takes as it moves along with the liquid waste. At top left, house and street are seen in cross-section. Each of the various utilities—gas, electricity, water, and sanitary sewers—leads from the street to the house. The largest of the conduits found under the street is the main or lateral branch of the sewage system that collects domestic waste from many houses on the street. A cross-section of the inside of the house is depicted at top right. Connections and flow from sink, tub, and flush toilet are seen leading to the street sewer.

The street sewer joins large trunk sewers from other neighborhoods, through which the waste flows directly to a treatment facility.* The unit at far left in the middle row represents the trunk line arriving at the treatment plant. Wherever practical, sewers are built to allow sewage to flow by gravity; when this is not possible, pumping stations are strategically placed to pump sewage through pressure conduits to points where they can discharge into a gravity sewer.

As the sewage flows along through the many miles of piping, biological activity engendered by the extensive microbial flora naturally present in human waste (together with additional microbial forms from soil, street washings, dead animals, fruit skins, and whatever else falls into sewers progresses at an ever-increasing rate. The longer the sewage remains in the system, the greater will be the activity. If the sewers are extensive and the rate of flow low, the biological activity will be so advanced that the waste can be considered as having received partial treatment before it reaches the plant. The key points here, and as the waste continues on, are biological activity and treatment. Both are concerned with rendering this highly putrescible organic material innocuous; that is, preventing water pollution, odors, and unsightly conditions.

At this point, a digression may be in order. Most piping used to transport liquid waste is relatively inexpensive concrete. However, improperly ventilated sewers can undergo severe corrosion as a consequence of microbial activity. Under anaerobic conditions (poor ventilation with insufficient oxygen) hydrogen sulfide (H_2S) is produced. The sulfur-oxidizing bacterial present in the

*Many cities have combined sewers in which both sewage and water runoff from street-washing and rain are collected and flow to-gether to the treatment plant.

waste can, under proper conditions, convert the H_2S to sulfuric acid, which in turn reacts with the lime in concrete to form calcium sulfate. Calcium sulfate, having little structural strength, crumbles. To avoid this, more expensive, acid-resistant, vitrified clay pipes must be employed, if adequate ventilation cannot be achieved.

At the treatment plant, sewage generally flows through a series of coarse and fine screens to remove large floating objects; the lost ring would most likely pass through the coarse screen, and possibly through the fine screen. From the screens the waste passes through a comminutor, which shreds the remaining solids to a size calculated to prevent clogging at points farther along in the plant.

After sewage has been screened, the next step is removal of the easily settled suspended matter, such as sand, gravel, and ashes, in grit chambers. When a sewage system collects both liquid waste and storm-water runoff, grit chambers are usually provided at the treatment plant to remove these coarse materials, which can cause clogging of moving parts (sludge-collector mechanisms and pumps), pipes, and drains.

From the grit chamber the liquid waste passes to the primary settling or sedimentation tanks (Figure 16) at low velocity. This method is widely used as either preliminary treatment or as is too often the case, as the sole treatment of sewage before it is emptied into a stream or river. In such cases, raw sewage is placed in the watercourse with the hope that its dilution with large volumes of water will prevent pollution or nuisance conditions. All too often, this hope is unjustified.

The velocity of flow through the primary settling tanks is adjusted to achieve a thirty- to ninety-minute detention time, depending on the strength of the sewage and on whether any additional treatment is to be given. The purpose of primary settling is removal of a minor portion of the suspended solids—the carbohydrates, fats, and proteins that are the major contributors to the pollution-nuisance complex. It is quite likely that the ring originally lost down the bathroom sink will settle out in the primary tanks as a result of the decreased velocity and gravitational effects, and will finally be lost in the accumulated sludge.

During the course of flow thus far, the potentially putrescible organic compounds in sewage have been relatively unaltered. If the waste were dumped into a stream or river without additional treatment, the ability of the stream to purify itself would be seriously impaired, if not completely destroyed. To prevent this, secondary treatment of sewage is designed into the process to deal specifically with the organic compounds. Often, secondary treatment can remove up to 90 percent of the suspended organic compounds. This degree of stabilization can prevent most rivers from becoming polluted.

At this point, depending upon the type of secondary treatment to be given, the sewage will pass to either a trickling filter (biofilter) or an activated sludge aeration tank. Both are based upon the stabilization or neutralization of organic waste by biological action. That is, a host of biological species ranging in size from bacteria to snails and flies take part in the process that eventually produces an inoffensive effluent. It is in either the trickling filter or the aeration tank that the business of removing or physicochemically altering the remaining suspended matter occurs. From either the trickling filter or the aeration tank, the stabilized and clarified liquid flows, or is pumped, to a secondary settling tank for an additional short holding period.

Up to this point the second of the two major functions of waste treatment, the prevention of disease transmission by virus, bacteria, and protozoa, has been given only cursory attention. Although pathogenic microorganisms are partially removed in the settling process and others mechanically removed by filtration and aeration, it is in the chlorination tank that disease-producing organisms are killed. In addition, chlorine abets the stabilization of the remaining organic matter by its highly oxidizing character. After contact with chlorine for approximately thirty minutes, the clarified disinfected liquid is discharged into a watercourse.

This then is a generalized description of the trip sewage takes from home to stream or river. It is at the point of sewage outfall in some watercourse that water pollution begins, and it is at the point of water intake farther downstream that many of the problems of drinking water begin. Chapter 8 will be devoted to these questions. Figure 16 indicates the general path followed by water from point of intake downstream of the sewage outfall, through treatment, and back to the consumer.

The question that remains to be answered is: "If all sewage follows the path outlined, why do we have polluted rivers and streams?" As has been pointed out, the treatment of domestic and industrial wastes usually depends at some stage in the process upon the metabolic activity of microorganisms and some larger species. Microorganisms use the organic matter and minerals of sewage as a source of nutrients for growth and reproduction. The treatment system described effectively removes the available energy of the waste and neutralizes or stabilizes it. When the stabilized organic waste reaches a watercourse, it is no longer a source of nutriment for the many biological forms in the stream or river.

When microbes metabolize food, in this case sewage solids, oxygen is consumed. The more food available, the more oxygen used up; the more oxygen used, the less available for fish and other stream biota. Pollution or fouling occurs as a consequence of the removal of oxygen from the stream. Without an adequate supply of oxygen, life in the stream dies or is driven farther downstream.

A sewage-treatment plant that employs secondary treatment employs a form of biological treatment. Where biofilters are used, the liquid from the primary settling tank flows to the filter or percolation bed. Here, large rotary distributor arms spray the clarified liquid over a bed of stones. Figure 17 shows the entire unit; Figure 18 is a close-up view of the liquid falling upon the bed. As the liquid trickles over and between the stones, bacteria, protozoa, worms, snails, spiders, and flies utilize its protein, carbohydrates, and fats to make additional bacteria, protozoa, worms, etc. The waste is thus transformed to energy-free particles that do not need the oxygen dissolved in the stream; with little or no oxygen demand, pollution cannot occur. Thus, the main purpose of secondary treatment (or even tertiary treatment, if it is used) is to reduce the amount of dissolved oxygen withdrawn from the stream. Since pollution of many waterways by sewage *is* occurring, it is clear that stabilized waste is not the only type of waste

FIGURE 17. Trickling filter in operation outside Paris

entering the water. It is well known that many communities pipe their effluents directly from primary settling tanks to a river or stream. This waste is loaded with energy-rich nutrients that provide food for aquatic microbes. In metabolizing these nutrients, the microbes utilize large quantities of dissolved oxygen, which are then no longer available for fish, aquatic invertebrates, and plants. As oxygen is depleted, the flora and fauna die or move away. The stream becomes anaerobic and offensive to the senses; in short, it is polluted.

Pollution can also occur in another way. Modern technology has produced chemicals that often defy microbial attempts at their degradation in the secondary treatment processes of the sewage plant. Thus, they pass unaltered into the river. Many of these chemicals are toxic to fish and other species. When dumped into a watercourse, they bring about pollution by killing the biological species that aid in the purification process. Additionally, toxic industrial chemicals, when combined with sewage wastes at the treatment plant, can kill the microbes in a trickling filter or aeration tank, thereby destroying the filter's stabilization capacity. Thus, energy-rich waste with a large oxygen demand passes

FIGURE 18. Close-up view of a section of a distributor arm of a trickling filter

through the treatment plant virtually untreated and, with its great potential for pollution, gains access to streams.

One of the newest, low-cost methods for stabilizing the sewage emanating from small communities is the oxidation pond or lagoon, known in Europe as the oxidation ditch. Like the other methods described, it is based on biological degradation. The sewage which is not subjected to any preliminary treatment is pumped directly from a collecting point to the pond, which is essentially a shallow ditch two to six feet deep. The area of the pond is usually dictated by the available land.

The name *oxidation pond* indicates that the process is aerobic—making large amounts of oxygen available to the microbes. As the raw liquid waste enters the pond, the heavy particles settle out, leaving the suspended organic matter to be attacked by bacteria, algae, and protozoa. After a rather long retention period, thirty to forty days, the stabilized effluent is released into a nearby waterway. From time to time the accumulated sludge must be removed in order to keep the lagoon in operation.

Such industries as dairies, food canneries, and breweries are turning to oxidation ponds for the economical handling of their high-oxygen-demand wastes and to prevent overloading of already overburdened municipal treatment plants.

Another means of sewage disposal widely used in the United States, which often contributes to pollution of streams and drinking water, is the septic tank. This is an individual system used where water is available to carry waste from a home which is not served by municipal sewer lines. The system is composed of three simple elements: the septic tank, a distribution box, and a disposal field.

Liquid waste is conveyed by pipe from a dwelling to a waterproof concrete or metal container. Figure 19 shows the general plan of the system and a cross-section of the primary con-

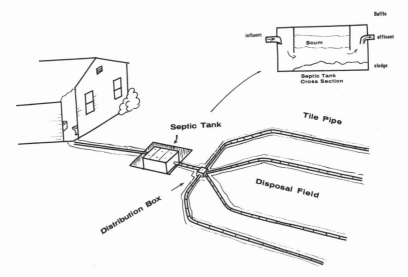

FIGURE 19. Schematic view of a septic-tank system

tainer. The tank usually contains two baffles to prevent the heavier solids and the buoyant scum from passing out with the effluent to the distribution box and into the disposal field.

During the retention period in a properly operating system, from 50 to 70 percent of the suspended solids are removed by sedimentation, which forms a sludge that must be removed periodically. Failure to remove the accumulated solids often results in discharge of solids in the absorption field, with resultant clogging and ponding.

The principle is relatively simple. Because this is a closed system with little ventilation, anaerobic conditions prevail. This implies that the bacterial metabolism will be carried out by anaerobic species. The process is one of digestion in which both floating scum and the settled solids are reduced in volume and transformed to liquids, gas, and an irreducible minimum of biologically inert solids. The gas diffuses into the atmosphere and the liquids containing organic acids pass into the fields and percolate through the soil, where aerobic bacterial species complete the stabilization.

The distribution box provides a means for even dispersion of the liquids to the perforated tiles. An integral part of the system is the disposal or absorption field, which should be carefully designed. Inadequate field size and too compact a soil prevents percolation of the liquid sewage and results in ponding. As a result, nuisances occur. In areas with sandy soil, contamination of ground water can result.

Although septic tanks are a direct evolutionary offshoot of cesspools, they are not the same. Cesspools have been described as "wells in reverse." Untreated domestic waste is allowed to run into a hole or pit in the ground from which seepage or leaching through soil occurs. This stabilizes the waste through bacterial action. All too often the depth of the cesspool places the raw sewage in contact with the water table, with the result that gross contamination of the drinking-water source occurs.

The lack of any disinfection procedure in either the septic tank or the cesspool does not recommend them from the community health standpoint. Although some of the pathogenic microbes are removed during sedimentation and digestion in septic tanks, a significant number do enter the disposal fields. Cesspools are even more hazardous, as they place disease-carrying organisms in close proximity to wells and ground-water acquifers. Public health agencies are quite correct in attempting to eliminate their use.

Although farmers and rural populations generally have used septic tanks since their development around the turn of the century, it is the rapid expansion of residential areas into formerly rural communities in recent years that has greatly accelerated the number of private sewage-disposal systems.

Of our 200 million people, some two-thirds, or 132 million, are served by municipal sewers. The remainder use septic tanks. Of those 132 million using city sewer lines, about 10 percent live in communities that discharge untreated sewage directly into streams. Another 25 percent live in communities where raw sewage is discharged after a short retention in primary settling basins. Recall that primary treatment includes screens to remove large floating objects, a comminutor for shredding, a grit chamber, and a sedimentation basin for settling of the heavier solids. Little stabilization occurs up to this point.

It has been estimated that the sewage discharges from communities giving primary treatment or none at all corresponds to the raw waste of almost fifty million people. Figures published in 1966 revealed that among the 11,420 communities in this country that have sewer systems, 2,139 still discharge untreated waste. Many treatment plants are old, inefficient, and overloaded, so that a substantial portion of the sewage is only partially stabilized. Thus, there are ample reasons for pollution of water by domestic and industrial wastes.

It was noted earlier that many of the new industrial wastes are not fully metabolized by the organisms of the secondary treatment facilities and that some of these chemicals coming into the treatment plants in high concentration prove toxic to the stabilizing organisms. The saga of synthetic detergents (syndets) is a good example of the dislocations created by new products. Bear in mind that sewage-treatment plants were originally designed to treat human excretal waste, not industrial chemicals.

Both soap and syndets have detergent properties, that is, the ability to clean by emulsification of particles of dirt. Syndets, however, have the added advantage of being able to accomplish this in both hard and acid waters, where soaps precipitate and require large amounts to achieve little if any cleaning. Syndets are molecularly different from soap, and their molecular configuration does not allow bacteria to "eat" them, whereas soap is easily metabolized.

Since bacteria in streams and rivers cannot metabolize syndets, little if any oxgen is used up by their presence. Thus, contamination of waterways by syndets is not accompanied by oxygen depletion. The pollution in this case consists of the inordinate amount of foam produced and the fact that the syndets appear in drinking water after having passed intact through sewage treatment plants, and often disrupting the efficiency of the trickling filters.

Another interesting aspect of sewage treatment makes use of the many nutrients in sewage to increase food supply. Although the need for protein supplementation of diets is greater in Asia, Africa, and South America than in the industrialized nations of Western Europe, the huge sewage system in Munich, Germany, utilizes fish ponds to both purify sewage effluent and increase the supply of fish.

Instead of being discharged into a river, the effluent is sprayed into a pond stocked with rainbow trout or carp. The fish rapidly increase in weight on the luxurious diet, and at the same time purify the waste, which is then discharged into the Yser River; the fish are sold for a smart profit.

After the introduction of the water-carriage method of waste disposal in the 1850's and the widespread introduction of sewerage systems shortly thereafter, little additional progress in waste disposal was made until the introduction by Corbett in 1893 of large-scale trickling filters in Lancashire, England. This was followed by the introduction of septic tanks in 1905 by Cameron in Exeter, England. Just prior to World War I, Avdern and Lockett, two English scientists, published accounts of their work on the oxidation of sewage, thereby laying the basis for the activated sludge process of sewage stabilization.

The fact is that although modifications have occurred from time to time, they have been concerned with increasing the loading. But even this has about reached its limit. No completely new methods for treating sewage have been produced for over fifty years. Perhaps even more pertinent may be the fact that while engineers attempt to design more efficient waste-treatment facilities and units to receive greater and greater hydraulic loadings, the biological basis for stabilization remains virtually unknown. Thus, although advanced waste-treament procedures such as electrodialysis, reverse osmosis, solvent extraction, eutectic freezing, and distillation are being investigated by scientists in industry, government, and the universities, there has been little interdisciplinary effort to achieve a much-needed breakthrough. The time is ripe for development of completely new ways of treating human waste.

8

WATER POLLUTION AND ITS CONTROL

I am convinced that although water pollution is a subject that invites wide general discussion, and heated discussion at that, few people know how to define or measure it, or have any idea to what extent it may be tolerated. Since widespread opinion holds that water pollution can be caused by the addition of *any* human (not necessarily fecal) or industrial waste, the public must be prepared to recognize and accept the fact that there are degrees of pollution; and that the mere statement that a body of water is polluted does not necessarily imply that it is *in extremis*.

Although microbiologists and sanitary engineers consider water pollution as the depletion of oxygen, with all its attendant consequences, the general public takes a broader view. To some, water pollution means the coliform index, a bacteriological test of water quality used to ascertain the numbers of bacteria of intestinal origin present, which will be discussed later in this chapter. To others, water is considered to be polluted when anything extraneous is placed in it. Figure 20 typifies this attitude to pollution. The empty champagne bottles, metal tins of caviar, and wooden cigar boxes are certainly unsightly and thus constitute an aesthetic pollution, but they have little or no effect on the dissolved oxygen in the stream. To still others, water pollution refers to anything other than chemically pure water, which, of course, has never existed on this planet.

FIGURE 20. "It's pollution all right, but it's pollution of rather a high order."

Stevenson; copyright © 1965 The New Yorker Magazine, Inc.

If pollution is taken to mean the depletion of oxygen, with consequent septic conditions, such as offensive odors, floating masses of sludge, and death of fish and other aquatic life, then pollution is undoubtedly older than recorded history.

Even before the presence of man's communities, the fall of leaves into streams at certain periods of the year produced significant sags in the oxygen content when microorganisms converted the complex organics of the leaves to simpler molecules. As man cleared the land and cultivated it, surface water runoff increased and brought with it large amounts of organic material, with similar depletions of oxygen. As soon as settlements arose in river valleys, human wastes began to be emptied into streams. The course of history leads in a straight line from the Stone Age tanner who scraped his furs into a stream to the river-polluting oil refinery, tannery, or plating plant of the twentieth century. There is, however, an important difference. As recently as a century and a half ago, next to nothing was known of the consequences of dumping human and factory wastes into rivers. Today, we no longer have this excuse.

When a river receives regular or continuous supplies of organic matter, the river tends to purify itself; that is, it can overcome or adequately handle the waste load in the course of time. "Running water purifies itself" is an old adage that had much truth to it, but one that may no longer be true, as the magnitude and types of waste presently being discharged frequently overwhelm the recuperative capacities of the stream and thus stall recovery. Self-purification, which leads to the stabilization of the imparted organic matter, depends primarily upon the biochemical activities of bacteria, which, when given sufficient dissolved oxygen, utilize the organic matter as food and break down (metabolize, neutralize, stabilize, digest) compounds to simpler and innocuous end-products. Other factors, such as dilution, sedimentation, and the energy of sunlight, also play a role in the self-purification scheme. Some waterways undergo self-purification in fairly short distances from point of sewage outfall, while others require twenty-five, fifty, or more miles in which to accomplish this. The process is complex, and each stream or river is a unique ecosystem with its own specific capacity for purification and recovery. If oxygen is removed faster than it can be replaced by natural aeration or by photosynthesis, conditions worsen and pollution of virtually an entire river may result.

Water pollution, the availability of acceptable drinking water, and sewage disposal are inextricably bound together. The realization that waste disposal and water use is a cyclical process will aid in any benefits a community or region will obtain when considering their own needs, and the needs of the neighboring communities downstream.

A city not uncommonly locates its water pumping stations up-stream on a river and discharges its sewage effluent downstream into the same river. The next city downstream repeats the process, as does the next and the next. Distances between discharges of sewage effluents and raw water intakes are being squeezed closer and closer together because of the outward expansion of communities as a result of increased population. Figure 21 indicates the progressive intake-outlet re-use condition that prevails on so many rivers today.

Today's communities and modern industry are both elephantine users of water. The average city-dwelling family of four uses about six hundred gallons of water each day. Industry requires some five gallons of water to produce a gallon of gasoline, ten gallons to produce each can of vegetables, twenty-five thousand gallons to process one ton of steel, and fifty thousand to produce one ton of paper. After use, the spent water, loaded with organic waste, is often dumped directly into a stream or river with the generally mistaken idea that dilution with fresh water will prevent pollution locally or further downstream. Unfortunately, however, the available water resources are unevenly distributed; many sections of the country are forced to re-use the available supply long before the river from which they draw it has had a chance to purify itself. It has been estimated, for example, that the thirteen-hundred-mile stretch of water of the Ohio River is used from three to eight times before it joins the Mississippi at Cairo, Illinois.

The present state of development of our technological society makes it mandatory that we accept a certain degree of pollution. We are still far from developing new methods of liquid-waste disposal that will make dumping in rivers obsolete. The fact is that industry and residential communities alike would be forced to shut down if unified public opinion demanded pollution-free water-ways. It is, therefore, in the best interests of the community to support research investigations aimed at discovering the degree of waste a stream can adequately tolerate without the initiation of noisome conditions. Decisions as to what constitutes a tolerable degree of pollution must be reached after considering the water's

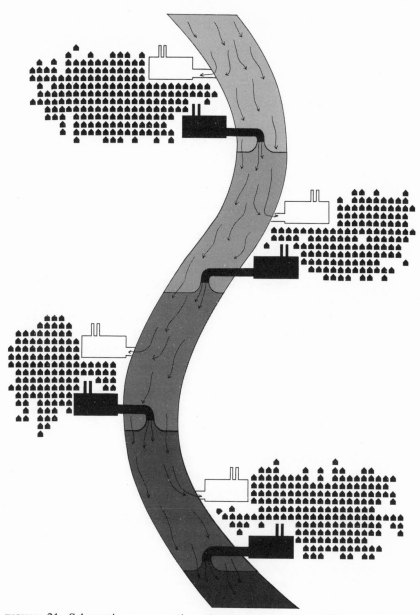

FIGURE 21. Schematic representation of water reuse by four cities

natural purification capacity and the purpose for which it is to be used.

The people concerned with investigating water pollution have categorized pollutants as chemical, physical, biological, and physiological.

The chemical pollutants include both inorganic and organic compounds, such as dairy, textile, cannery, brewery, and paper-mill wastes, ensilage, laundry wastes, manure, and slaughterhouse wastes. These essentially contain proteins, carbohydrates, fats, oils, resins, tars, and soaps. If these pollutants are not excessive, they will be stabilized by the self-purification process. If they are excessive, death of fish and offensive odors can result. In addition, such plant nutrients as phosphates, nitrates, and potassium have the ability to aid weed growth and promote algae blooms, which further deplete oxygen. Inorganic salts, particularly toxic heavy metals not removed by the standard sewage-treatment processes, can produce water unsuitable for industry, irrigation, and drinking.

Biological pollutants include the many types of microscopic animal and plant forms, such as bacteria, protozoa, and viruses that are associated with disease transmission. These come from domestic sewage, farms, and tanneries.

Physiological pollution manifests itself as objectionable tastes and odors. These may be imparted to the flesh of fish, making them inedible, or water itself may become unfit to drink owing to its odor and taste. Odors and tastes occur in water as a consequence of the presence of inorganic chemicals, such as hydrogen sulfide, or the extensive growth of certain species of algae. Some impart musty odors, while others give fishy, pigpen, spicy, or chemical tastes to it.

Various physical effects, such as foaming, color, turbidity, and increased temperature are also considered forms of pollution.

Elevated temperature also plays a part in water pollution. Water from a nearby stream or river is pumped into a plant to cool a machine or process that normally generates heat. The transfer of heat to the cooling water raises its temperature several degrees. When this heated water is discharged back into the stream or river whence it came, it can disrupt ecological relationships within it. A rise in temperature of only a few degrees can be lethal to a variety of aquatic plant and animal forms, which, like most living things, are sustained only within a narrow temperature range. The death of certain species removes the food supply of species which prey on them; without this food supply they in turn will die or be forced to move downstream. Furthermore, the warmer the water, the less oxygen it will contain; oxygen, as has been pointed out, is vital for the prevention of deterioration. At elevated temperatures all chemical and biological activity proceeds at a more rapid rate than would normally prevail, and this in turn depletes the sensitive oxygen balance of the stream. This series of events can result in the loss of self-purification capacity by altering the stream community.

Recently, the Ohio Department of Natural Resources reported the first case of an industrial firm being fined for thermal pollution. The Ohio Sugar Company of Freemont was required to pay the state approximately thirty-two hundred dollars for the loss of fish because of discharges of hot water from its plant. Perhaps this laudable precedent will help discourage similar pollutional activities.

One of the most widely used measures of the concentration of biologically oxidizable matter in a river or stream is the biochemical oxygen demand, the B.O.D. Although used as a chemical test, it is in fact a biological procedure, depending for its activity on the microorganisms in the sewage. The B.O.D. test is a quantitative measure of the oxygen used up by a sample of sewage effluent or river water during a five-day incubation period at 20° C. The sample is diluted with fully oxygenated water and the initial amount of oxygen determined. After five days in the dark, the oxygen content is determined again; from the difference between the initial value and the five-day value, the B.O.D. or strength of the original sample can be calculated. Several state health departments have set their water conservation policies by limiting the B.O.D. to a stipulated maximum, while others attempt to control added pollution by limiting the B.O.D. of effluents.

Several random B.O.D. values may be helpful: the B.O.D.

of the sewage of a residential community generally varies between 150 and 250 milligrams per liter (mg/l). (The B.O.D. of the sewage produced in the five boroughs of New York City averages about 100 to 200.) Milk processing and cannery waste range from 5000 and 6000 mg/l, while the liquid discharged from pulping operations, which contains large amounts of wood sugar, casein, and starches, often has a five-day B.O.D. of 10 to 15,000 mg/l. Among the strongest wastes going into rivers and streams is that which comes from the wool scouring industry; its waste can have a B.O.D. above 20,000 mg/l.

Probably the most useful single indicator of the overall condition of a river or stream is its content of dissolved oxygen (D.O.). This value, more than any other, determines whether self-purification is likely to proceed satisfactorily and whether the stream community or ecosystem is adequately balanced. University, government, and industrial laboratories are currently pressing research investigations dealing with induced re-aeration by mechanical aerators and flow augmentation schemes as a means of maintaining D.O. contents compatible with maintaining sound or healthy waterways. Theoretically, under conditions of standard temperature and pressure (20° C, 760 mm Hg) 9 mg of oxygen can be dissolved in a liter of water; this is said to be the saturation concentration for this particular temperature. Healthy streams and rivers generally yield D.O.'s of 5 to 7 mg/l. Values consistently below 4 mg/l tend to indicate organic overloading, developing sepsis and migration downstream of fish species. Neither the B.O.D. nor the D.O. indicates the presence or degree of human fecal matter in a river, stream, or bathing area.

In June, 1967, Frank O'Connor, then president of the City Council of New York, publicly chastised Mayor Lindsay for, as he charged, blatantly disregarding the health of New York's citizens. Mr. O'Connor indicted the mayor for permitting the people to bathe in the "grossly polluted" waters of the city's beaches. Replying to this charge, the mayor contended that he would close the beaches only if the Department of Health indicated a need to do so.

On July 6, Mr. O'Connor repeated his charge and further noted that the unusually heavy rains preceding and during July

4 had greatly intensified the pollution. This further note clearly indicated a lack of even rudimentary understanding of the idea and meaning of water pollution as measured by the coliform index, a bacteriological test used as an indicator of fecal matter in water supplies.* However, Mr. O'Connor is not alone in this: several recent books attempting to persuade the public of the severe fecal pollution existing in our waters have made the same inept pronouncement.

The typical aquatic microflora and the bacteria that decompose the organic constituents of sewage have no sanitary or public health significance. That is, they are not found in the intestinal tracts of either human or animal species, nor are they pathogenic agents. Since most streams and rivers used as sources of drinking water have been contaminated by sewage effluent, the presence of fecal matter must be considered a distinct possibility; as a consequence, the presence of agents of infectious disease is not unlikely.

Because it is only an assumption, but one to be ignored at our peril, water for domestic use must be subjected to regular and continuous bacteriological examination. The tests involved are not employed simply to determine the numbers and types present, but rather are specific for those whose natural habitat is the human bowel. As epidemiological evidence has established beyond a doubt a cause-effect relationship between water-borne illnesses and certain microbes of intestinal origin, the value of these bac-

---

* With regard to Mr. O'Connor's statement that after the intense rains "pollution" increased, two possibilities remain: he could have made a lucky guess or he could have been correct. Because of the large diameters of the sewers, wastes move slowly during periods of low or normal flow. As a result, the heavier excretal solids settle out. During periods of heavy rains, large volumes of water tend to flush out of the settled material. This acts to increase the coliform index of the water samples taken for analysis.

If, as noted later in the discussion, tests to establish the fecal or non-fecal nature of the coliforms were not carried out, Mr. O'Connor could only have made a lucky guess. Right or wrong, he had no business making the statement. Political considerations should have no place in matters of the public's health.

teriological examinations in evaluating the safety of the water supply has been solidly substantiated. Certainly, no bacteriological test is performed more frequently than that for the determination of water quality.

The tests for water quality seek primarily to verify the presence or absence of recent fecal contamination. If intestinal discharges have contaminated the water, large numbers of coliform bacteria are certain to be present. These organisms are benign types, living a saprophytic existence as part of the natural flora of the large intestine (the colon). They incite no illness and are always present in feces; thus their presence in water testifies to the fact of fecal discharge. As natural inhabitants of the human bowel, they do not find environmental conditions in natural waters suitable for multiplication and, in fact, begin to die off rapidly. Their presence in water samples, therefore, permits a diagnosis of recent origin.

If fecal matter is of recent origin it can correctly be assumed that, along with the harmless coliforms, there may also be pathogenic organisms such as *Salmonella typhosa,* the organism associated with typhoid fever; *Shigella dysenteriae,* the organism associated with bacterial dysentery; *Vibrio comma,* the cholera organism; and *Entamoeba histolytica,* a protozoan associated with amebic dysentery, to mention a few. Pathogens such as these, if present in water supplies, are usually few in number and exceedingly difficult to detect. Accordingly, no effort is made to test for them during routine examinations, instead, an indicator organism is used.

The concept of an indicator organism is well established among public health microbiologists and engineers, and the biochemical reactions and growth characteristics have been studied extensively. Basically, the indicator's presence in routine tests indicates the presence of excretal material and the possible presence of pathogens. In addition, its numbers usually vary with the degree of fecal pollution. Its absence indicates that intestinal discharges are not present and that the water is presumably free of pathogens. In addition, it is hardier than most pathogens: its survival and presence in a sample of water indicates the potential hazard of the supply. Here again mature, professional judgment, combined with standardized criteria, is needed to determine when a water supply is unfit to drink or bathe in. Such decisions cannot be made lightly or be based on political expediency.

Although several groups of bacteria have served as indicators, no group is so well established as the coliforms. The routine test for determination of coliform density requires that samples of water be inoculated into a series of tubes containing a medium specific for its growth, followed by incubation at $35°$ C $\pm 0.5°$ C for 48 ± 3 hrs. Gas production, in the form of bubbles of CO_2 rising in the tubes of liquid, is positive evidence of the presence of coliform organisms. A coliform index, or a count of the most probable number of organisms present in the original water sample, can be calculated on the basis of the amount of sample inoculated into a stated number of tubes. Criteria for the acceptance or rejection of a water supply are based on a long record of correlation of this parameter with the occurrence or non-occurrence of waterborne disease outbreaks.

Often, after prolonged or torrential rains, the coliform counts of water samples rise precipitously. Does this reflect the fact that human fecal matter has been washed into waterways as surface runoff? In the U.S. or Western Europe, this could hardly be the case. How then can this rise in coliforms be interpreted?

By definition, coliforms include all rod-shaped, non–spore-forming Gram-negative bacteria that can ferment lactose with gas production within forty-eight hours at $35°$ C. Unfortunately, this encompasses organisms that are non-fecal in origin. That is, although they are called coliforms, a group of them do not live in the colon of human or animal species. This group is widely distributed in nature, being found in grasses, in soil, and on plants. Accordingly, since these organisms are carried into water sources that are intended for drinking or bathing, and since they are not indicators of fecal contamination or the possible presence of pathogens, a means of distinguishing between fecal and non-fecal coliforms is necessary and desirable.

To distinguish *Escherichia coli* a major fecal coliform species, from *Aerobacter aerogenes* a major representative of the non-fecal coliforms, simple, straightforward, but accurate biochemical procedures have been developed. If members of the genus *Escherichia,* particularly *E. coli,* are present, then gas production is a positive indication of fecal contamination, with all its attendant implications; if organisms belonging to the genus *Aerobacter,* particularly, *A. aerogenes,* is producing the gas, then fecal contamination can be ruled out. Thus, Mayor Lindsay was quite correct in replying to Mr. O'Connor that he would close the beaches to bathing only on the advice of the Department of Health. Presumably, they had carried out the differentiation tests and found the coliforms to be non-fecal types.

Two additional points are worthy of note. The Atlantic Ocean is the "old swimming hole" for the most of New York City's residents. It has a salt content of approximately 3.5 percent. This is not conducive to the survival of disease-transmitting pathogens, which are among the most fragile and sensitive of all microbes. Furthermore, the ocean has never been incriminated as a vehicle for any waterborne disease. French scientists studying the problem of waterborne poliomyelitis found that the prevalence of clinically manifest paralytic poliomyelitis was not higher in bathers who swam regularly in the Mediterranean Sea near Marseilles, France, than in non-bathers. Speaking at a symposium entitled "Transmissions of Viruses by the Water Route," in December, 1965,[1] Dr. Joseph Melnick of Baylor University Medical School noted that small doses of virus in water supplies may serve to immunize rather than produce disease. He noted that sewage workers had the lowest rate of absenteeism among all occupation groups studied. "It appeared that sewage workers were regularly immunized by their exposure to small amounts of infected material," he said.

Historically, the primary reason for water-pollution control was prevention of waterborne disease. If public health authorities in the U.S. and Western Europe were asked to point to their single greatest accomplishment, it would undoubtedly be eradication of the classical waterborne diseases. Nevertheless, many infectious waterborne diseases remain endemic in other areas of the world, particularly, the non-industrialized nations of Asia, Africa, and Latin America.

In addition to cholera, typhoid, and dysentery, the developing countries contend with bilharziasis, commonly contracted when bathing in fecal- and urine-polluted streams and canals; urban filariasis, transmitted by the bite of an insect vector that breeds in polluted water; and infectious hepatitis, which was responsible for a recent major epidemic that included approximately thirty thousand cases in New Delhi, India.

Because of the rapidity of human migration from endemic areas, coupled with the possibility that certain disease agents may adapt to new habitats in new environments, constant vigilance and surveillance of water supplies must be maintained.

That proper treatment of raw water can substantially reduce illness resulting from the ingestion of water contaminated with fecal matter is seen in Figure 22. In Philadelphia, there were from six thousand to ten thousand typhoid cases each year between 1890

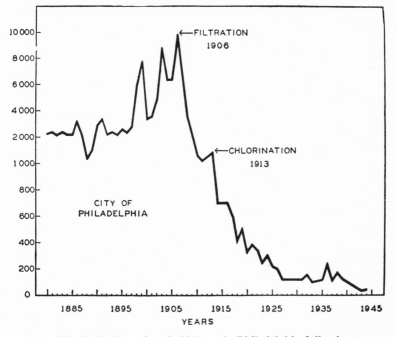

FIGURE 22. Reduction of typhoid fever in Philadelphia following treatment of the water supply

Adapted from W. G. Smillie and E. D. Kilbourne, *Preventive Medicine and Public Health,* 3rd. ed. (New York: Macmillan, 1962)

and 1907. With the introduction in 1907 of so simple a device as sand filtration of drinking water, a precipitous reduction in illness was achieved. Six years later, the introduction of chlorination, over the strident protests of those opposed to the addition of synthetic chemicals to water, another abrupt drop in typhoid cases occurred. Clearly, mechanical and chemical treatment could control waterborne disease. As if to remind us that we cannot wear our laurels lightly, and that vigilance cannot be relaxed, an epidemic of waterborne typhoid involving some eighteen thousand people occurred in Riverside, California, in 1966. As yet, conclusive evidence as to the mechanism of its entry and transmission has not been obtained.

Three years earlier, a classical explosive outbreak of typhoid occurred at one of the most affluent playgrounds of Europe: 437 cases, and 3 deaths, occurred in Zermatt, Switzerland. Months after the epidemic had passed, a leakage of sewage into the chlorination tank was found. Because of the additional burden of organic matter, the chlorine concentration was precipitously reduced, and with it, its disinfecting action.

Another example illustrating the ability of water to convey infectious material is bilharziasis, also known as schistosomiasis* and snail fever. This is considered to be the world's worst disease; estimates of the number infected range between 120 and 250 million. It is primarily a disease of tropical and subtropical areas, but because of the ease and rapidity of world travel, it is also found in other regions. For example, New York City has an estimated forty thousand cases imported from Puerto Rico and Cuba. There is little danger that the disease will spread here, as it is not directly communicable and our ecological conditions hinder its establishment in a new habitat.

Bilharziasis, while seldom directly fatal, is debilitating and eventually contributes to the death of its victims. While the afflicted endure the illness for years, their ability to work is severely restricted. The economic loss to a country such as Egypt, with 47

* In 1851 Theodor Bilharz discovered the parasite in the blood of victims. The disease is often called bilharziasis in his honor. *Schistosomiasis,* another name for the disease, refers to the type of parasite that causes the disease, a schistosome or flatworm.

percent of its population (fourteen million people) infected, has been calculated as approximately $560 million per year.

Over a hundred years passed from the time of Bilharz's discovery of the flatworm in the blood of a patient to the complete untangling of the complex life-cycle of the human illness, which includes a snail, three growth stages in the development of the miniscule worm, and man.

A crop of eggs laid by the worms gains entrance to irrigation canals and streams via urine or feces. The eggs hatch out as pear-shaped, ciliated miracidia which must find a snail host within twenty-four hours, or die. Those that locate a suitable snail host burrow into it and undergo a two-month period of incubation. During this period the miracidia are transformed. They become fork-tailed cercariae that leave the snail and seek another host, usually a warm-blooded one, human or animal. In countries where streams, canals, ponds, or any other watery area such as rice paddies serve as latrines, laundries, and recreational areas, it is the rare cercaria that cannot locate a human host. Thus, the cycle is completed—and oft repeated.

These free-swimming cercariae appear to fasten themselves by a sticky secretion to human skin, then penetrate with the aid of proteolytic enzymes, which dissolve a path for them. Upon reaching a blood vessel they pass to their ultimate sites, the veins of the upper and lower intestinal tract, or the veins of the bladder and rectum. After several months the cercariae develop into adult schistosome worms. At the height of the disease hundreds of worms can be found in a victim; each lays as many as three thousand eggs per day. The number and size (approximately two centimeters) of the adult worms causes mechanical blocking of hepatic circulation, which produces the fluid-filled, swollen abdomen characteristic of biharziasis.

After three to six weeks, an explosive onset of fever occurs, along with generalized aches, diarrhea, and extreme weakness. During the chronic stage the victim grows emaciated and steadily weaker. Thus far, treatment has been "worse than the disease."*

* Recent reports indicate almost 100-percent effectiveness of niridazole (Ambilhar, Ciba) in curing schistosomiasis by preventing egg-laying.

Because drug therapy proved unsuccessful, attempts have been made to rid canals and streams of the host snail by chemical molluscicides such as copper sulfate and sodium pentachlorophenate. Unfortunately, this has not proved successful.

Although snail fever was first described in a four-thousand-year-old Egyptian papyrus, it has been given added impetus by man in the name of progress. The construction of huge irrigation projects in the underdeveloped countries of the world has caused the disease to spread into areas where it was previously unknown. The construction of the Aswan High Dam, for example, will now control the annual silt-laden floods that in the past reduced the snail populations. Cautious estimates suggest that 55 to 70 percent of the population in the reclaimed areas can be expected to become infected as the water backing up behind the dam spreads the snails and worms over greater and greater areas. If only 55 percent of the population becomes infected, an additional 2,650,-000 new cases are anticipated after the completion of the dam. This will bring the total number of cases in Egypt alone to over 17,000,000. While the Aswan project will make new land available for cultivation, the medical costs may offset the agricultural gains.

As was noted above, although there are some forty thousand known cases in New York City and some additional cases spread around the country by returning servicemen and tourists, bilharziasis is not expected to establish itself here. However, two of our native snails, both of the genus *Pomatiopsis,* are potential hosts of the fluke. One is limited to Louisiana, the other is more widespread: its range is from the Great Lakes to Kentucky and from Iowa eastward to the coast. Public health authorities appear fully convinced that our system of sewage disposal and our personal hygiene habits do not offer the necessary ecological facets for the infection to become established. Again, vigilance and regular surveillance are expensive but necessary precautions.

It is of interest to note that cercarial dermatitis, also known as swimmer's itch and clam digger's dermatitis, are the result of an infection by an avian form of schistosome worm. The eggs reach the water in bird droppings, and the miracidia locate suitable host snails in which to develop into fork-tailed cercariae. The cercariae invade human skin, producing pustules that itch intensely. The itch is well known in such diverse states as Michigan, Minnesota, New York, Rhode Island, Florida, and California.

A type of water pollution that affects man only indirectly is entirely man-made. I refer to the growing menace of poisoning in grazing ducks who eat lead shot.

Many water birds, particularly ducks, feed by harvesting a varied fare from the bottom of lakes, marshes, and ponds. In areas that are heavily hunted, waste lead shot accumulates in large amounts at the bottom of these waters. The feeding birds pick up the shot—which resemble seeds—only to have it lodge in their gizzards. The grinding action of the gizzard on the shot, coupled with the action of acidic digestive juice, erodes the lead from the surface of the pellets. The soluble lead salts pass into the digestive tract and initiate a complex of symptoms. The first manifestation of toxicity is a reduction of food intake resulting from a paralyzed gizzard. This leads to starvation and ultimate death. Large numbers of birds have been known to ingest such large quantities of waste shot pellets that death resulted from a highly acute form of lead poisoning.

In 1966, the Bureau of Sport Fisheries and Wildlife estimated that each year tens of thousands of ducks and geese fall victim to spent shot. Fortunately, the lead, toxic to the birds, does not appear to affect people who unknowingly eat the meat.

To the credit of the arms industry, major American and Canadian producers of sporting firearms have financed a ten-thousand-dollar study at the Illinois Institute of Technology to investigate the possibilities of developing a substitute for lead shot or so modifying it that it will not pose a threat to water birds. Thus far, no substitute that possesses lead's ballistic characteristics has been found.

Perhaps it is too much to expect that the tragic experiences of one country, still within memory, will not be repeated by another. Unfortunately, it appears that the Soviet State Timber Industry Committee has not heard of "Albany beef."

At the turn of the century, the Hudson River supported a thriving caviar industry. The fish-roe delicacy obtained from the giant sea sturgeon that frequented the clear waters of the Hudson River was exported to Russia by the barrelful. Sturgeon meat, another high-priced appetizer, was often called "Albany beef." Unfortunately, commercial sturgeon fishing in the Hudson River lives only in the memory of old men and in newspapers yellowed with age. The large volume of sewage and industrial wastes discharged into the Hudson has profoundly altered life in the river.

Lake Baikal, in Soviet Siberia, its southern tip just a few miles from the Mongolian border, may be headed for a fate similar to that of the Hudson River. By any limnological standards the Hudson River and Lake Baikal are hardly comparable. Baikal is the largest freshwater lake in the world. With a volume of 5,520 cubic miles and a maximum depth of 5,314 feet, it is twice the size of Lake Superior and five times as deep. It also has the distinction of being the oldest lake in the world, roughly twenty-five million years old.

According to recent reports,[2] Baikal is being polluted by the waste from a huge new pulp mill. To limnologists—scientists who study freshwater lakes—this is a disaster because of the lake's purity and its diversity of biological species. Over one thousand varieties of plant and animal forms are found only in Baikal. Over millions of years many of them have evolved unique physiological processes permitting them to thrive in its peculiarly cold, mineral-free water.

It is feared that the large volume of high–oxygen-demand pulp waste will remove a great part of the existing biota, while the thermal pollution will raise the temperature of the normally frigid water high enough to permit predators, heretofore barred by the extremely cold water, to invade and annihilate other forms.

At present, the lake supplies 35 percent of Siberia's edible fish supply, including trout, perch, pike, and sturgeon. Because Baikal is over a mile deep in places and 395 miles long, water flowing into the lake remains there about four hundred years. Although this implies that pollutants may accumulate, it also implies that a good deal of time will pass before the input equals the output. This does not mean that the Soviet government has time to do nothing. If it fails to heed the warning signals, an irreplaceable natural resource could be headed for extinction.

When the American-owned tanker *Torrey Canyon,* bound for Britain with 117,000 tons of crude oil in her tanks, foundered off the southwest coast of England in March, 1967, a grave national crisis developed: at stake were the beaches that line the Cornish coast as well as the abundant flocks of sea birds and marine animals that could be lost by suffocation and drowning from the oil slick that would blanket everything.

The incident of the *Torrey Canyon,* while grim, had great instructional value. With the initial shock came all manner of "scientific" suggestions about how best to deal with the threat. Because the Royal Navy had built up a backlog of experience dealing with oil spills in harbors, its advice was sought. The Navy suggested that detergents were the answer. Accordingly, 2.5 million gallons were sprayed on beaches and at sea. This proved to be more toxic and damaging to the aquatic flora and fauna than the oil. The greatest toll was exacted from among the many species of diving birds that breed in this area; a total of twenty-five thousand dead birds were reported. Fortunately, because northerly winds blew two months after the ship discharged its oil, at a time when winds usually blow from the southwest, less than half the anticipated amount of oil ended up on the beaches.

For us, the important lesson was the lack of adequate knowledge about the effects of chemical pollutants on marine life. Such a lack should not exist. This is an area of research that should be vigorously pursued, especially if we are to plan for proper and reasonable pollution control and prevention.

Although modern technology is thought only to plunder and pollute, it can also be the means of preventing and controlling environmental pollution. For example, since the invention of paper by the Chinese some nineteen hundred years ago, the process had remained virtually unchanged. With it, pollution of waterways usually occurred wherever paper-pulping plants were located. Recall that these are high-B.O.D. wastes. In 1967, however, Karl

Kroyer of Denmark informed the world of an entirely new process for assembling cellulose fibers. A dry process of papermaking has long been the dream of many; this is what Kroyer has invented. He has indicated that his process resembles the setting of women's hair. Each hair (fiber) is positioned where it is needed and the whole is finally sprayed to set it more or less permanently in position. Because fibers can be positioned as desired, many types of paper can be prepared. But, most important, the waste emanating from paper manufacture can be drastically reduced.

In considering the future of water pollution generally, however, the World Health Organization is not terribly optimistic. They note that "population growth in seventy-five developing countries was 40 percent greater than the average for the world as a whole, which probably means that it is at least double that in some of the older industrial countries. Water supply and pollution problems may, therefore, double or more than double every ten years for some decades." They also note that the increasing population is seen largely in the urban areas and they predict that "the world rate of urban growth is 2½ times greater than the rate of rural growth. Since it is urban growth that causes the most intense pollution problems, it would appear that a doubling of the problem every ten years may well be a gross understatement of the problem."

Accordingly, piecemeal solutions to abate and control water pollution are doomed to failure. In fact, they are wasteful of a community's limited financial resources. Ecological or regional schemes are more reasonable and offer some certainty of success. They include planning for adequate sewage treatment throughout a watershed and the course of a river, and planning for land use, agricultural and industrial requirements and their byproducts, and recreational needs. Of course, this implies some loss of local authority, which is never palatable to local business interests and politicians. More will be said about this problem in Chapter 16.

CHAPTER

9

SOLID-WASTE DISPOSAL

For the ten thousand citizens of Wilton, Connecticut, 1967 began much too dramatically. The town simply ran out of space to dump its garbage. The nightmare of many city officials around the country had come true for Wilton. By the time Dr. Henry Applebaum, Wilton's health officer, declared a health emergency, many residents had gone without garbage and refuse collection for almost ten days.

Until January 1, 1967, Wilton's refuse was dumped in an open pit provided by the neighboring town of Weston. A ruling by the Connecticut General Assembly stopped this practice because of the unsanitary conditions created. Wilton then purchased seventy acres of land to use as a sanitary landfill. Residents of the area around these seventy acres went to court to prevent this, and won their case. However, Wilton was granted use of the land only until May 15, 1967. After that date they would either have to find another solution or try to have the court decision reversed. In

November, 1967, I learned from Dr. Applebaum that the use of the present disposal site would be permitted until a decision was handed down by the State Supreme Court.

In what was sure to be a precedent-setting ruling, the State Supreme Court in 1968 ruled that because of the medical urgency confronting Wilton, the injunction would be set aside, permitting free use of the seventy acres as a sanitary landfill. The judges implied that with the formation of megalopoli, many communities will sooner or later be confronted with the same dilemma. Accordingly, they gave precedence to life over property.

Although Wilton has yet to solve its present and future garbage and refuse disposal problem, the question of how to do so, is not limited to Wilton. It is a national concern.

In March, 1967, Samuel J. Kearing, Jr., commissioner of sanitation of New York City, indicated the seriousness of the problem for New York. He said: "The city has only about eight years left before it uses up the sites presently designated for dumping refuse. The city is in a real crisis."

On October 22, 1966, the world read of the awful tragedy in Aberfan, Wales. For almost a hundred years, slag—made up of shale and the other inert residue that originates from the processing of coal—had been dumped on the side of a mountain. On Thursday, October 21, the four-hundred-foot-high pile began to slide. As it slid, it picked up momentum, until a sea of slag came crashing into the village. Engulfed beneath the two million tons of coal waste were a schoolhouse, a farm, and a dozen miners' cottages. One hundred forty-four people died that day. Wilton, New York City, and Aberfan have a common problem: what to do with the solid waste produced by home and industry.

Ever since people began living in communities, there has been the problem of waste disposal; the removal of garbage, rubbish, and litter from their living areas. Moreover, disposal had to be conducted in a manner that did not generate unsavory conditions. As cities have grown, so has the problem. There was a time when people or communities could always find someplace to throw their trash. This is no longer possible. That "someplace" has been or is rapidly becoming urbanized. In addition, both the quantity and the variety of solid wastes generated by today's urban communities are cause for concern. The typical city-dweller discards four to five pounds of solid waste daily. This is double the amount of trash discarded by his parents. But, more important, the type of waste has changed considerably. The shift has been toward materials whose disposal is much more difficult, more costly, and perhaps more hazardous to health. Today, our large cities have astronomical quantities of trash to dispose of. In New York City, for example, whose more than eight million inhabitants are augmented each year by millions of visitors and whose commerce and industry generate all manner of solid waste, approximately five million tons of garbage and refuse are collected yearly. Throughout the United States, each year, we must dispose of forty-eight billion cans, twenty-six billion bottles and jars, and sixty-five billion metal and plastic caps. Add to this millions of junked automobiles, refrigerators, bedsprings, bathtubs, and a myriad of miscellaneous objects totaling some 130 million tons per year and you begin to perceive the dimensions of the problem. The bill for collecting and processing this waste is now in excess of three billion dollars annually. Only a small portion of the waste is salvaged for reuse. The unsalvaged remainder represents a vast potential for illness, pollution, and accidents.

I've used several, different terms in talking about solid waste: *rubbish, refuse, garbage,* and others. Strictly speaking, the terms are not synonymous. According to the classification developed by the American Public Works Association, each term refers to a specific type of material. For example, *rubbish* includes two groups: combustible items, such as cartons, boxes, paper, grass, plastics, bedding, and clothing; and non-combustibles, such as ashes, cans, crockery, metal furniture, glass, and bathtubs, to name a few.

Garbage is classified as waste resulting from growing, preparing, cooking, and serving food. Included in this category are market wastes. Together they account for approximately 10 percent of the volume of solid waste collected.

A third class is *dead animals,* such as the cats and dogs found on roads and streets, victims of encounters with automobiles.

This group also includes rabbits, skunks, porcupines, cows, horses, and deer, whose dead and decaying carcasses must be disposed of because of the potential health hazard.

Demolition waste includes some of the most persistent substances, such as bricks, masonry, piping, and lumber.

Sewage-treatment residue, such as septic-tank sludge and solids from the coarse screening of domestic sewage, is another category of solid waste.

The term *refuse* has no official or quasi-official definition. It is a more pleasant word than *garbage* and as such has been used to denote all types of waste, but, no matter what it is called, the critical problem of disposal remains.

Often geographical location dictates or suggests a means of disposal. For coastal cities, dumping at sea solved the problem for many years. In 1933, however, the state of New Jersey sought relief in court from the nuisance created by New York City's garbage, some of which washed ashore on her beach property. The Supreme Court's decision in favor of New Jersey has virtually eliminated barging and dumping at sea.

But it didn't rule out dumping on land. Open dumps, as such sites are called, are nothing but areas where community wastes of all types are indiscriminately collected. Certainly this is an easy means of waste disposal for the city fathers who want a cheap answer to a nagging problem. Dumping requires little planning, little maintenance, and unskilled personnel—all particularly appealing to budget-minded administrators.

Open dumping is an unsanitary practice that should be discontinued. Not only is it an uncontrolled process, but it also allows raw garbage to pile up without treatment. Figure 23 is a close-up view of a hill of refuse and garbage. Dumps offer excellent harborages for disease-carrying rats and highly favorable breeding conditions for flies and mosquitoes, both potential carriers of diseases of public-health significance. When exposed waste is dumped in coastal areas near airports, the thousands of seagulls that come to dine are a hazard to aircraft. In the summer months, spontaneous fires are common occurrences in open dumps, and the surrounding communities must live with the smoke and odor. Dur-

FIGURE 23. A refuse dump near San Francisco

ing 1965–66, fires in old, half-buried dumping areas of the New Jersey marshes near Newark Airport burned for weeks. The inaccessibility of the refuse defied all attempts to extinguish these fires and the surrounding area was blanketed under a pall of low-lying smoke, with its accompanying noxious odors, for days at a time.

In order to conserve dumping space, refuse is periodically set afire deliberately. Burning can be a solution for combustible refuse. However, it increases the load of particulate matter (smoke) and volatile chemicals in the already overburdened air and thus, of course, contributes to air pollution. Burning dumps are a major contributor to air pollution in most large cities. Figure 24 depicts

FIGURE 24. Dense smoke from the Kenilworth dump, Washington, D. C. This dump is a major contributor to air pollution in the Washington area.

the dense smoke typical of a burning dump.

For too long, the attitude to solid waste has been: dump it; barring that, burn it or bury it. Burying waste can be a satisfactory solution as long as there is public land available for this purpose, and as long as the waste does not leach out and contaminate water supplies.

An outgrowth of the open dump is the sanitary landfill. Unlike the open dump, it is a planned and supervised procedure requiring trained personnel. Nuisances are at a minimum and rodents are practically nonexistent.

Sanitary landfills can be described according to the shape and location of the space filled. Three methods are employed: area, trench, and ramp methods. With the *area method* refuse is deposited in horizontal layers on relatively flat ground, compacted, and covered over, sides and top, with soil or another inert material, in the fashion of a layer cake. With the *trench method* land is excavated in the shape of a trench to a depth, length, and width commensurate with the tract and its particular characteristics. Depths of ten to fifteen feet and widths up to twenty feet are widely employed. Refuse is deposited in the trench and compacted by bulldozer; then the trench is filled in with earth. In both the area and trench procedures, the depth of the soil between refuse and the compaction acts as a barrier to prevent fly-eggs from hatching and rats from boring. Another important feature is that the separation of refuse by walls of soil, as shown in Figure 25, prevents fires from spreading beyond a single cell. The soil cover of from eighteen to twenty-four inches virtually eliminates odors.

Both these procedures usually require about one acre per ten thousand people per year. Therefore, it is necessary for a community to set aside large tracts of land. In the face of the increasing demand for living space, the two needs come into conflict. The *ramp method* of filling land usually employs existing ravines or quarries in which refuse is deposited on an angle, against the side of the ravine or quarry. As with the area and trench methods, inert cover is placed on the sides and top at regular intervals. When refuse is buried and covered, chemical changes take place as a result of microbial activity. Refuse conveyed to a fill site ordinarily contains a lively flora of saprophytes and, at times, pathogenic bacteria, viruses, yeasts, and fungi, which are a potential source of disease to the community.

In a controlled, properly designed landfill, the energy released by the chemical changes taking place is so great that there is a precipitous rise in internal temperature. Recordings after seven to

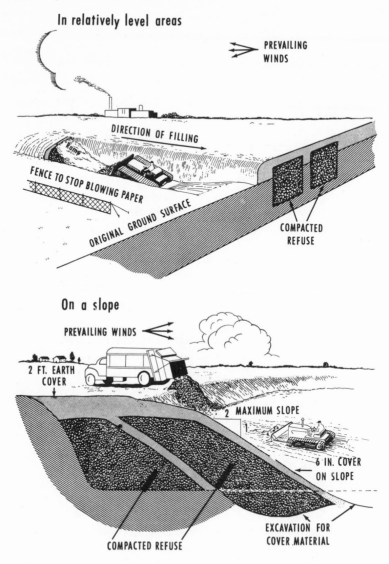

FIGURE 25. Schematic representation of a well-planned sanitary land-fill

ten days have been as high as 150° to 160° F, well above the temperature needed to kill the heat-sensitive pathogens. This offers a fair degree of assurance that the fill is not a health hazard.

Microbial activity of a newly filled area is primarily that of aerobic bacteria, and it will continue until the residual oxygen contained in crevices of the refuse is exhausted. At this point, anaerobic organisms continue the degradation. The generalized expressions of these two reactions are:

(1) organic matter + oxygen + organisms $\longrightarrow$
$$CO_2, H_2O, NH_3 + energy$$
(2) organic matter + organisms $\longrightarrow$
$$CH_4 + H_2S + CO_2 + H_2O + energy$$

A more specific example linked with the production of heat energy is seen in the degradation of the amino acid leucine, present in the protein of many foods:

$$(CH_3)_2 - CH - CH_2 - \overset{\overset{\textstyle H}{|}}{\underset{\underset{\textstyle NH_2}{|}}{C}} - COOH + 15O \longrightarrow$$
$$6CO_2 + 5H_2O + NH_3 + 755 \text{ Cal.}$$

The greater the amount of organic matter present in refuse, the higher will be the temperature reached. (See Table 9 for an analysis of typical municipal refuse.) When the anaerobic organisms enter the scheme, their metabolic reactions yield different end products. Such gases as hydrogen sulfide (H_2S) and methane (CH_4) are produced. These can have an effect in a way that I will shortly discuss.

In 1961, researchers reported their findings on the relationship of sanitary landfills to water pollution. They noted that rain and snow percolating through landfills can leach out chemicals from the refuse and thereby contaminate ground-water acquifers and nearby wells. This problem deserves increased technical and scientific study in order to elucidate any health hazard and perhaps to modify or control leaching. If this were accomplished, sanitary landfills could become a wholly acceptable method of waste disposal.

Leaching and subsequent seepage or runoff of water-soluble chemicals is a real possibility.

When Dr. William Westlin, mayor of Chatham Township, New Jersey, ordered all dumping of garbage on its dump stopped, he was guided by the fact that seepage from the dump had been shown to be a potential hazard to the wildlife of the Great Swamp National Wildlife Refuge Wilderness. Mayor Westlin's order was based on the data recently collected by the U.S. Fish and Wildlife Service. One wonders how many other mayors would have had the courage to act as Mayor Westlin did.

While chemical tests of a water supply for chemical pollutants is standard procedure, biological tests can be more sensitive and more revealing. For example, a chemical released into a stream or river one day frequently will be carried away or so diluted by the next that it will be virtually undetectable. On the other hand, had the biological "fingerprints" of that specific watercourse been catalogued—that is, if the many species of fish, aquatic insects, and microscopic flora and fauna had been recorded, and if some of these known species had been killed by a chemical passing through, their absence would have been detectable for many days or even weeks. The absence of marker species would signal the recent presence of a toxic substance.

This was, in fact, the case in Chatham. Biologists of the Fish and Wildlife Service, examining samples of water from the Great Swamp, found marker species missing in one area but not in another. "Direct observations revealed that there was a paucity of small organisms within the area influenced by the dump, as contrasted with identical areas of aquatic environment not subject to that influence."

Another case in point, from which a different lesson may be drawn, occurred in Philadelphia. Recently, the city fathers believed they had the answer for disposing of the tons of refuse collected each day: it would be shredded, packed, and shipped upstate, for burial in abandoned strip-mining coal pits. It seemed like the ideal solution to a vexing problem. However, almost as soon as the operation got underway, it was vetoed by a state authority as having the potential to cause water pollution through leaching.

Unfortunately the issue in this instance, as lofty as it may seem, was surrounded by hints and suspicion of skullduggery. Charges of personal, political, and financial gain have been hurled back and forth. It remains to be seen how this challenging contemporary problem will be solved.

As long as landfills were publically owned and sufficiently isolated from town or city to prevent the erection of dwellings on them, no problems occurred. With the growth of urban areas and the mass migrations to the suburbs, however, filled land has been developed by private interests for home sites. Two problems have resulted:

1. In too many instances, the settling of fill has caused houses to develop large cracks. A sad example of the consequences of erecting homes on fill occurred in New York City in 1966. In 1959, twelve three-story row houses were erected on filled land in the East Bronx. Six months after occupancy, cracks developed in the walls. By 1965, the floors were severely tilted and large cracks had opened along the length of the brick walls. In December, 1966, Housing Commissioner Charles Moerdler ordered the houses demolished as unsafe and hazardous. The twelve owners lost their homes and investments.

2. In 1966, First, Viles, and Levin [1] reported on the danger of toxic gases and explosive hazards in buildings erected on landfills. This brings us back to our discussion of bacterial activity. You will recall that a half-dozen gases can be produced by both aerobic and anaerobic metabolism of refuse. Dr. First and his group at Harvard found that the principal hazard associated with erecting homes on filled land arose from anaerobic production of methane. They also noted the impossibility of creating gas-tight structures because of the continuing production of gas. In addition, they found unsafe levels of gas in many buildings. The possibility of explosions was great unless suitable venting and aerating were employed.

Perhaps a better solution would be to set these lands aside

for much-needed parks and playgrounds.

One of the major uses of landfill is for the reclamation of otherwise unusable land, particularly marsh. However, the loss of marsh areas, which may serve as recreational sites and sources of fish, may not be completely desirable. This situation serves to highlight the interrelatedness of man and the biosphere. The report of a recent White House Conference on Environmental Pollution noted that the "filling in of marshes to make real-estate must be recognized as the most threatening danger to marshes." In Long Island, New York, between 1954 and 1959, over 13 percent of the wetlands were destroyed by landfill projects.

At the present rate of utilization, New York City will have used up its major sanitary landfill area at Fresh Kill, on Staten Island, by 1975, which is just six years away. Then the city will have to find other disposal sites. Are any available? A look at the map quickly shows that New York is facing a real problem.

The planners responsible for such decisions think they have a solution—to fill in Jamaica Bay.* If, they say, some four to five-thousand of Jamaica Bay's nine thousand acres could be filled in with solid waste, New York City will have solved its waste-disposal problems for the next sixty years. Is this the answer to the problem? And when Jamaica Bay has been filled, under what new rugs will the wastes be swept? This type of piecemeal, crisis-to-crisis solution is not the answer. This is a dilemma of staggering proportions that will require the creative imagination of our best scientific and technical people to solve, and it must be solved.

A method of waste disposal particularly suitable for urban areas is incineration. It may also be the solution for suburban areas that have no available sites for burying their waste.

---

* That this is not just idle speculation became evident on November 1, 1967, when the *New York Times* reported Sanitation Commissioner Kearing's remarks on the proposed $110-million refuse-disposal plant to be constructed on the site of the Brooklyn Navy Yard: "Kearing warned that the project was necessary to save the city's remaining wetlands in Pelham and Jamaica Bay from being turned into dumps."

Shortly after this article appeared, Kearing resigned.

Incineration is the reduction to ashes of combustible material by controlled burning at high temperature. Incinerators generally offer the most efficient, hygienic means of disposing of all types of combustible waste. As a result, they can be located closer to communities than landfills. This lowers haulage costs and permits nearby industry to utilize the steam byproduct, which also aids in lowering the cost of operation.

Incinerators usually operate at temperatures between 1600 and 1900° F. Temperatures in this range produce only inert ashes and smaller particles that leave as stack effluent. The ash must be hauled away for burial, usually to landfill operations. The stack effluents can increase the load of particulate matter in the air. In New York City, for example, the contribution of the eleven municipal incinerators has been estimated to be 10 to 15 percent of the total air pollution load. During 1967–1970, the planned installation of electrostatic precipitators on incinerator smokestacks should reduce their pollutional activity precipitously. Ninety-percent removal of particulate matter is commonly obtained in European installations.

One of the major needs of incineration is new design criteria. Too few engineers are engaged in this type of research. Incinerator design must be based on knowledge of the type and quantity of material to be burned. In our affluent communities today, we throw away more than ever before, and the kind of waste has changed considerably since many of the present incinerators were designed and constructed twenty-five years ago. A city that produces waste of which more than 50 percent is noncombustible has completely different requirements than a city producing refuse of which 10 to 30 percent is noncombustible. Tables 9 and 10 indicate the composition of typical municipal waste and the ranges to be found. Design criteria must be developed for each city; this has been done in only a fraction of our cities, and yet new incinerators and combustion equipment are being built without this needed data.

An ever-increasing number of communities are turning to incineration to solve their solid-waste disposal problems. A recent

TABLE 9.

Chemical composition
of typical municipal waste

		Range
Moisture	21.	0–65
Carbon	28.	16–77
Total hydrogen	3.5	2.4–10.35
Oxygen	22.35	4–45
Nitrogen	0.33	0.05–10.0
Sulfur	0.16	0.01–2.0
Non-combustible	24.93	1–72.30
C:H Ratio	39.4	9.1–131
BTU/lb.	9,000.	7000–16,000

TABLE 10.

Organic analysis of typical waste	%
moisture	21.
cellulose sugar, starch	46.6
lipids (fats, oils, waxes)	4.5
protein, 6.25N	2.0
other organics (plastics)	1.15
ash, metal, glass, etc.	24.93

study by the New York State Office of Local Government revealed the following relationship between population and method of disposal:

Sanitary landfills: 60 municipalities totaling 892,000 people
Incinerators and related fills: 66 municipalities totaling 12,200,000 people
Open dumps or private disposal: 1,420 municipalities totaling 3,659.000 people

Although this suggests that the larger municipalities utilize inciner-ation, smaller ones will be turning to it as available fill land disappears.

The most controversial but potentially the most desirable method of solid-waste disposal is composting. It is particularly advantageous because it has a threefold usefulness: The disposal of many types of refuse, the disposal of sewage sludge, and the end-product can be utilized to enrich depleted soil as a soil conditioner.

Composting is the controlled microbial degradation of organic materials to a sanitary, nuisance-free, humus-like material. The breakdown of refuse by microorganisms is probably the oldest biological waste treatment method. Unwanted waste has been buried by peoples for centuries, and our allies the microbes have split the complex organic compounds into simpler substances, which are then used by plants and converted back to complex organic matter. Refuse disposal by microbial action occurs both in the sanitary landfill and in composting. Although composting is not new, it is only within recent years that major improvements in the process have been made that allow its use for large-scale dis-posal. Basically, the production of compost results from the break-down of organic matter by bacteria and fungi under aerobic conditions. Sanitary landfills, you will recall, degrade waste via aero-bic and anaerobic metabolism. For rapid aerobic metabolism to occur, it is necessary only to ensure an optimum balance between available air and moisture. This can be enhanced by grinding the refuse to a size that will create optimum surface area for the organisms.

A primary requisite to proper functioning of a composting operation is the removal or separation out of such non-compostibles as glassware, metals, and ceramic items. Oxygen needs are provided by tumbling or aerating the compost. Figure 26 is a

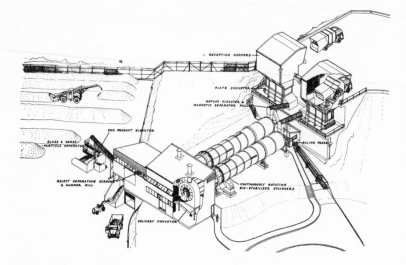

FIGURE 26. Schematic diagram of a a compost plant

schematic representation of a typical composting apparatus. The moisture requirement of not less than 30 percent can be provided by sewage sludge, which simultaneously provides a means for its disposal. Temperatures within the compost range above 150° F, which is sufficient to destroy pathogenic bacteria such as the streptococci, *Mycobacterium tuberculosis,* fly larvae, and parasitic worms, which are often found in human waste and garbage. Some dozen composting methods are available, each offering some unique modification. In spite of this, however, every attempt to compost municipal refuse on a large scale in the U.S. has failed. Apparently, one of the important reasons for failure has been the inability of the compost producer to dispose of the final compost. Another reason be the inability of the producer to operate the plant profitably. The large volume of non-compostible material is also difficult to dispose of, and it increases the cost of the operation. Hopefully, research in this field in the coming years may provide a viable method of waste disposal. With the increasing demand for food and with decreasing soil fertility, the use of compost to improve agricultural production becomes critically important. The nutrients and humus obtained from composting of waste can be conserved for agricultural use, while at the same time sanitary disposal and protection of the environment are accomplished. Curiously enough, although composting has not taken hold in the larger cities of the U.S., European cities make good use of it. One of the largest composting plants in the world, with a capacity of six hundred tons of refuse per day, is in successful operation in Rome. Similar plants employing Dano Biostabilizer Composting Units operate profitably in such cities as Ghent, Belgium; Leicester, England; Jerusalem, Israel. Figure 27 shows a Biostabilizer Unit in operation in Aukland, Australia. Figure 28 is a cutaway sketch of the Tollemache Composting System in operation in Southern Rhodesia.

Another major means of disposing of certain types of refuse, particularly garbage, is feeding it to hogs. Such hog farming is an attempt at conservation in which food waste is converted into

FIGURE 27. Biostabilizer unit in operation in Aukland, New Zealand

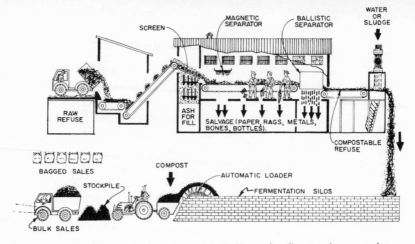

FIGURE 28. Schematic diagram of a Tollemache System in operation in South Africa

food. Feeding garbage to hogs is of some economic importance in a few areas of the U. S.: one thousand pounds of garbage produces fifty pounds of pork! The economics may be sweet, but the public-health aspects are often foul. The feeding of uncooked garbage to swine can be an important means of transmitting trichinosis to those who eat the infected meat. The farms are often so unsanitary that they become major harborages of rats and breeding areas for flies and mosquitoes. The odors in communities surrounding hog farms can be appalling.

Between 1953 and 1955 a virus disease of swine, vesicular exanthema, prompted the U.S. Public Health Service and many state departments of health to develop legislation requiring the pasteurization of garbage (exposure to a temperature of 212° F for thirty minutes) before it could be fed to hogs. The cost of this additional treatment and the increased cost of garbage collection have made hog farming only marginally profitable. As a consequence, fewer farms operate each year. Despite this, the feeding of garbage to hogs is currently a significant method of disposal; about 25 percent of the total garbage produced in the U.S. is fed to hogs. Since garbage must be collected separately or separated after collection, additional costs are involved. As municipalities shift to single collections, hog feeding may be reduced even further.

An important but little-considered type of waste is that generated by farm and domestic animals—manure. It has been estimated that the farm animal population in the U.S. is three times the human population. The wastes from swine, chicken, and cattle alone are equivalent to ten times the wastes from the human population. It has been calculated that seven to ten chickens produce as much waste as one person. Thus, a chicken farm with one hundred thousand birds produces as much waste as a town of fifteen thousand people. Additional studies have shown that one hog produces as much waste as two people, and one cow as much as ten people. The number one technical problem facing livestock producers, and, indirectly the rest of the population, is manure management. The encroachment of urban areas on previously rural areas, the scarcity of land for disposal, and the characteristics of manure make for some particularly difficult problems ahead. In addition to this is the problem of how to dispose of thirty million dead chickens each year.

In December, 1963, a National Conference on Solid Waste Disposal was held in Chicago to bring together people from many diverse fields of interest in order to evaluate the state of technology in the field and to discuss future needs. One of the major conclusions that emerged from the three-day conference was that we need a change in attitude as to the importance of engineers and scientists who are concerned with this aspect of environmental health. This means that we must attract the best brains to a field that has not had its share. Little status is attached to sewage and waste-disposal research. A second conclusion was that completely new ways of handling our waste must be developed.

On October 20, 1965, President Johnson signed into law the Solid Waste Disposal Act. Public Law 89-272 empowered and authorized the Department of Health, Education, and Welfare to invest over ninety-two million dollars during 1966–69 for solid-waste research and development activities, demonstration projects, surveys, and technical and financial aid to state, local, and regional agencies for the purpose of promoting interest in solid-waste disposal programs. Hopefully, this will be the spark that ignites the much-needed interest in some of our top scientists and engineers to conduct investigations in this neglected area.

As our society becomes more affluent and more people have more money to spend, we generate great mountains of waste. It is far cheaper to buy a new item than to repair an old one, so the old one is thrown out. Technological advances create new products that are extremely difficult to degrade or dispose of by the established methods. Much of our clothing, toys, dinnerware, hardware is now made of microbial-resistant plastics. These items are not made to last, but they can't be disposed of easily. The manufacturers who produce them give little thought to their disposal.

As the developing nations of Asia, South America, Africa, and the Middle East also become more affluent, they too will have to contend with disposing of mountains of waste—unless they profit by our experience.

AIR POLLUTION

On December 17, 1963, President Johnson signed into law the first Clean Air Act. Public Law 88-206 was an historic milestone for the control of community air pollution. It provided for federal interposition and for the establishment of a program to meet the steadily growing demands for cleaner air. With the signing of Public Law 89-272, an amendment to the Clean Air Act, on October 20, 1965, President Johnson indicated that the federal government would assume a greater role in guiding and planning for the prevention and control of pollution in the air over our cities.

On fixing his name to this document, the President remarked, "We have now reached the point where our factories, our automobiles, our furnaces, and our municipal dumps are spewing out more than 150 million tons of pollutants annually into the air we breathe—almost one-half million tons a day."

In December, 1966, Dr. William Stewart, Surgeon General of the United States Public Health Service, sponsored a National

Convention on Air Pollution in Washington, D.C., to focus greater public attention on the need to control air pollution. The battle was joined.

Stretching from the surface of the earth toward outer space is a relatively thin layer of air. This troposphere, some five to eleven miles deep, contains the air we breathe and the air we foul. From the day we are born we start contaminating the air around us with every breath, cough, and sneeze. As the years roll by, we add the byproducts of cigarette, cigar, and pipe smoking, cooking, driving our cars, and heating our homes. While man has only himself to blame for the magnitude of the pollutants present in the air, a truly unpolluted atmosphere never existed. The restless molecules of air carry with them many particles and gases flung up by the forces of nature. Decaying animal carcasses, ozone, bacteria, soil dust, nitrogen dioxide, salts, pollens, volcanic dust (including sulphur dioxide, hydrogen sulfide, and hydrogen fluoride), and the smoke and gases of forest fires would pollute the atmosphere even if man had never appeared on the scene. However, man lost little time in aggravating the problem. With his first technological advance, the discovery of fire for cooking and warmth, man-made atmospheric pollution began. Current estimates of the annual amount of aerial garbage poured into the air above our cities are between 125 and 150 million tons, a greater tonnage than our annual steel production.

Air pollution is the presence in the air of substances in amounts great enough to interfere directly or indirectly with our comfort, safety, and health, or with our enjoyment of property. Public and governmental concern with air pollution is generally considered to spring from the fact that the average person inhales approximately a half liter of air with each breath. As most of us breathe some twenty-two thousand times every twenty-four hours, we inhale about two thousand gallons of air per day. Each liter (approximately one quart) of air in our urban centers has been estimated to contain several million particles of foreign matter. Thus, in a day a city dweller can inhale some twenty billion particles of . . . what? These particles, it is claimed, must certainly impair human health. After all, we can clearly see the ill effects on ornamental plants and crops, as well as the corrosion of buildings and building materials. How can human tissue withstand the onslaught? Does it? Let us defer discussion of the effects of air pollution on health until the total problem has been more fully discussed; but let us keep this point in mind as we define such things as pollution, dirty air, and foul air. Are these necessarily linked with illness and disease?

As a prelude to a discussion of air pollution it may be well to ask the question, Is pollution of air, over and above the natural level, a necessary consequence of our style of life? It is well recognized that a major cause of air pollution is the congregation of large numbers of people in industrial city centers—the sources of affluence. Affluence and pollution appear to increase simultaneously.

In our country (and in other countries as well) hundreds of new chemicals and products are created each year. They are used to kill insects and bugs, clean our clothes, run our automobiles and machines, and wash our dishes. Some of these new chemicals even fight disease; but when their usefulness is ended, they often find their way, as waste, into the air we breathe and the water we drink. Often invisible—air pollution is not always seen as dark smoke—these materials can blanket an entire community in clouds of potentially hazardous vapors.

In order to supply vast numbers of people with electricity to light their homes and offices, schools and businesses, and to power television sets, radios, washing machines, air conditioners, toasters, vacuum cleaners, and the host of other devices that have become an integral part of our daily lives, huge amounts of fuel must be burned. It is this burning of fuel that constitutes one of the primary sources of waste products discharged into the air.

The effluent or exhaust from millions of automobiles, trucks, and buses needed for commercial and private transportation is another major chemical pollutant. The evaporation of solvents and the burning of mountains of paper and other solid wastes add still more to the overburdened air.

In May, 1966, Mayor Lindsay's Task Force on Air Pollution specified the sources of pollution in New York City:

1. New York City's eleven municipal refuse-disposal stations, with their forty-seven furnaces and smokestacks, operate with inferior smoke-control and gas-control equipment.

2. The city's public housing projects have 2,666 incinerators and 2,500 heating furnaces, most without effective pollution-control equipment.

3. Privately owned apartment houses and office buildings, use some 10,000 incinerators and 135,000 heating furnaces, all totally lacking in pollution-control devices.

4. Approximately six hundred thousand single- and double-occupancy private dwellings employ fuel oil for heating furnaces of varying degrees of efficiency.

5. Consolidated Edison operates eleven power-generating stations. In this network, 116 boilers and 49 smokestacks operate under inefficient conditions of pollution control.

6. Approximately eighty-five hundred manufacturing establishments are in operation, producing all manner of noxious gases and particulates.

7. The construction of new buildings and demolition of old ones produces large quantities of airborne dust and dirt.

8. Large quantities of street dirt which is inaccessible to streetcleaning procedures is blown into the air.

9. Approximately thirteen thousand public eating establishments operate in New York City. A large number emit smoke and odors at street level.

10. Approximately 1.5 million trucks, automobiles, and buses are operating in the city without any devices for control of effluent fumes.

11. Each year some four hundred thousand takeoffs and landings by jet aircraft at New York's airports contribute large volumes of exhaust pollutants.

12. Steamships in port. Each year the city records the operations of some twenty-five thousand steamships in New York Harbor,

apart from those of an undetermined number of engine-run harbor craft.

13. There is also pollution by invasion: dirty air drifts in from other states, especially New Jersey.

TABLE 11.

Types and Quantities of Pollutants
Produced in New York City

particulate matter (soot, fly ash *)	230,000 tons per yr
sulfur dioxide	597,000
nitrogen oxides	298,000
hydrocarbons	567,000
carbon monoxide	1,536,000

* Soot is composed of black particles in smoke resulting from burning wood, coal, and oil. Fly ash is composed of the solid un-burnable particles from .003 to 0.1 inch in diameter resulting from burning of fossil fuels.

These materials are not unique to New York City. Many are shared by cities all over the world.

It is not just industries and municipalities that contribute to air pollution. Few individuals stop to consider that in the course of their daily activities they too are polluters. How many people burn leaves in their backyards, blanketing the neighborhood in smoke? How many burn trash and refuse in inefficient home incinerators? And how many leave their car motors running while they do errands? When these activities are brought to their attention, they are shrugged off as worth nothing, and as certainly making no difference. To the polluter, there can be no great harm in his bit of pollution. Affluence contributes to pollution in still other ways. In hot climates we build our houses without the large roof overhang that would decrease the amount of air conditioning needed to make the house cool. In northern areas, we build houses with enormous picture windows, thereby increasing the amount of fuel needed for heating. In short, individuals and industry are the culprits together, and, apparently, our way of life is far too comfortable to give up. Table 12 shows the magnitude of the

---

TABLE 12.

*Air pollution in New York City
on an average heating day (tons per day)*

Space Heating	21
Vehicular Exhaust	695
Refuse Combustion	120
Miscellaneous Losses	
AUTOMOTIVE EVAPORATION	120
SOLVENT EVAPORATION	
DRY CLEANING	24
SURFACE COATING	350
ALL OTHERS	176
Miscellaneous, Other	74
Overall Total (Rounded)	1550

SOURCE: *Air Pollution in New York City,* Council of the City of New York, Report M-970, June 22, 1965.

---

pollution load in New York City from all measurable sources for one day. Will we consider making changes in established habits and patterns of life as a price for cleaner air? I wonder. There is good reason why such countries as India and Mexico, and many of the countries of Africa and South America, for example, still have clean air. They have not as yet reached our state of affluence. When they do, if they fail to profit from our experience, air pollution will be their lot also. Unfortunately, this is already becoming so in some of the developing countries, as they rush to gain the benefits of industrialization without concern for its unwholesome byproducts.

I noted two major sources of air pollution: fuel for heating and electricity and fuel for automotive transportation. These two different fuels produce dissimilar types of air pollutants and, depending upon prevailing geographical and meteorological conditions, produce two dissimilar types of air pollution. The Los Angeles or smog type of pollution is a characteristic of automotive effluents acting in concert with the location of the city. The New York or London type of air pollution, on the other hand, results from burning huge quantities of fossil fuels—coal and oil. Since the effects of both types of air pollution are notably worse during a meteorological mixup, called an inversion, it may be appropriate to describe this condition before discussing the pollutants themselves.

Pilots and mountain climbers are quite aware of the reduction in temperature that occurs the higher they climb. With each thousand-foot rise, the temperature drops about 5.5° F (1.8° C). When this normal condition is reversed, that is, when there is a temperature *increase* with increasing height, the condition is called an inversion. Inversions occur more often in the autumn and winter months and during the early morning hours.

On a clear, calm night, the surface of the earth cools quickly. In response to this surface cooling, the air in contact with the earth's surface is also cooled. During the hours between evening and morning, this air has cooled considerably, while the upper atmosphere (air) has remained relatively unchanged. The result is a layer of warm air sandwiched between two cold layers—an inversion. The feature that all inversions have in common is the damping action of the warm layer on the cool bottom layer. This damping action acts like a lid on a pot. It prevents or severely reduces the air's natural upward movement. With such a condition prevailing, the air over a community, city, or region is literally trapped. If the air is trapped over a large industrial or urban area, pollutants emitted from smokestacks or tailpipe exhausts cannot be blown away (diluted) but remain fixed in the area, to pile up to higher and higher levels—sometimes to dangerous levels. Figure 29 shows the increases in pollution levels of four byproducts of both fossil fuel and gasoline which actually occurred in New York City in 1962. Figure 30 depicts an inversion and a normal pattern.

The Los Angeles Basin is an area of about four hundred square miles, with the Pacific Ocean to the west and hills on the other three sides. This geometry inhibits horizontal air movements. Thus, air masses have little opportunity to escape from the basin.

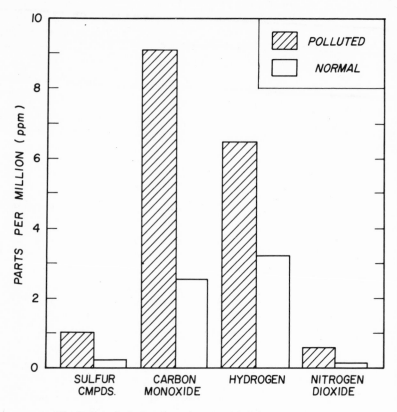

FIGURE 29. Polluted air levels and normal levels

In addition, temperature inversions, prohibiting vertical air movement, occur 260 to 270 days a year. During prolonged inversions, pollutant concentrations increase precipitously as the air mass shifts back and forth—from the city to the ocean during the night, when land breezes prevail, and back over the city in the morning, when sea breezes prevail. The predominantly sunny weather of Los Angeles adds to the problem: In the presence of nitrogen oxides and the sun's energy (in the form of ultraviolet irradiation), organic chemicals undergo a photochemical reaction that

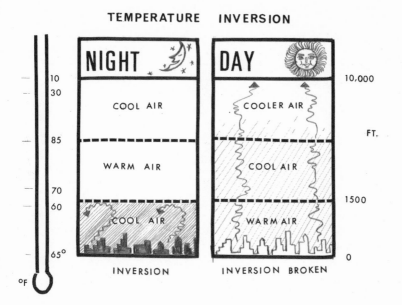

FIGURE 30. Inversion and normal condition

can produce entirely new compounds, reduces visibility, and produces eye irritation, crop damage, and characteristic noxious odors. This peculiar reaction was first noticed in Los Angeles and is, therefore, referred to as Los Angeles or photochemical smog. An important part of the photochemical problem is our transportation system's almost total dependence on gasoline, and on the internal combustion engine, which is the principal source of the hydrocarbons (some 130 have already been identified), carbon monoxide, and oxides of nitrogen present in the atmosphere. The concentrations of these compounds emitted by an individual car are insignificant. However, when multiplied by millions of cars in city traffic, the emissions can be measured in tons. Even these large amounts are not hazardous until the air masses over a community stagnate as they do during an inversion. Table 13 indicates the estimated amounts of a series of pollutants emitted during one week in New Jersey. The statistics for California, with over 8.5 million registered automobiles, more than three times the number registered in New Jersey, would be considerably greater.

TABLE 13.

Estimated Weekly Amounts of Pollutants Emitted in New Jersey

Pollutant	Tons per week *
Carbon monoxide	64,800
Hydrocarbons	6,480
Oxides of nitrogen	2,160
Aldehydes	108
Sulfur compounds	162
Organic acids	43
Ammonia	43
Other solids	6.5

* It should be noted that tonnage may not be as important as concentration.

Besides its engine, the automobile has two additional emission sources: evaporation from the fuel tank and the carburetor. It has been estimated that for every thousand gallons of gasoline put into gas tanks, five leave unburned, two leave the crankcase ventilation pipe, and one is lost through evaporation. These evaporative losses are hydrocarbons. Neither carbon monoxide nor oxides of nitrogen are involved.

To reduce the automobile's contribution to atmospheric pollution, electric cars are being reinvented. Although electrically powered vehicles do not produce hydrocarbons, carbon monoxide, sulfur compounds, or aldehydes, they do produce ozone. Curiously enough, few reports have called attention to this or calculated the degree of concentration of ozone in urban atmospheres that might be expected as a result of the operation of millions of electrically driven vehicles. However, with advances in switching design, motor and control design, and transistorized switching circuits, an electric car suitable for moderate-speed urban use would be feasible.

Impetus for the eventual mass-production of electric cars was provided by a cross-country race that began on August 26, 1968. Two great engineering schools agreed to race the products of their electrical skills, the California Institute of Technology using a vehicle containing a lead-acid battery and the Massachusetts Institute of Technology using a racer powered by a nickel-cadmium battery. Although the winner of this race has yet to be decided (the MIT entry crossed the finish line first, but since it had to be towed across, CIT was declared the nominal but tenuous winner), the race did indicate that mass-production of a high-speed, battery-powered electric car is a long way off—at least twenty-five years, if not longer.

It also highlighted the fact that while universities and some few industrial firms are trying with quite limited financial backing to develop a suitable energy source to power the kind of automobile the public will accept, the utility companies, who stand to profit the most from such developments, have done nothing to advance these expensive investigations. As an electric car will have to be recharged each night by plugging it into a 110-volt outlet, use of electricity in homes and factories will rise precipitously. It would be a welcome change if these huge corporations invested in the community by diverting a portion of their substantial profits into research—or the support of research—that would aid in the control of air pollution.

On April 29, 1967, the Ford Motor Company, in conjunction with the Mobil Oil Company, announced that they planned to begin a seven-million-dollar research program to develop fume-free, gasoline-powered automobiles. This projected investigation will concentrate on all elements of the engine: fuel and lubricant composition, catalysts, afterburners that would help oxidize unburned gasoline, and methods of removing nitrogen oxide from the exhaust and of controlling evaporation from the fuel tank and carburetor. This type of research is eminently desirable, and its initiation may be due in part to the mounting public outcry against air pollution.

That they have made a point of specifying research on after-burners and catalysts to aid in the oxidation of unburned gases, may be of distinct value. Apparently, it has been conceded by both public and private sources that none of the proposed after-burners has proved workable. After approximately five years of effort, an effective and efficient unit has not been produced.

In the New York and London type of pollution, which is the predominant type of atmospheric contamination found in most large industrialized communities, vertical inversions are not as frequent as in the Los Angeles type, nor is horizontal air passage usually impeded. Dispersal of pollutants is thus not frequent as in the Los Angeles type, nor is horizontal air passage usually impeded. Dispersal of pollutants is thus not generally restricted. Although vertical inversions do occur, they are relatively infrequent. Restrictive topography, however, is not a necessary condition for extreme pollution levels if contaminants are being discharged into the atmosphere at a sufficiently high rate. New York City, for example, is not hemmed in by hills on any of its borders, but nevertheless, was blanketed by a mass of stagnant warm air above a layer of cool air for several days during the Thanksgiving weekend of November, 1966. The effects on human health of the pile-up of sulfur dioxide and particulates is still being studied.

The pollutants in areas that burn fossil fuels are primarily sulfur dioxide and particulate matter; oxides of nitrogen and hydrocarbons are present, but to a lesser degree. These substances are all the byproducts of manufacturing, electric-power generation, burning of refuse, and space heating.

Much of the available and usable knowledge concerning the effects of air pollution on human health has come from acute exposures during prolonged inversional episodes or accidents. Two of these acute episodes occurred in areas where large amounts of fossil fuels were used and where heavy industry also contributed its special pollutants. These two areas were further handicapped by restrictive topography. A third acute episode occurred in a large city with no restriction on air flow. It has been only under the extreme conditions in these three episodes, described below, that fairly strong causal links between air pollution and acute upper respiratory illness has been established.

The Meuse Valley of Belgium, scene of some of the bloodiest battles of World War I, is a heavily industrialized area. Blast furnaces, glass factories, lime furnaces, and sulfuric acid and artificial fertilizer plants spew a variety of contaminant chemicals into the atmosphere. During the first week of December, 1930, a thick fog blanketed most of Belgium. The air was especially stagnant in the river valleys, particularly along a fifteen-mile stretch of the Meuse. Three days after this abnormal weather condition began, residents began to report shortness of breath, coughing, and nausea. Thousands became ill; the exact number was never ascertained. About sixty people died. Again deaths were primarily among the elderly and those with longstanding illnesses of the heart and lungs. Once the fog lifted, no new cases occurred.

Because this was the first notable acute air pollution episode of the twentieth century, public health scientists were unprepared. A study of the area after the incident suggested that the effects on health had been caused by a mixture of the sulfur oxides, sulfur dioxide gas, and an aerosol of sulfur trioxide. This has never been fully substantiated, and such an episode has not recurred in the Meuse Valley.

The episode in Donora, Pennsylvania, took place during the last week of October, 1948. Donora is located some thirty miles south of Pittsburgh in a highly industrialized valley along the Monongahela River. On the morning of October 27 the air over Donora became very still and fog enveloped the city. The air over the city was trapped, and it remained so for four days. In addition to sulfur dioxide, nitrogen dioxide, and hydrocarbon from the burning of coal for heating and electricity, the air contained the effluents from a large steel mill and a large zinc reduction plant, where ores of high sulfur content were roasted. During the period of the inversion these pollutants piled up. As they did, severe respiratory-tract infections began to occur in the older members of the population. Eye, nose, and throat irritations were common. Twenty people died; the normal expectation of death rate for a four-day period was about two. Autopsies of many of those who died showed chronic cardiovascular disease. This finding confirmed the opinion that preexisting heart disease increased the chances of serious illness and death during an air pollution episode. Before the weather changed and broke the inversion, 5,910 of the 12,000 inhabitants had become ill. This episode has never recurred in Donora.

The highly inefficient burning of soft coal in open grates by the citizens of London was primarily responsible for the fog that blotted out their capital on December 5, 1952. The city, located on a gently sloping plain, is not hemmed in by hills, unlike the Donora and Meuse Valley communities. The flow of air over London is not impeded by topography. For five days a strong inversion and fog enveloped the city to such a degree that the "ceiling" was some 150 feet high. Within twelve hours after the fog had settled over London, residents began complaining of respiratory ailments. By the time the inversion lifted on December 9, four thousand deaths in excess of the normal rate for a four-day period had been recorded in the Greater London area. Some striking differences between this episode and earlier ones were noted. The increase in mortality was not confined to the very old. Although the highest increment was among those over age forty-five, deaths occurred in all age groups. Another difference was in the rapidity of onset of illness: twelve hours, as compared to forty-eight and seventy-two in the earlier episodes. A third difference was the increased death rate in London compared with Donora and the Meuse Valley. Perhaps Londoners were more susceptible.

London experienced a second episode in 1956 that was responsible for the deaths of one thousand people and a third episode in 1962 that caused seven hundred deaths. The reductions in mortality are believed to be due to the preparations made after the 1952 experience. Sulfur dioxide from the burning of coal was implicated as the irritant mainly responsible for illnesses and deaths.

As I noted earlier, accidents can also yield valuable information. In November, 1950, the Mexican village of Poza Rica was subjected to an unusual pollutional experience. Tanks of waste hydrogen sulfide accidentally released their contents and blanketed the entire village in a yellow haze. People of all ages were hospitalized, and twenty-two died.

It becomes increasingly clear that air pollution is an extremely complicated process: the degree and type are influenced by climate, weather, industry, traffic density, heating practices, and topography. Yet there is another, perhaps more critical, problem that requires elucidation.

I noted earlier that these acute episodes and accidents have strengthened the hypothesis that there is a causal relationship between air pollution and illness. I think it fair to say that acute air pollution can be lethal. As a result of these dramatic periods of abnormal pollution, it has become mandatory to investigate whether higher death and illness rates occur during periods of less intense pollution. I refer, of course, to the long-term, low-level, "normal" pollution to which urban dwellers are regularly subjected. This returns us to a question posed earlier: Is it conceivable that air contaminated with a host of chemicals can be lethal at high concentrations, yet be benign when exposure is of long duration but concentrations are low? This question is the real basis for the present agitation for control or prevention of air pollution. Present research investigations, whether with animals or man, seek to uncover evidence on the effects of repeated exposure to less than lethal concentration of air pollutants over an extended period.

Another question being studied stems from a similar concern. We have seen that most deaths during the acute episodes were among persons with preexisting illnesses. Thus, it is of prime importance to learn if the effect of certain pollutants or a combination of pollutants during "normal" periods initiates new lesions or aggravates old ones, or both. It is also important to know which pollutants of the myriad present in the air are, in fact, the culprits and at what levels they produce their effects.

Before discussing current research and what has been learned, a brief digression may be in order. Recall that in most acute episodes only a small fraction of the population at risk succumbs. The great majority do not become ill. This implies either that those who do are more susceptible or that their defenses were overwhelmed. In either case, the presence of some physiological defense mechanism is suggested. Although most writers concerned with air pollution either do not know of its existence or choose to ignore it, there is an efficient natural defense mechanism combatting this environmental stress.

Recall again that in the course of a day, we inhale some two thousand gallons of air—and if we are urban dwellers, this air contains billions of foreign particles. Each breath consists of about half a liter of air*, 20 percent of which is molecular oxygen. The air swirls briefly through a maze of branching ducts leading to tiny sacs (alveoli), a gas-exchange apparatus in which some of the gaseous oxygen is dissolved in the bloodstream. I am, of course, describing the lungs. Do the billions of foreign particles actually enter the alveoli? What protects the lungs and the air ducts leading to them from contamination? As a prelude to examining the body's defenses, a glance at the respiratory system may be helpful (Figure 31 is a cross-section of the respiratory tract).

The nose can be compared to an air-conditioning unit because it controls the temperature and humidity of the air entering the lungs and filters out foreign particles. External respiration begins and ends with the nose. The nose filters, warms, and moistens the air. The interior of the nose is divided by a wall of bone and cartilage, the septum. On both sides of the septum are a series of scroll-like bones, the turbinates or conchae. The purpose of the turbinates is to increase the amount of tissue surface so that inhaled air will be further "conditioned" before continuing towards the lungs. The surface of the turbinates is covered with a mucous membrane secreting a continual supply of mucus, which drains slowly into the throat. The mucus gives up heat and moisture to incoming air. It also helps dilute any irritating substances contained in the inhaled air. The mucous membrane is coated with cilia—hairlike filaments that undulate back and forth approximately twelve times per second. These millions of cilia help clean the inhaled air. The inhaled air passing through the nasal cavity passes into the pharynx (a common passage for both air and food), which leads to the esophagus (the food tube) and the larynx (the voice box or Adam's apple). When food is swallowed, a

* Approximately half a quart, or a pint

THE RESPIRATORY SYSTEM

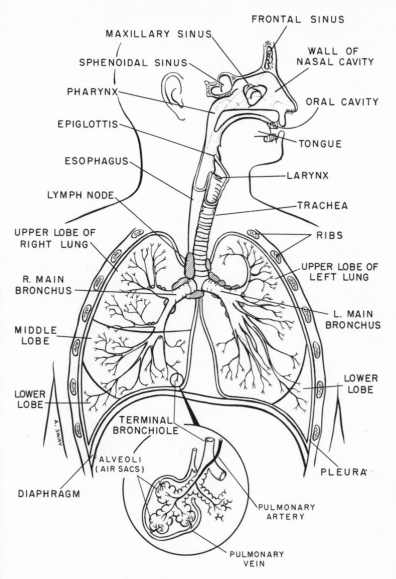

MAXILLARY SINUS

FRONTAL SINUS

SPHENOIDAL SINUS

WALL OF NASAL CAVITY

PHARYNX

ORAL CAVITY

EPIGLOTTIS

TONGUE

ESOPHAGUS

LARYNX

LYMPH NODE

TRACHEA

UPPER LOBE OF RIGHT LUNG

RIBS

R. MAIN BRONCHUS

UPPER LOBE OF LEFT LUNG

MIDDLE LOBE

L. MAIN BRONCHUS

LOWER LOBE

LOWER LOBE

TERMINAL BRONCHIOLE

DIAPHRAGM

ALVEOLI (AIR SACS)

PLEURA

PULMONARY ARTERY

PULMONARY VEIN

FIGURE 31. The respiratory system

flap of cartilage—the epiglottis—folds over the opening; at the same time, the larynx moves up to help seal the opening. On the side of the pharnyx are the tonsils, an additional filtering device that guards primarily against microbes entering through the mouth and nose. The larynx is at the top of the trachea, the column that passes the air to the lungs. The trachea continues down the neck into the chest and branches into the right and left bronchi. This is the end of the upper respiratory tract.

Each bronchus divides and subdivides; between twenty and twenty-two bronchial subdivisions have been counted. The smallest bronchi in the depths of the lung are called bronchioles. They end in some three hundred million air sacs, called the alveoli, which are seventy-five to three hundred microns* in diameter. The alveoli are balloon-like structures that give the lungs their spongy quality.

In the upper respiratory tract the hairs in the nose block the passage of large particles. Beyond the hairs, the involuted contours of the turbinates force the air to move in many narrow streams, so that suspended particles tend to come into contact with the mucous surfaces. The filter system of the nose almost completely removes particles larger than 10 μ in diameter. Particles from 2 to 10 μ usually settle on the walls of the trachea bronchi, and bronchioles. Only particles between 0.3 and 2.0 μ are likely to reach the alveoli. Particles smaller than 0.3 μ, if not taken up by the blood, are likely to remain in suspension as aerosols to be blown out of the lungs with exhaled air. Foreign matter that settles on the walls of the nose, pharynx, trachea, bronchi, and bronchioles may also be expelled by the explosive blast of air generated by a sneeze or cough; more often it is removed by ciliary action. In action, each cilium makes a fast, forceful forward stroke, followed by a slower, less forceful return stroke that brings the cilium into starting position again. The strokes of a row of cilia are precisely coordinated so that the hairs move together as a wave. The cilia of the human respiratory tract do not beat in the open air; they operate within a protective sheet of mucus

---

* The micron, μ, a unit of the metric system, is 0.001 mm, or 1/25,400 of an inch. A three-quarter-inch-long firefly is to the 1,472-foot Empire State Building as one micron is to an inch—twenty-five thousand times smaller.

secreted by glands in the trachea and bronchi. The effect of their wave-like motion is to move the entire sheet, and anything trapped on it, up through the tract to the pharynx, where it can be expectorated or swallowed. This ciliary escalator is in constant operation.

In spite of all these preventive measures, inhaled particles, particularly those suspended in fluid droplets, manage to pass into the alveoli. However, in the deep tissues the lymphocytes—amoeba-like white blood cells—and the macrophages—closely related forms—engulf and digest these foreign particles. The lymphocytes and macrophages surround particles in the air ducts and ride the muco-ciliary escalator up to the nasopharynx. Some particles do remain permanently attached to lung tissue, as the darkened lungs of coal-miners and city dwellers demonstrate. Many of these particles are essentially harmless; others, such as particles of silica, asbestos, and beryllium, for example, can result in the formation of tough, fibrous tissue that causes serious pulmonary disease (see Chapter 13).

Thus, the filtration mechanism of the upper tract has several important functions. It is responsible for the interception and removal of foreign particles. It can remove bacteria suspended in the air and also dispose of bacteria, viruses, and even irritant or carcinogenic gases when they are adsorbed onto larger particles. Unless the filter system becomes overloaded, it keeps the alveoli practically sterile.

This is not the only protection the lungs possess. Among the reflex responses to chemical or mechanical irritation of the nose are cessation of breathing, closure of the larynx, constriction of the bronchi, and even slowing of the heart. These responses are aimed at preventing potentially harmful gases from reaching the alveoli and, through the alveoli, the pulmonary circulation.

When specific chemical irritants penetrate beyond the larynx, the reflex response is usually a cough, combined with bronchial constriction. This reflex is less active in old people—this is why they are more likely to draw foreign bodies into their lungs and why they are usually the first to become ill and even die as a result of an acute air pollution episode.

Exposure to pollutants that produce severe bronchial constriction can result in excessive secretion of mucus, reduction in ciliary activity, obstruction of the fine air paths, and in some cases cell damage.

Heavy smokers often exhibit depressed ciliary activity as a consequence of prolonged contact with tobacco smoke. As a result, their defense against air pollutants is markedly decreased. These circumstances enable bacteria to penetrate to the alveoli and remain there long enough to initiate infectious lung ailments. They are probably also one factor in the development of such tracheobronchial diseases as chronic bronchities and lung cancer.

One of the most difficult facts to uncover about the many chemicals released into the air has been which, or how many, are associated with or directly responsible for a specific illness or disease. At the present time it is believed (but is by no means firmly established) that air pollutants contribute to or aggravate such acute and chronic respiratory diseases as bronchial asthma, sinusitis, chronic generalized emphysema,* chronic coughing, eye irritation, chronic bronchitis, ** the common cold, and skin roughening.

Air pollution is strongly suspected of aggravating cardiac and circulatory ailments. In addition, some medical scientists believe that long-term, low-level exposure reduces resistance to other diseases.

Certain experiments have shown that the susceptibility of white mice and golden hamsters to the bacteria related to pneumonia can apparently be increased by exposing these animals to pollutants before, during, and after exposure to the bacteria. Another experiment showed that mice exposed to ozonized gasoline developed large lung abscesses and pneumonia. Examination of lung tissue revealed the presence of a specific microbe. Since no deaths occurred among the untreated control animals, it was concluded that the ozonized gaso-

---

* Emphysema is by far the most common chronic disease of the lungs. It is the enlargement of a portion of or the whole lung due to loss of elasticity. The main elastic system of the lungs is contained in the bronchi, bronchioles, alveolar ducts, and blood vessels. It is now a matter of record that more than 90 percent of emphysematous patients are heavy smokers.

** Chronic bronchitis is characterized by excessive mucus secretion in the bronchial tree. It is commonly seen as a recurrent cough with sputum. The Surgeon General's Report, *Smoking and Health,* indicates that cigarette smoking is the most important cause of chronic bronchitis in the U.S.

line had activated a dormant infection. That is, the microbe had been present in a quiescent condition until mice were exposed to the gasoline.

In 1965, Pearson and Skye reported [1] that lichens (plants consisting of an algae and a fungus in a mutually beneficial relationship) grown in atmospheres of sulfur dioxide of from 100 to 100,000 ppm* showed abnormalities similar to those seen in Swedish industrial centers. They suggest that certain lichens may be absent from cities because of the presence of sulfur dioxide. When one considers the average sulfur dioxide level around the United States—0.06 ppm, with a range of from 0.01 to 0.38 ppm —one can only wonder at the reliability of the study.

In March, 1966, Myrvik and Evans reported [2] to the Conference on Air Pollution sponsored by the American Medical Association that nitrogen dioxide could immobilize macrophages obtained from rabbit lungs. However, at this meeting Corn and Burton of the University of Pittsburg noted that no substance is present in air in sufficient concentrations as a community air pollutant to produce the classical picture of human tissue inflammation. They added that present sampling procedures do not allow prediction of the irritating capacity of air pollutants. Dr. S. W. Tromp of the Biometeorology Research Center in Leiden, The Netherlands,[3] rejected current views that relate air pollution to bronchial asthma. He maintained that the rapid onset of cold weather was the critical factor.

Between 1959 and 1961, Dr. Warren Winkelstein and his group at the Medical School of the State University of New York at Buffalo [4] carried out a statistical study of the effects of air pollution on men age fifty to sixty-nine in Erie County, New York. One of the most striking observations was the lack of association between air pollution and deaths from cancer of the trachea, bronchus, and lung. Although the study also found a lack of association between air pollution and deaths from cancer of the large intestine

---

* Most people have no conception of what constitutes one part per million (ppm). A few examples may help:
    one inch is one part per million in 16 miles
    one part per million is one minute in two years
    a postage stamp is one part per million of the weight in a person

and rectum, an association was found between air pollution and deaths from cancer of the prostate, esophagus, and stomach.

Addressing the Eighteenth Annual Meeting of the California Branch of the American Cancer Society in October, 1964, Dr. E. Cuyler Hammond, Director of Statistical Research for the Society, noted that his four-year study in three smog-ridden counties of California failed to yield evidence that air pollution seriously affected illness or death rates.

He found that coughs, loss of appetite, and nausea were almost as common outside the smog areas as in it. Furthermore, death rates for men were almost identical in smog and non-smog areas. Strangely enough, the death rates for women were lower in the smog areas.

It is curious indeed that many of the same people who eagerly accepted Dr. Hammond's statistical studies correlating cigarette smoking with cancer of the lungs received his air pollution report with studied coolness.

In a particularly cogent report,[5] Anderson and Ferris, in December, 1965, noted that "we have failed to show any increased risk of disease for a twofold increase in dustfall and a threefold increase in SO_2 across three residential areas at Berlin, New Hampshire, and for a sixfold difference in dustfall and a tenfold difference in sulfation rate between Chilliwack, British Columbia, and Berlin, New Hampshire.

In 1966, Dr. Mary O. Amdur, a toxicologist at the Harvard School of Public Health, reported her studies [6] dealing with the physiological responses of guinea pigs to sulfur dioxide. Dr. Amdur concluded that at concentrations found in urban atmospheres, SO_2 could have no harmful effect on the health of man.*

At the October, 1967, National Meeting of the American Public Health Association, Dr. Eric Cassell and colleagues of the Department of Community Medicine, Mt. Sinai School of Medicine, reported that their three-year study of air pollution levels and death

---

* Addressing a senate committee in May, 1967, A.J. Clark and G.N. Stone of the Central Electricity Generating Board, London, said that after twenty years of intensive study, the British National Medical Council could not implicate SO_2 as a cause of illness or death.

rates in New York City failed to establish a significant correlation between these two conditions, since their data showed several associations: periods of high pollution and low death rates; low pollution and high death rates; and high pollution and high death rates.

The report of the Environmental Pollution Panel of the President's Science Advisory Committee (White House Conference, 1965) said: "While we all fear, and many believe, that long-continued exposure to low levels of pollution is having unfavorable effects on human health, it is heartening to know that careful study has so far failed to produce evidence that this is so, and that such effects, if present, must be markedly less noticeable than those associated with cigarette smoking. Attempts to identify possible effects of ordinary urban air pollution on longevity or on the incidence of serious disease have been inconclusive."

This evaluation was substantially buttressed by a report made public by the California State Department of Health in December, 1967. Its main conclusion condemned cigarette smoking as the primary factor in the generation of lung cancer.

Results of a study of some seventy-thousand deaths over a five-year period specifically ruled out smog as a cause of cancer. Accounting for such variables as length of residence, age, and smoking habits, the researchers found that the lung-cancer death rate was significantly higher in the San Francisco Bay and San Diego areas than in Los Angeles county, the major smog-ridden area of California. The study also showed that heavy smokers were five times more likely to die of lung cancer than non-smokers. These findings tend to support Dr. Hammond's earlier study.

Recently, Walborg S. Wayne of the U.S. Department of Health, Education, and Welfare, in collaboration with Dr. Paul F. Wehrle, a pediatrician at the School of Medicine of the University of Southern California, reported the results of their year-long study of absenteeism in two Los Angeles elementary schools.

Analysis of their data showed that "absence rates were highest in the winter and usually greater on Monday and Friday than on other days of the week. They also found that " . . . in contrast, oxidant levels were lowest in the winter and usually higher in the middle of the week than on Monday and Friday." As a result, they concluded that "no evidence of statistically significant associations between absence rates and oxidant levels could be found."

Despite the singular lack of evidence and the inconclusive nature of many studies relating air pollution with human illness, there seems to be a widespread attitude that air pollution is "bad" and must be causing illness and death. Perhaps it is, but it remains, as the Scots say, "unproven."

There is also agreement among air pollutionists that air pollution control programs should not be held up pending more substantial evidence of a cause-effect relationship. Perhaps not, but the noticeable lack of hard evidence during the past ten years seems to indicate that certain assumptions, and control programs based on them, may be unwarranted.

One wonders whether the untoward effects of air pollution may come from a heretofore unsuspected direction.

Recently Dr. John Ott of the Environmental Health and Light Research Institute (Sarasota, Florida) reported [7,8] that air pollution, which filters out certain wavelengths of the sun, may affect man sexually. His studies with animals indicate substantial changes in the sex ratio of animal litters as a result of exposure to certain colored lights which simulate the filtering effects of air pollutants.

For example, in the presence of bluish light, chinchilla produced offspring that were 80-percent female, in contrast to litters that are normally 25-percent female. If light and hormone production are as intimately related as this experiment suggests, perhaps it would be instructive to check the sex ratios for the past twenty-five years in the City of Los Angeles. Perhaps the 260-odd days of smog per year are reflected in an unusually large crop of females. Of course, the Los Angeles male-female ratios would have to be compared with sex ratios in areas of the country that are free of smog or pollution and with those in areas of intermediate pollutant concentrations. My guess, however, is that little if any correlation would be found; the sex ratios of human beings are probably controlled by more complex mechanisms that those of chinchillas.

That there is an obvious gap between what we know and what we believe is apparent. Yet scare tactics in the press and on radio and television regularly exhort the community to greater vigor in combatting pollution lest horrible death or disease be our lot. This is uncalled for. For reasons yet unknown, there is a desire on the part of some for quick action—any kind of action so long as something is done. While it is tempting to motivate people by appealing to their distaste for illness and injury, Dixon [9] has shown that such continuous reference produces an opposite effect.

In such an atmosphere even thoughtful people are misled and frightened, and feel that they must assume that illness and death as the consequences of community air pollution are well-established facts. Of course, they must also wonder why, if this relationship is true, there is any delay in getting the clean-up job done.

At this point, I would suggest that all concerned people—air pollution researchers, administrators, clinicians, politicians, and citizens—take time out to read what is probably the most cogent critique of the air pollution morass: "Air Pollution Epidemiology," by Dr. John R. Goldsmith.[10] In this short but incisive essay, he indicts, albeit in an amicable way, the concerned parties for attempting "to deal with a manageable part of the problem while ignoring the bulk of it."

One would hope this article obtains wide circulation and consideration. Perhaps then many of the questions will get satisfactory answers and much of the murkiness shrouding the subject will be dissipated.

Before his untimely death in 1964, Dr. Frank Princi of the University of Cincinnati College of Medicine wrote an article [11] that should be widely read. Perhaps a few paragraphs from the introduction to his paper, *Air Pollution—Facts and Fables,* will provoke you to read the entire piece:

> The thoughtful physician who is charged with the responsibility of providing proper medical advice and care for his community must have some objective means of obtaining adequate information concerning contemporary medical developments and scientific achievements. Traditionally, this **information has been provided by scientific journals and through the medium of medical meetings and professional agreement.**

If the question of the health effects of air pollution were confined to these scientific forums, in a professional and dignified fashion, they could be resolved by scientific experts who recognize each other as peers in a specific area of specialization. This orderly and logical type of scientific evaluation is impeded, in our present society, by the eagerness of popular magazines, newspapers, and self-styled authorities to explain glibly and denounce with righteousness. The thesis is a simple one—we are being destroyed by private interests who have a callous disregard for the human race and who can become rich by spreading death and disaster. Illogical perhaps, but totally effective as propaganda.

Some years ago, Senator Abraham Ribicoff, speaking on air pollution, said, "The facts are in. Now is the time for action." Are the facts really in? What kind of action do we need? I shall say more about this in Chapter 16, The Politics of Pollution.

CHAPTER 11

ACCIDENTS

On a crisp September day in 1899, Mr. H. H. Bliss stepped from a trolley car in New York City and was struck down by a horseless carriage, thus becoming the first person to be killed by an automobile. Since that day, more than 1.5 million men, women, and children have been killed by motor vehicles.

Somebody's home catches fire every fifty-seven seconds of the day and night. Literally, millions of injuries, both fatal and non-fatal, occur each year in the home, at work, and at play. In 1965, 107,000 of our citizens died as a result of accidental injury. By 1968, the yearly toll of dead had risen to 114,000. Today, accidents constitute a greater threat to the public than do all communicable diseases combined; only heart disease, cancer, and stroke have higher annual death rates.

Our rapidly changing environment is the prime reason for these statistics. New scientific advances are being applied in industry, in agriculture, and in the home faster than ever before in history.

Employing unfamiliar fuels, machinery, chemicals, and household paraphernalia creates new hazards. In industry, potential sources of accidents are constantly arising as a result of the introduction of new processes and materials (see Chapter 13), while in the home, new patterns of living engender new accident risks. Approximately thirty thousand accidental deaths in the home were recorded last year and over twenty million disabling injuries occurred within and around the home. Table 14 indicates the frequency and distribution of accidental

TABLE 14.

Accidental deaths in all age groups, 1964

Motor vehicle accidents	48,000 *
Home accidents	28,200
Work accidents	11,100
Fires and burns	8,000
Poisoning	2,100
Drowning	1,500
	98,900

* By 1968 this figure had risen to 55,100.

deaths in the United States in 1964. Perhaps even more dramatic is the number of disabling accidental injuries that do not result in death. Exclusive of motor vehicle injuries, over forty-two million * injuries from all causes are reported each year. This means that just about one person in four can expect a disabling injury during the year.

These grim statistics are not unique to the United States. In June, 1967, for example, the Supreme Court of the Soviet Union ordered a legal crackdown on officials whose neglect of safety rules leads to accidents at Soviet factories and farms.

In economic terms, sixty-eight thousand hospital personnel and fifty thousand hospital beds are needed each year to care for accident

* In a world of large numbers, I fear that a figure such as forty-two million, rather than conjuring up the calamitous conditions now existing, will be shrugged off as just another large number.

victims. Accidents cost the community approximately fifteen billion dollars a year in lost earnings and productivity, medical expenses, property damage, and insurance overhead. The president of a leading industrial concern recently said that "off-the-job accidents alone cost more than seven billion dollars a year." *

Accidents are usually measured in terms of the frequency and severity of injury and the cost of property damage or medical care or man-hours lost from work. Indices such as these are of practical value for insurance, engineering, or legal purposes. However, why a driver, for example, sustained a fractured skull is not the same question as why he drove his car into a tree. The question that is being asked more and more today is, Do accidents occur by chance alone, or do they occur because we set up certain conditions? Are accidents accidental?

In common usage, the word *accident* is defined as a suddenly occurring, unplanned, unintentional event which leads to personal injury death, or property damage. However, experts in this field say that less than 10 percent of all "accidents" are unplanned, unintentional, chance events. If this is true, then 90 percent of all accidents must be attributed to purposeful acts; that is, they are the result of acts of omission or commission on the part of some of the people involved. This puts the problem in a new light.

Americans put up with the nationwide slaughter on highways and with all manner of "accidental" injuries because they believe that accidents are fortuitous events—strokes of bad luck beyond one's control. In fact, it is being revealed time and again, as more accident research is conducted, that human failure is a component of most accidents. Human failure can manifest itself as inattention, distraction, haste, and preoccupation, which in turn are often related to anxiety, anger, fear, hate, frustration, and guilt.

At the University of Michigan, a study of ninety-six drivers involved in traffic accidents showed that 20 percent had been subject to emotional disturbance just prior to the event. Dr. Melvin J. Selzer,

* How much is a billion dollars? If you had one billion dollars on the day Christ was born some two thousand years ago, and if you spent one thousand dollars every day from that time until the present, you would still have over two hundred million to spend.

a psychiatrist at the University said that most of the victims "had had violent quarrels, for the most part with women." Most accident researchers also agree that teenagers are particularly prone to driving accidents. As both drivers and victims, teenagers have nearly twice the average rate of traffic fatalities. Another study at the University of Michigan found that teenage problem drivers drove to express a need for recognition, to vent antisocial urges, and to escape authority.

According to Professor Ross A. McFarland of Harvard University, accidents must be studied as a non-contagious mass disease of epidemic proportions; research, he believes, should concentrate on the interactions between the host (the individual), the agent (the object involved in the accident), and the environment. Accidents can be controlled only by analyzing their incidence in relation to complex causal factors throughout the environment, not just by searching for loose boards or faulty steering wheels.

There are five steps in the strategy used to attack any public health problem. These steps are as applicable to designing an attack on accidents as they are to attacks on diseases such as typhoid or smallpox:

1. Collection and analysis of data: place of accident, time, age of victim, sex, season of year, etc.

2. Examination of apparent relationships to discover possible causative factors.

3. Establishment of a hypothesis regarding causation and testing of the hypothesis under controlled conditions.

4. Development of control measures and testing to determine their effectiveness.

5. Incorporation into accident prevention programs of control measures which prove to be effective. To apply this methodology to a problem national in scope, the nationwide collection of data is essential.

When accident reports from around the country are collected and analyzed, graphs such as Figure 32 can be constructed. Figure 31 shows that accidents are the leading cause of death for all

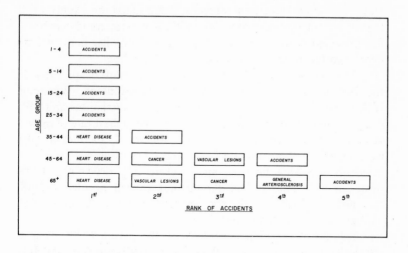

FIGURE 32. Accidental death

age groups from one to thirty-four years of age. Among older people, deaths from accidents are also quite high. Although less than 10 percent of the national population is over sixty-five, more than 25 percent of all those who die in accidents are sixty-five or over. Older people are particularly prone to falling, and since their bones are less resilient than those of younger people, they often suffer serious fractures requiring longer recuperative periods.

The statistics clearly point to the excessive risk of motor-vehicle deaths among males aged fifteen to twenty-four and strongly suggest the need for probing more deeply into the underlying reasons for this correlation. The research at the University of Michigan mentioned above is a step in this direction.

The collected data highlight the difference between the sexes. Up to age eighty-five, the accidental death rate is 2:1 in favor of men. Either men are at greater peril in our society or they are more susceptible to accidents than women. Between twenty and twenty-four years of age, the ratio climbs to 6:1. It is now well documented that the motorcycle is the deadliest vehicle on the nation's highways. In 1966, 2,043 cyclists were killed on our highways. The chances of a motorcyclist being killed are twenty times that of an automobile driver. By 1970, if present trends continue, five thousand deaths per year are anticipated. Similar findings have been reported from England and Western Europe.

Interestingly enough, the highest accidental death rates in the U.S. occurred in four western states—Montana, Wyoming, Idaho, and Nevada—and two southern states—Arkansas and Mississippi. These western states also reported the highest rate of motor-vehicle fatalities. Among the causes for which the death rates were higher in these states than in the country as a whole were accidents involving firearms and aircraft, and drownings. Curiously enough, Alaska had the highest overall accidental-death rate and the highest rates for accidents involving aircraft, fire, explosions, and firearms, and drownings.

Significant variation depending on the season of the year is also well documented. The peak accident months are June and July and November and December. Increases in drownings occur in June and July, while sharp increases in motor vehicle accidents, falls, fires, and explosions occur in November and December. With this type of information, the emphasis of an accident control and prevention program can be modified as required.

What of environment as a variable? More than a quarter of all accidental deaths occur in the home. Farm work is a definite threat to safety; a third of all farm deaths are attributed to the misuse of farm machinery.

The danger to life and limb in our homes and places of work is dramatized by the fact that during World War II, the casualty lists (death and injury) for the armed forces of England averaged 8,126 per month for the six-year period 1939–1944. During this same period, there were 22,000 industrial casualties per month. The armed forces of the United States averaged 23,000 casualties a month during World War II, while industrial casualties averaged 161,000 during the same period.

On the basis of the collected data, experts suggest that there can be no simple solution to the accident prevention problem. Accidents result from the reaction of man to his environment. From moment to moment the accident susceptibility of individuals changes, depending upon as yet poorly understood physical, physiological and psychological factors. Man constantly moves from one environment to another: he leaves home, proceeds to a place of work, and engages in various recreational activities. The very environment in which he customarily moves changes, often imperceptibly, sometimes radically. The environment changes with the seasons and with the time of day or night, and it often is changed by the actions of other people—skates left on a staircase, a cupboard door left open, competitive traffic, or faulty machinery. There is very little if any stability to any of these multiple factors.

As noted earlier, it is now believed that 10 to 15 percent of all "accidents" are solely fortuitous events to whose causation the victim made no contribution whatever. On the other hand, the remaining 80 to 90 percent appear to have been brought about by the victim himself.

A trailer truck, traveling at night, goes off the road and turns over in a riverbed. The accident report reads: "asleep at the wheel."

An eight-year-old boy is struck down by a city bus. The accident report reads: "Ran in front of vehicle."

A lawyer, homeward bound from a late party, misses a turn and rams a culvert buttress. The accident report reads: "Driver inattention."

A garage worker pins another employee against a wall while testing a car. The accident report reads: "Shifted the wrong gear."

Let's look at the four accidents just cited. In the first one, further probing revealed that the dead driver, in order to earn more money for meeting debts, had driven for three nights without sleep and was keeping awake on amphetamine. An autopsy on the eight-year-old boy disclosed a tumor that deprived him of sight on the side on which he was struck. The garage worker admitted that he had been under severe emotional stress after his physician had informed him that his child was mentally retarded. The lawyer recalled that he had reached for the cigarette lighter in his new car and had turned out the headlights instead.

Researchers seeking to isolate all the tangled components

that go into the making of any single accident have suggested a useful tool: the accident syndrome. A syndrome is usually understood to be a group of related symptoms that together characterize a disease. The components of the accident syndrome as put forth by Schulzinger [1] are depicted in Figure 33.

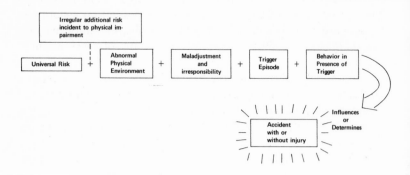

FIGURE 33. The accident syndrome

SOURCE: M. S. Schulzinger, *The Accident Syndrome* (Springfield, Ill.: Charles C. Thomas, 1956)

The universal risk is considered to be a constant factor. From the day of his birth an individual lives in continual peril; anything, including death, can occur at anytime. For the most part, the universal risk becomes part of the syndrome because of fear of injury. Many accidents are brought about because of a state of mind induced by knowledge that danger exists; the dread of an accident may well be a factor in its cause. A nervous, jumpy, nagging passenger may, for example, upset an otherwise reliable driver to the point where he has an accident, when ordinarily no accident would have occurred.

Irregular additional risk is set above the other components of the syndrome, as it does not have to enter into the equation. It can enter the syndrome as an individual's physical defect or handicap. The fact that a person is a diabetic, which would be an irregular additional risk, would enter the syndrome only if insulin deficiency initiated a series of metabolic events resulting in coma. Similarly, epilepsy and cardiovascular disease can increase the risk of accident. However, many physically handicapped persons compensate for impairments and may in fact have fewer accidents.

In the May, 1967, issue of the *(British) Medical Journal,* an English physician reported [2] that about 9 percent of all automobile drivers studied had some form of disability. Among the disabilities found were eye defects, coronary conditions, epilepsy, and severe hypertension.

Not so obvious are those without "true" handicaps. An individual of 6'3" or over does not have the line of vision needed to readily observe overhead traffic lights. In many automobiles, windshields are tinted more heavily at the top. At night, very tall people experience restricted vision in their line of sight. On the other end of the scale, short people have difficulty reaching automobile pedals. Individuals at the extremes in stature have difficulty with entrances, furniture, machinery, tools, and household appliances.

Abnormal physical environment, the third factor in the syndrome, is a rather mercurial area, not at all sharply defined. Nevertheless, certain points can be noted. Extremes in weather, such as heavy downpours, can sufficiently obstruct vision and make conditions ripe for skidding. Poor ventilation, upsetting odors, sudden startling noises, and excessively hot weather, as well as sustained periods of cloudiness and rain, may contribute to accidents. In-depth probing by teams of experts has elicited this sort of information from accident victims.

Although abnormal physical environment remains an evanescent area, it is clear that maladjustment and irresponsibility, which lead to the blunting of good judgment, are at the core of the accident syndrome. The main psychological or physiological elements that abruptly increase the probability of accidents in maladjusted persons are anxiety, fear, hostility, worry, fatigue, frustration, and a host of other states resulting from pressure in the home, on the job, and in the community. Some 250 factors contributing to the blunting of good judgments and accidents have been suggested. Experts in the field of accident prevention look to this area as the most promising for reducing accidents now that mechanical devices and educational programs appear to be achieving less and less.

The most readily observable portion of the syndrome is the "trigger episode." The nail that is stepped on, the blown tire, the fire that burns, and the bullet entering the body. To those who are studying accident prevention, these are the least important symptoms of the syndrome, since the prospective victim almost invariably will reach some accident trigger. The maladjusted person ready for an "accident" may find his trigger anywhere: at home, at work, on the street. The trigger is only the detonator of a far more powerful cause or combination of causes. Consider for a moment how you would appraise a blown tire in the light of the syndrome theory. Check your ideas with Figure 33.

A particularly important aspect of the syndrome is the individual's behavior in the presence of the trigger. An individual's pattern of behavior when confronted with a sudden decision or with danger will frequently determine whether the forces set in motion will result in a near miss or an "accident." In addition, behavior may affect the severity of the accident. For example, if clothing is ignited, one person may try to smother the flames by wrapping himself in a coat or blanket. Another person, in stark panic, may run aimlessly, and as a result may die or suffer severe injury. Behavior in such a case is determined, at least in part, not by the immediate situation, but by long previous adjustment —one's life situation—that paves the way for disastrous mishaps or survival. Perhaps, in the diagram of the syndrome (Figure 33), this factor should be related directly to maladjustment rather than be linked to the trigger episode.

Given all these factors making up the syndrome, it does not follow that an accident with or without injury is inevitable. In the main, however, it does occur.

Viewed in this manner, accidents appear to be set in motion by a constellation of events. And it may well be that this type of theorizing offers means to break the links at various points in the accident chain. Hopefully, the accident syndrome theory may be a tool that will lead to significant reductions in "accidents."

Accidents are the primary threat to the life and safety of children. Each year about fifteen thousand boys and girls under the age of fifteen die as a result of accidents. About seventeen million, or one in three, are injured each year. Although most of those accidents are non-fatal, many children are maimed for life. The suffering, the schooldays lost, and the expenses involved are never reflected in the statistics; perhaps they should be.

In the one-to-four age group, motor vehicles are the chief cause of accidents. In most of these accidents, children are run over in driveways and streets. Drownings account for another large number of deaths, and, curiously enough, do not always occur at the beach or in pools. Many children, left unattended, drown at home or close to home in fishponds, cesspolls, wells, creeks, and brooks.

Surprisingly, it is now a well-documented fact that injury rates among children are highest for those whose parents are college graduates. Could it be that college graduates (particularly mothers and teachers) give these children credit for having better judgment than they actually possess? Perhaps this hypothesis is worth investigating.

Over half of the non-fatal accidents to children under fifteen occur at home. The part of the body most frequently injured is the head. This is in contradiction to the statement often made by parents that hands and arms are most frequently injured. Figure 34 shows the parts of a child's body that are most often injured.

As in the case of the infectious diseases that affect a community, the occurrence of accidents in a specific portion of a population involves important, though at present poorly understood, interrelationships between host, agent, and environment. An analysis of the causes of childhood accidents can be attempted by studying the interrelationships between the host (the child at risk), the agent (the tool or instrument involved), and the environment (the external circumstances). From the physician's point of view, the injured child is of primary concern, whereas to the epidemiologist the number of accidents, their time and place of occurrence, and the possible relationship of these events to

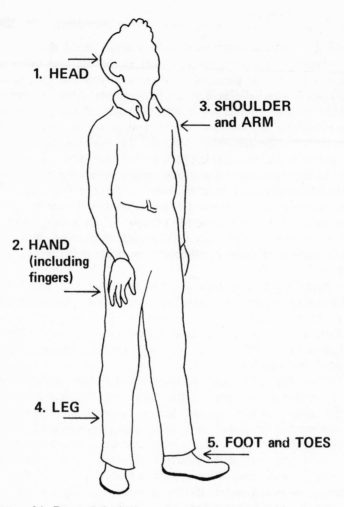

1. HEAD

3. SHOULDER and ARM

2. HAND (including fingers)

4. LEG

5. FOOT and TOES

FIGURE 34. Parts of the body most often injured

the group at risk are of greater concern. These may lead him to an understanding of the cause of an accident and ultimately to means for prevention and control.

A particularly fruitful area of study may be the narrowly averted accident. It might reveal "carriers" of accidents. Reports from time to time have hinted that there may be children who involve others in dangerous games or activities. While these human infectors manage quite well to avoid harm to themselves, they appear to involve their playmates in accidents resulting in injuries or narrow misses. A good example of this type of individual was reported from England, where "last across the road" was played for some time until the authorities put a stop to it. In this game, the bigger, more agile boy ran across a road or street in front of oncoming traffic; of course the smaller, less agile boys were often caught in the path of onrushing cars. Concerted instruction in the schools to make children traffic-conscious has all but eliminated this "game."

Everyone is familiar with the child who shouts, "I dare you do it," and the children who take the dare and all too often wind up with an injury. The absentminded child who manages to inflict injury upon himself or others through lack of awareness of his surroundings is also well known. What is not well known is the reason he does this. Investigations of the host as a personality problem may be a means of controlling these types of induced accidents.

From the collection and interpretation of epidemiological data it has been learned that accidents are the leading cause of death in the one-to-thirty-four age group. In childhood, mortality from accidents is highest at the preschool age, lowest among schoolchildren and higher among adolescents. The fifteen-to-twenty-five age group is the greatest contributor to accidents with motor vehicles. These facts suggest where control and prevention programs might best be directed, given (as is too often the case) a limited budget.

Because of its unique culture, climate, geography, and general environment, each country must study its own population to ascertain its peculiar accident patterns. Perhaps then "accidents will happen" less frequently.

Alcohol has a profound effect on behavior. It also has a major impact on traffic deaths. The evidence for this has been obtained largely from postmortem examinations of fatally injured drivers, which show that some 60 percent of them had alcohol levels of more than .05 percent in the bloodstream; some 35 to 40 percent of the victims had levels of more than .15 percent.

In New Jersey, recent tests conducted under the state's Alcohol Determination Program showed that for four successive years more than 50 percent of drivers killed had an alcohol content in their blood of .15 percent or higher. A 150-pound man, drinking an ounce of whiskey or a bottle of beer, will have a blood-alcohol concentration of .02 percent. The same individual will have a concentration of .15 percent after consuming ten ounces of eighty proof liquor; this concentration is sufficient to cause loss of balance, emotional instability, and a slowing of responses to external stimuli.

Studies conducted over the past ten years clearly indicate that alcohol is not only a very significant contributor to fatal accidents, but also increases the risk of all types of accidents, particularly in the home. As yet, researchers are not certain why drivers drink so much. It may be due to a generalized pressure in society generated by our faster-paced way of living, or it may be that the drunk drivers are pathological drinkers. Before prevention programs can be instituted, however, these alternatives will need a great deal of additional study.

Although the riddle of alcohol and accidents may not be solved in the near future, safer car design and road engineering may help reduce motor vehicle injuries and fatalities.

If accidents cannot be eliminated, it may be necessary to build "crashworthy" cars that are so constructed as to minimize injuries when an accident does occur. Although there will never be a fully crashproof car, surely a vehicle can be designed so that in a collision its occupants will not be hurled about by the sudden deceleration.

A major area on current research is the "second collision": the impact of a passenger against the interior of his vehicle after its collision with an exterior object. The concept of the second collision goes back to a chance observation by Hugh De Haven, who had been a Canadian aviation cadet during World War I. De Haven, the sole survivor of a two-plane collision, rejected the notion that good luck alone saved him. Studying the problems of accident-induced injury, he noticed that such unlikely items as clotheslines saved people who fell from great heights. He was one of the first to show that seat belts could greatly reduce injuries from the second collision. Pilots in World War I used seat belts but unhooked them when crashing seemed imminent; they believed the belts would cut them in two.

Experiments by Lt. Col. John P. Stapp in the 1950's, using the rocket-powered sled, showed that the toughness of the human body had been highly underestimated. He found that a sled moving at 175 mph could be brought to a full stop within twenty-seven feet without injury to the passenger.

Speed is not necessarily a major factor in collisions: most collisions occur in fair weather, on good roads, within twenty-five miles of the driver's home, at speeds less than fifty mph.

On our overcrowded thoroughfares, how well are we naturally equipped with vision, hearing, judgment and speed in response to stimuli to perform the intricate task of driving?

Given the complexity of several simultaneous, split-second circumstances that converge to cause an accident (rain, inattention, fatigue, drunkenness, foot placed on accelerator instead of brake pedal, etc.) what chance does a driver have? If, as has been assumed, accidents cannot be eliminated, it may be necessary to design cars with the express purpose of minimizing injury in the event of a collision. For the most part, research is being directed at controlling the injury of the second collision.

Milliseconds after a vehicle comes to a crash halt, there is a collision between the passengers and the inside of the car. If a passenger is not restrained by a seat belt or harness, he will be hurled upward and forward toward the point of impact with tremendous force. It has been calculated that at the moment of impact, a 175-pound man in a car traveling 50 mph will be hurled against the front of the car with a force of almost four tons.

At the Institute of Transportation and Traffic Engineering (University of California, Los Angeles) studies are under way to ascertain the effects of impact on vehicle and passengers, as a prelude to improved vehicle design.

Figure 35 shows the result of a head-on collision of two schoolbuses of different design. Using anthropometric dummies

FIGURE 35. Experimental collision. On the left is a 1965 school bus with thirty-six occupants; on the right is a 1944 school bus. Each was traveling at thirty miles per hour at the moment of the head-on collision.

to simulate schoolchildren, the type and extent of injury can be determined. The complete accident is filmed by strategically placed motion picture cameras; the film is used to study the impact and its results. From Figure 35 it is obvious that a 1944 model bus with a front-mounted engine protected the children far better than one with a rear-mounted engine. Additional studies under way at the Institute of Transportation and Traffic Engineering deal with the measurement of collision impact forces on passengers and with finding new ways to design the interior of vehicles in order to limit injury. Studies such as these should go a long way toward reducing collision injuries and fatalities.

A completely different approach to solving the motor-vehicle accident problem is concerned with human behavior and employs electronic driving simulators in a newly created Public Health Service laboratory in Rhode Island.

The new laboratory, the first of its kind in the country, is devoted to the study of behavior patterns that may relate to accidents.

The electronic simulators create the illusion of actually driving a car. Each simulator has the usual driving controls, so that a subject seated in an actual car can react just as he would in his own car to various driving situations programmed on analog computers and presented to him on a huge television screen.

Figure 36 shows a twelve-by-eighteen-foot model of a portion of Akron, Ohio. Because of the angle of the lens on the camera, it appears to the driver that he is looking across the replica and not down on it. As the driver presses down the acceler-

FIGURE 36. Model of a portion of Akron, Ohio, and an electronic TV camera.

ator, electronic impulses move the camera forward over the "road." Figure 37 is a close-up view of the TV camera suspended above a point on the road.

With the aid of the simulators, research can be undertaken which would not be feasible on the highway. Drivers can be exposed to the most hazardous conditions, an accurate record of their responses can be compiled, driver behavior in many different situations can be observed, and many different drivers can be observed in an identical situation.

If a disease were to threaten every tenth person in this country (particularly our young people) with illness or death, there would undoubtedly be a tremendous popular outcry to check the havoc. Diseases such as tuberculosis, poliomyelitis, cancer, and heart disease have provoked such a public response. As a consequence, the incidence of several of these diseases has been reduced, and others are being intensely studied. Yet the epidemic on the highways, which has taken over 1.5 million lives, permanently crippled four million people, and cost ninety billion dollars in property damages, continues unabated. Why is this? Why don't people seem to care about death and injury resulting from accidents?

Some people may spend a great deal of time and effort agitating against an elusive hazard such as fluoridation of water supplies, but give no thought to the proven, daily slaughter on our highways. Did you ever hear anyone asking an automobile dealer or manufacturer for a guarantee of safety before purchase? Consider this: someone eagerly pays three to six thousand dollars for a car, without so much as a comment about its safety, yet the same person demands a guarantee of safety each time he purchases a twenty-five-cent loaf of bread. Why this inconsistency? Perhaps research in this area will uncover information that will lead to greater safety in our lives.

There is one aspect of the problem of preventing and controlling motor vehicle accidents that cannot be attacked through the creation of tools such as the accident syndrome, nor through epidemiological considerations, nor through the use of computers that simulate potential road and highway accident patterns. This is

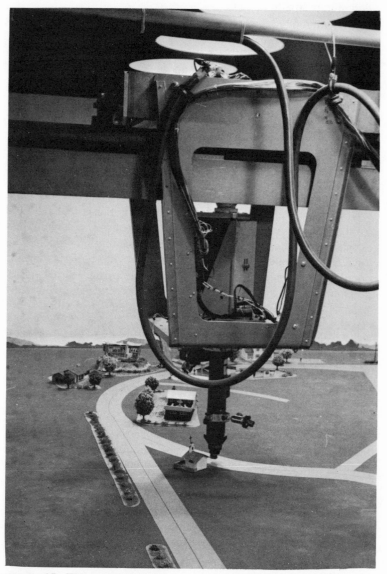

FIGURE 37. TV camera focusing on a point in the Akron model

community apathy.

Community apathy, a catchall term for a host of current environmental problems, needs definition within the context of motor vehicle accidents, and, more specifically, accidents within the fifteen-to-twenty-four age group.

Motor vehicle accident cases are generally adjudicated in a police court at the local level. Accordingly, in any specific case, the community representatives involved are: the police, in the person of the arresting or complaining officer; the parents of the youngster; lawyers for the defendant and the township; witnesses for the township; and the presiding judge. The community at large is represented only indirectly, by the prevalence of a general attitude; it either cares for the safety of its members or it does not.

I categorically suggest that the handling of cases at the local level is directly related to the type and frequency of a community's accident record. I suggest further that a significant reduction in vehicular accidents can be rapidly effected by abruptly halting the coddling of offenders, which is presently the practice in too many communities across the country. Consider for a moment who really benefits from a verdict of "Careless driving—ten-dollar fine." Apathy is in fact complicity.

This attitude was forcefully brought home to me recently as I sat in the Princeton (New Jersey) Township Police Court for several hours observing the inglorious proceedings. Up to this time, there had been a steadily mounting accident rate, particularly among the high school population.

A charge of "reckless driving" had been brought by the police against a seventeen-year-old boy who had received his driver's license only six months earlier. The community representatives were in their places. I would shortly be introduced to a form of apathy I hadn't realized existed in my community. Unfortunately, it indicated that the representatives cared little for the safety of its members.

The central figure in a case of this type is the judge. Not only do his attitude and actions set the tone of the proceedings, but he alone weighs the evidence and determines the fine and the ultimate charge that will appear in the legal records. It is, therefore, virtually through him alone that the accident rate can be affected—up or down.

The lawyer for the defendant is in a unique position: If the police charge is generally correct, he must try to mitigate the circumstances in any way possible, for, after all, that's what he is professionally trained to do. The fact that he may abet in upping the accident rate is not his concern. Or is it?

The prosecuting attorney, perhaps the father of a young son or daughter himself, is not anxious to pursue these cases overmuch. After all, "They are really good kids and only young once." Whatever the judge says is all right with the prosecutor.

The police, a much-battered lot, damned if they do and damned if they don't, are harried and hamstrung by parents, lawyers, and judges. It became blatantly clear at the trial I attended that the community representatives have little respect for the minions of the law. In fact, they are treated with obvious disrespect. All this is obvious to a young defendant, who is gathering experiences and learning values that are supposed to serve him as a member of the community.

If motor vehicle accidents are to be significantly reduced, researchers will eventually be forced to come to grips with parents. On learning that their son or daughter was to blame for an accident, the initial reaction of too many parents is indignation at the police for daring to suggest such a thing, and for meddling. Their next action is to get a lawyer, in order to get the youngster out of trouble and right back behind a wheel, lest his social life become dislocated. Little or no thought is given to the accident and its consequences, or the near miss, or the next time. Are these parents really helping their children? Are they at all concerned with the community? The answer to both questions must be a firm no.

As the trial in Princeton progressed it was all too clear that the judge's thoughts were elsewhere, and that he brought himself back to the business at hand only when forced to do so by the intrusion of the lawyer's questions. The policeman, given short shrift by both the judge and lawyers, stood weakly by, unable or unwilling to press his case. Experience had conditioned him well.

When both sides agreed they had gone on long enough—after

summations by both, with the prosecuting attorney affirming he had amply proved the charge of "reckless driving"—the judge took over.

"Young man," he began, "I'm glad to see your record is clean, no previous convictions." Was that meant to be a joke? The boy had been licensed only six months before. "It's clear to me that you were a bit careless—a little too heavy on the gas pedal. You've got to leave some margin for error." With those stirring words ringing in our ears, we heard the verdict: "Careless driving—fifteen-dollar fine."

Leaving the courtroom, I heard the policeman say to his witnesses: "I told you how it would go. We were lucky to get that much. It's usually less. Our hands are tied; it's just a waste of time. The word gets around fast. The kids know what they can expect. That's the law." I had to agree with Dickens's Mr. Bumble that "the law is a ass."

In Table 15 I have set forth a comparison of the number of motor vehicle deaths and deaths of U.S. military personnel in Vietnam.

No, computers and syndromes alone will not effect a major change in the automobile and motorcycle accident rate. Reductions will come when community pressure wills it, not before.

TABLE 15.

Comparison of number of motor vehicle deaths and Vietnam deaths

	Motor Vehicle Deaths	*Vietnam Deaths*
1968	55,100	14,000
1967	52,900	9,378
1966	53,000	5,008
1965	49,000	1,369
1964	47,000	147
Totals	257,770	29,902

Not only is the yearly death toll from motor vehicle accidents appalling, but worse, it has become a fact of life that apparently is acceptable to most people. The yearly figures have been over forty-five thousand for the past six years. In the face of such carnage, it is difficult to comprehend how great numbers of people can become incensed over the loss of life in Vietnam, yet remain insensitive and silent about death on our streets and highways.

CHAPTER

12

NOISE

On April 21, 1966, Theodore Kupferman, representative from Manhattan's Seventeenth Congressional District, rose to address his colleagues.[1] As he spoke, it became obvious that an insidious environmental problem created by modern technology has inspired a champion who would assume responsibility for the political action necessary for its control and prevention. He said: "Another serious environmental problem which demands our immediate attention is that of excessive noise. I call it 'noise pollution.' Accordingly, I have introduced a comprehensive bill to provide for a study of the complex noise situation in the United States with a view toward finding ways and means of eliminating unnecessary noise in general on the inhabitants of our cities and towns." With these words, political involvement was initiated: community pressure had seen to that.

It had been argued that because noise produces no dramatic ill effects that we are yet aware of, the public has been largely uninterested in its suppression. It may be more to the point to say that the degree of annoyance and discomfort that people will endure is astonishing.

Although noise, within limits, is a necessary and probably unpreventable adjunct of our machine civilization, it would appear that unless definite steps are taken to reduce the present inordinate levels in industry and in the community generally, increasing numbers of the population may become auditory cripples.

Fortunately, in the past few years, large segments of the population have expressed an increasing determination to revolt against noise. A measure of this resentment is seen in the number of articles that regularly appear in newspapers and popular magazines. In New York City, one of the most cacophonous of cities, concerned citizens have banded together to assure that their voices are heard above the din. In fact, Citizens for a Quieter City, Inc., was the motivating force behind Congressman Kupferman. KEEP NEW YORK PLASTERED: To the uninitiated, these clever signs in buses and subway trains may at first appear to be supporting wholesale inebriation. The fact is, New Yorkers are opting for thick plaster walls as a means of reducing noise levels in multi-unit dwellings, instead of the currently employed thin sheetrock.

Although Ramazzini (see Chapter 13) mentioned the deafness of coppersmiths in his book *Diseases of Workmen,* published in 1700, the range of adverse effects of noise are of relatively new interest. Some hundred years ago isolated references were made to the hearing losses among blacksmiths and, later, boilermakers.

During the past twenty-five years, the increasing mechanization and industrialization of our society has sharply increased the frequency and magnitude of noise-induced hearing loss, and this problem has been drawn to the attention of the medical profession, industrial leaders, governmental agencies, labor unions, and, workmen's compensation boards. Lack of interest in the past was due in part to the fact that accurate means of measuring noise and hearing loss were not available.

The magnitude of the problem may be inferred from the fact that conservative estimates place the number of Americans who need hearing aids at eight to ten million; the rate of hearing-aid use in urban communities is believed to be about seven per one thousand people. Estimates place at 170,000 the number of men age fifty to fifty-nine who are eligible for workmen's compensation because of hearing impairment. Industrial surveys have shown that 20 percent of the people who are given hearing tests for employment have hearing losses; factory workers appear to have double the rate of hearing loss of office workers in comparable age groups. Because there is a loss in hearing acuity associated with the process of aging, it is often difficult to distinguish between noise-induced hearing loss and natural loss. In addition, there are differences in the ability to hear of men and women. Generally, women have better and less variable hearing than men of the same age. The major break in the audibility curves of men occurs at about age thirty-two; in women it occurs about five years later.

While it is well known that sudden, severe exposure to loud noise can cause deafness, it is the insidious loss of hearing due to chronic, long-term exposure to critical noise levels in industry and the community that needs extensive investigation.

We could define noise in terms of particle displacement, variations in pressure, and particle velocity in an elastic medium, or we could accept the concept advanced by the British Committee on the Problems of Noise, who, with characteristic British pithiness, defined noise as "unwanted sound." It has also been defined as any sound regarded as a nuisance. While wholly satisfactory, these definitions imply a measure of subjectivity: that is, responses to what may be considered annoying are largely personal, depending upon individual thresholds. To some people, even certain weak sounds may be offensive. Generally, however, nuisance increases with frequency and pitch.

Sound (noise) in industry, in the home, or in traffic is a byproduct of the conversion of energy. No process using power is completely efficient; some energy is inevitably wasted. Most of this is converted into heat, some into sound, as when surfaces vibrate or turbulence is set up in air. All noises send out sound waves, which vibrate at various frequencies. The number of vibrations per second—the number of times per second that the sound waves emitted exert a pulsating pressure (sound pressure) on the ear—is the frequency of the sound, usually described in cycles per second (cps) or Hertz (Hz) or vibrations per second (vps).

A cannon shot roars out its sound waves, while the drop of a pin is hardly audible. Thus, sound is also characterized by its pitch, its degree of highness or lowness. Low pitch implies a slower rate of vibration, or fewer cycles per second, than high pitch, in which the same type of pulses strike the ear more often each second. Thus, although pitch depends in part upon the frequency of the sound stimulus, it is primarily a function of the amplitude or depth of the sound wave.

Another essential characteristic of sound as it affects the perception of noise is loudness or intensity. However, loudness is a sensation that is decided by the nerve stimulus which reaches the brain. It is a highly subjective perception. Each person experiences his own degree of loudness because the stimulus received depends on the intensity of the sound energy reaching the nerve and the sensitivity of the nerve. Here again, wide ranges of individual difference are found. The human ear can translate sound between approximately twenty and two thousand cycles per second into nerve impulses. This means that the ears of healthy young adults are sensitive to a wide range of frequencies. For the most part, our ears are most sensitive to the range of 500 to 4000 cps, which includes conversational speech.

The range of a piano may help to give an idea of the frequencies of various sounds. The keys range from the lowest note, A_0, which emits pulses that vibrate at the rate of 27.5 cycles per second, through middle C, with a frequency of 286 cps, to the highest note, C_8, which generates 4,186 cps. Men's voices range from 80 cps, for the lowest basso, to tenor, producing sounds at 300 cps—just above middle C. It is not uncommon for sopranos to reach 850 cps. Some few trained voices have been known to exceed this.

Few, if any, people can hear sounds above 20,000 cps. In these regions the ears of animals are particularly keen. "Silent" dog whistles are silent to human ears only because they emit vibrations with frequencies well above twenty thousand, to which dogs readily respond.

The ear is least sensitive at the low frequencies. For example, its sensitivity to a tone of 100 cps is only 1/1000th that to one at 1000 cps. Von Bekesy points out that this is a physical necessity. If it were not so, we would hear all the vibrations of our own bodies. He notes that "the ear is just insensitive enough to low frequencies to avoid the disturbing effect of noises produced by muscles, bodily movements, etc. If it were any more sensitive to these frequencies than it is, we would hear the vibrations of the head that are produced by the shock of every step we take when walking."

"What noise annoys an oyster?" Although no adequate way of measuring the annoyance level of noise has been devised, we know that the annoyance level is often directly related to loudness. Studies have found that loud sounds are more annoying than those that are of similar character but not as loud. To ascertain loudness level and to determine whether a noise is a potential hazard to the hearing mechanism, an accurate sound measuring system must be employed. Several general types are available.

For preliminary screening of a site for possible hazards, the sound-survey meter, as seen in Figure 38, is appropriate. For example, it is well suited for measuring noise levels in manufacturing plants as a means of locating areas where possibility of hearing damage exists. It is often used by architects, planners, and engineers to study possible sites for schools, hopitals, office buildings, and express highways in relation to existing homes. The sound-survey meter is small, simple, and relatively inexpensive. For more precise measurements, a sound-level meter (see Figure 39) is generally employed. This unit is more sensitive and far more accurate than its smaller counterpart.

Recall that sound is a transmission of energy in the form of vibrations which constitute variations in pressure in air, liquid, or solid media. Acoustical instruments for measuring variations in sound pressures are usually calibrated in dB, decibels.

The magnitude of these pressures is relatively small and is, therefore, measured in dynes per square centimeter. The standard reference level used in measuring sound levels in decibels is

FIGURE 38. Sound-level meter used for survey studies

equivalent to a sound pressure of 0.0002 dynes/cm². This is close to the faintest sound (the threshold) that can be heard by a healthy young adult in a quiet location, and is equal to zero decibels. The decibel is a dimensionless unit. It simply expresses a ratio between two sound intensities: the reference pressure *

* Often the term *microbar* (μ bar) is used as the reference, one microbar being equal to 1 dyne/cm².

FIGURE 39. Precision-type sound-level meter

and the source being measured, whether it be a pneumatic hammer, a speech, a food blender, or a subway train.

Between the threshold of hearing, the lowest pressure to which the human ear responds, and the greatest intensity that the ear can interpret as sound but not as pain, the average individual can distinguish about 130 steps in intensity. In other words, the range of hearing covers approximately 130 decibels. Figure 40 lists some commonly encountered sound-pressure levels.

The number of decibels, while indicative of the sound level, tells nothing about the frequency distribution of the component frequencies. Deafness, whether of a temporary or permanent na-

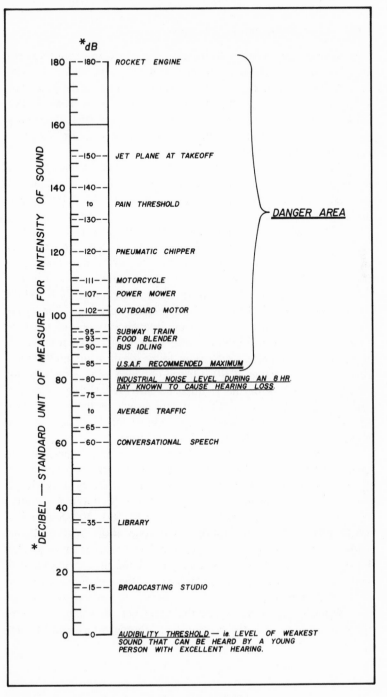

FIGURE 40. Noise levels in urban communities

ture, is better correlated with frequencies than with overall intensities. Whereas overall noise levels can indicate the need for noise reduction or control, it provides no information about the particular frequencies that are causing the noise problem. Most noises in our urban communities are complex, since the noise emanating from a single source is usually composed of sounds of many frequencies, varying in intensity.

The response of the human ear to a certain sound pressure depends upon the frequency of the sound. While sensitivity is greatest between 500–4000 Hz (cps), it falls off for both lower and higher frequencies.

When adolescents with good hearing are tested, a characteristic profile of the efficiency of hearing at several frequencies is obtained. This is portrayed in Figure 41. The curve shows that at low frequencies the sound-pressure level must be relatively high before the tone can be heard. By contrast, tones in the range 200–10,000 cps can be heard even though the levels are very low. This variation in hearing acuity depending on frequency is one of the reasons it is essential to know the frequency rather than the overall noise level, if a noise problem is to be dealt with intelligently. For example, a value of 90 dB was obtained near a steel-rolling machine. Analyses of the frequencies involved showed that the greatest intensity was in the low range—where the ear is least sensitive. The intensity was 81 dB, almost ten times less, in the higher ranges, where the ear is more sensitive.

To resolve the spectrum of frequencies of a sound, a frequency analyzer must be used. For the most part, an octave-band analyzer is employed. Octave bands are arbitrary spreads of frequencies in which the upper limit is twice the lower. Generally, the bands chosen are 20–75, 75–150, 150–300, 300–600, 600–1200, 1200–2400, 2400–4800, and beyond 4800. With both the sound-level meter and the octave band analyzer, reading should be taken at several points in and around the area being studied and, if in an industrial setting, as near to the ear of the operator as practically feasible.

When sound waves reach the outer ear, they initiate vibrations in the eardrum—the tympanic membrane, which can be seen

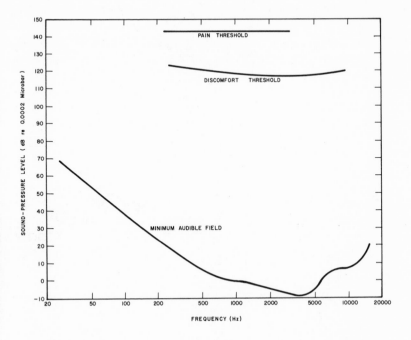

FIGURE 41. Thresholds of hearing and tolerance

SOURCE: *Handbook of Noise Measurement*
(West Concord, Mass.: General Radio Company)

in Figure 42. These vibrations are transmitted to three ossicles, the bones of the middle ear: the hammer (malleus), anvil (incus), and stirrup (stapes). Figures 42 and 43 show the relation of these three to the tympanic membrane. From the position and shape of the bones, it is not difficult to understand how they transmit vibrations to the inner ear.

The stirrup, a tiny bone weighing approximately 1/30,000 of

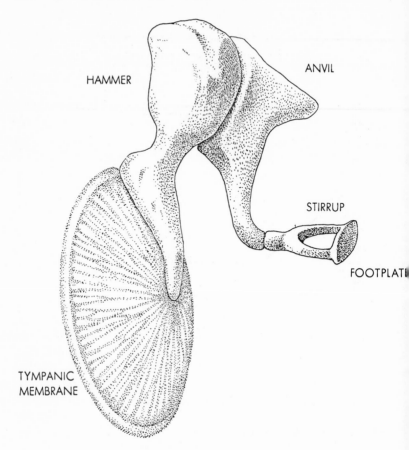

HAMMER

ANVIL

STIRRUP

FOOTPLATE

TYMPANIC
MEMBRANE

FIGURE 42. The middle ear

SOURCE: Georg von Bekesy, "The Ear," *Scientific American*

an ounce, drives the perilymph (fluid) of the cochlea back and forth, piston-fashion, according to the rhythm of the vibrating sound pressure. These movements of the stirrup, and particularly of its footplate, magnify the original vibrations some twenty times

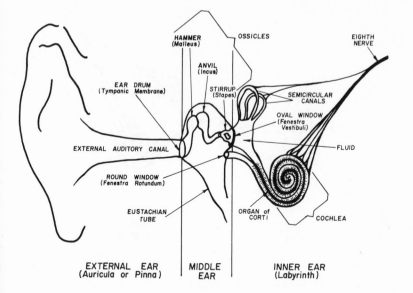

FIGURE 43. Schematic diagram of the ear

and initiate vibrations in the basilar membrane,* which in turn transmits the vibrations to the haircells of the organ of Corti, within the cochlea; the endings of both branches of the auditory nerve are also contained within the spiral cochlea. Here, mechanical motion is converted to nerve impulses. These impulses, carried by the auditory nerve to the brain, are then perceived as sound. It is in the inner ear that the vestibular and cochlear branches of the acoustic nerve receive its signals, and it is within the cochlea that translations of sounds are made. If the translations are muddled or weak, the acoustic nerve obtains and transmits faulty impulses to the brain. This is manifested in some degree of hearing loss.

It may be concluded, therefore, that noise-induced hearing

* Because of its filtering and analytical functions the basilar membrane is of interest in hearing research. Since, however it is embedded in the skull, direct study is extremely difficult.

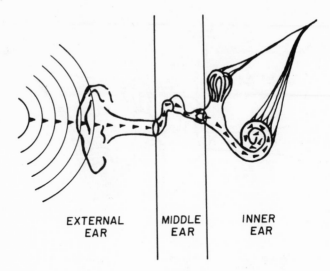

EXTERNAL
EAR

MIDDLE
EAR

INNER
EAR

FIGURE 44. Transmission of vibrations

loss is due not solely to ill effects on the eardrum, as so many erroneously believe, but also to damage to the internal ear—to the cochlea, the organ of Corti, and the acoustic nerves.

Incidentally, the eardrum is not the only avenue by which we hear. Sound energy can be carried to the inner ear by way of the bones of the skull. The sounds we hear when we click our teeth or move the tongue around the mouth come through the skull. Much of the sound we receive when the ears are plugged or covered also comes in this way. This distinction is an aid in diagnosing deafness. Von Bekesy notes that "if a person can hear bone-conducted sounds but is comparatively deaf to air-borne sounds, we know that the trouble lies in the middle ear. But if he hears no sound by bone conduction, then his auditory nerves are gone and there is no cure for his deafness. This is an old test long used by deaf musicians. If a violin player cannot hear his violin even when he touches his teeth to the vibrating instrument, then he knows he suffers from nerve deafness, and there is no cure."

Deafness is far from being solely of occupational origin. Any diagnosis of occupational deafness must first rule out the possibility of loss of hearing accompanying advancing age. Sensory presbycusis, one form of the natural aging process, is characterized by hearing losses in the high-frequency ranges. Other forms produce losses of hearing in all frequency ranges, as evidenced by flat audiometric curves. (This point will be discussed further on.) Thus, it is difficult to prove that a case of deafness is of occupational origin. In addition, tumors, infections, or blows on the head can also produce loss of hearing. In fact, before World War II, ear infections were the leading cause of deafness.

Progressive noise-induced deafness is known to occur through continuous exposure to sound levels above 80 dB, over an eight-hour day. Exposure to excessive noise is initially seen as a temporary threshold shift (TTS), which is the difference between the post-exposure threshold and the pre-exposure threshold.

Accumulating evidence indicates that levels of noise below 75dB are not dangerous. Levels about 80 to 85dB in the frequency range of 1200 to 4800 cps, however, seem to be unsafe. In fact, as noise-induced deafness progresses, the ability to hear the high-pitched sounds of speech is lost first. The most common complaint of people with noise-induced deafness is, "I can hear, but I don't understand." The first sounds to be lost by the nerve-deaf are the fricative consonants *f, s, th, ch,* and *sh.* It becomes increasingly difficult to discriminate between such words as *sick, thick, flick,* or *chick.* With greater hearing loss the explosive consonants *b, t, p, k, g,* and *d* become difficult to distinguish.

Recovery from a temporary shift of from 30 to 40dB may take several hours. For a shift of 50–60dB, even several days may be insufficient. Despite these figures, it should not be assumed that nerve deafness depends solely upon the noise level. A good deal depends upon the total noise exposure. This includes the overall noise level, the time distribution (whether the noise is continuous or intermittent), and the total duration of exposure during a lifetime. It is this combination of factors working in concert that constitutes the hazard of noise.

A step in the direction of controlling or preventing nerve deafness has been the development of damage risk criteria. Figure 45

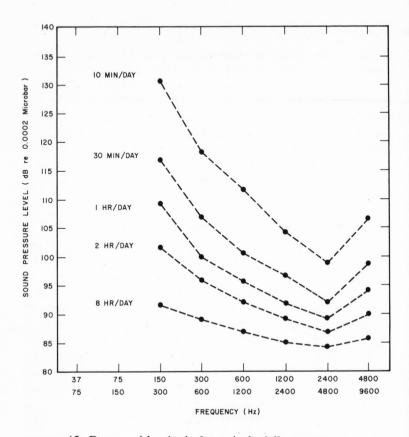

FIGURE 45. Damage-risk criteria for a single daily exposure

indicates the combination of sound-pressure level and frequency that may be tolerated without danger. From the graph, it is clear that the tolerable exposure periods decrease with an increase in decibels for the same octave band. For example, at 150 to 300 Hz, sound intensity is ten thousand times greater at 130dB than at 90dB. Thus, the difference between ten minutes and eight hours of tolerable exposure becomes understandable. Briefly, then, a damage-risk criterion specifies the maximum sound-pressure level

of a noise to which a person may be exposed without risk of
hearing loss.

E. R. Hermann,[2] an engineer at Northwestern University, has
developed a mathematical equation that may aid in explaining the
mechanism of noise-induced deafness. His calculations indicate
that the ill effects of noise follow a first-order differential equation. Simply translated, it suggests that the loss of hearing proceeds
as if the sound waves or pressures acted adversely upon one structure or organ or some cell within a critical organ. If, as current
theory holds, the conversion of sound from mechanical to electrical impulses occurs in the hair cells of the organ of Corti, then this
theoretical calculation fits nicely. Apparently, severe mechanical
stress on the hair cells causes them to become fatigued and unable
to transmit impulses to the auditory nerves. When physiologists test
this model, experimental evidence might unveil the actual mechanism of this failure, which might ultimately make it possible to
perform beneficial surgical or prosthetic intervention. Benefits
would accrue even if the organ of Corti did not prove to be the
primary site, because other experiments would follow naturally
and ultimately lead to a better understanding of noise damage.

In September, 1968, Dr. David M. Lipscomb[3] of the University of Tennessee's audioclinical center reported on the effects
of rock music on the ears of guinea pigs. Dr. Lipscomb and his
colleagues recorded music in a Knoxville discotheque and then
played it back to an audience of guinea pigs. After some ninety
hours of intermittent exposure to the music, the cells of the cochlea
(Figure 42) were photographed. They "had collapsed and shriv-
eled up like peas."

It is interesting that shortly after the report was published in
newspapers around the country, purveyors of this music quickly
pointed out that guinea pigs are not people and that the assumption
that damage occurs in human ears cannot be extrapolated from
animal studies. This is quite correct; but one wonders if the people
who cry "foul" in this instance are not among those who are so
quick to accept evidence of potential toxicity from animal feeding
studies as directly applicable to man.

Until the past few years, deafness was thought to be the only

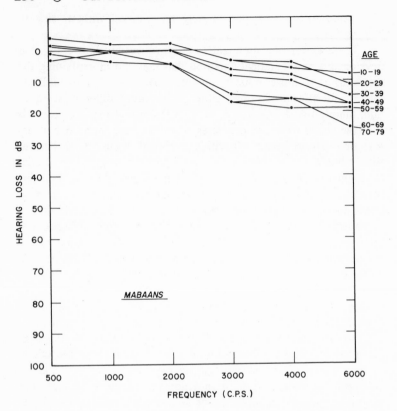

FIGURE 46. Comparison of hearing loss in Maabans and Americans
SOURCE: Dr. Samuel Rosen, *Archives of Otolaryngology*

ill effect of noise. Few, if any, reports even hinted at other effects.
In 1965, Dr. Samuel Rosen [4] of Mount Sinai Hospital, New York,
published the results of his studies of the Maabans of the Egyptian
Sudan, among whom he found an association between sustained
noise level and arteriosclerotic heart disease. In an earlier study,[5]
Rosen and his group had found that in primitive villages, compared with urban centers, there was very little noise. They also
noted that Maabans of age seventy had hearing acuity similar to
that of young boys, and that they also had low blood pressure.

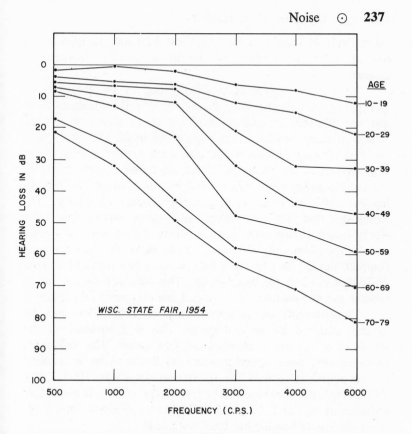

Dr. Rosen reported that the Maabans had better hearing than men and women of all age groups in the U.S. This comparison is shown in Figure 46. He explained that noise appears to cause a narrowing of the arteries that may affect the hearing mechanism. This point was corroborated by recent research in Germany which found that vasoconstriction persists as long as noise continues. Russian scientists also reported pain in the region of the heart and electrocardiographic changes in persons exposed to continuous noise at levels of 85 to 120 decibels. Dr. Rosen stated that "diminished hearing in people age fourteen to twenty-nine may be the beginning of the long process that eventually shows up as artherosclerosis or coronary artery disease." If this were to be demonstrated conclusively, it would be one of the most dramatic examples of the role of the technological environment in chronic degenerative disease.

An additional piece of evidence found by Dr. Rosen tends to support the noise-deafness theory. Among the Maabans there was no difference in auditory acuity between men and women. This is in sharp contrast to the populations in the U.S. and industrialized Western Europe, where men show greater hearing losses than women of the same age. Presumably, this is due mainly to the greater noise-levels encountered by the men on the job. In March, 1967, speaking to a group of concerned citizens, Dr. Rosen said that "the reflex effect which causes contraction of the blood vessels occurs with equal intensity during sleep as during wakefulness. Not only do noise signals make the blood vessels contract, but the skin becomes pale, muscles constrict and adrenalin is shot out into the bloodstream. This adrenalin output causes tension and nervousness. If chronic, it can elevate blood pressure."

Measurements of auditory acuity or hearing-loss can be quickly obtained by an audiogram. This is a measure of the threshold of hearing at standardized frequencies. The audiogram indicates how much sound-pressure on the eardrum is required for the sound at each of the six frequencies (500, 1000, 2000, 3000, 4000, and 6000 cps) to be just barely audible. If a standard sound must be raised 10 or 15 db higher to be heard, then a 10- or 15-db loss of hearing has been sustained.

An audiometer is an instrument that can produce sounds, usually pure tones at predetermined frequencies; part of the instrument is an attenuator that controls the intensity of the tone. The individual being tested dons a set of earphones and responds by pressing a button each time the test tone is heard. When both ears have been tested, a graph of threshold of hearing in dB versus frequency is plotted: this is the audiogram. It is particularly useful in being able to detect threshold shifts long before the individual notices difficulty in conversation, and it is useful in evaluating noise-control measures.

When it has been established, at least in the industrial setting, that a loss of hearing has resulted from exposure to excessive noise, it may be possible to reduce the level of noise at its source. Should this prove impracticable, exposure levels can be reduced by reassigning sensitive or susceptible individuals to a quieter area. If both of these measures are unsuitable, acoustical barriers can be imposed between the noise source and the ear. Individual acoustical barriers run the gamut from a wad of cotton placed at the entrance to the auditory canal to muff-type ear defenders, used with increasing frequency by airport mechanics.

Although dry cotton plugs provide little, if any, attenuation, many people continue to use them. Insert-type plugs made of rubber, plastic, or wax are far superior to cotton; muff protectors are better yet. Figure 47 shows the degree of attenuation achieved with a muff, with an insert-type plug other than cotton, and with cotton. Unfortunately, too many workers in high noise areas dis-

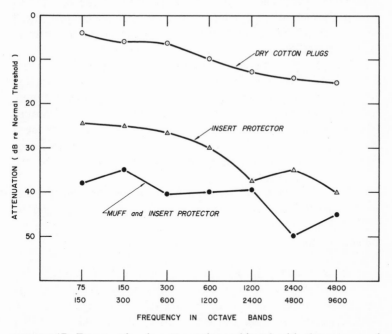

FIGURE 47. Degree of noise attenuation achieved with three types of ear protectors

card or fail to wear plugs or muffs. When asked, "Why don't you wear the ear protectors?" they may reply, "What's that, can you speak a little louder?"

In addition to employing barriers at the entrance to the auditory canal, environmental control can be instituted. This includes designing equipment so as to reduce its noise level, muffling apparatus with sound-absorbing materials, or isolating noisy processes or machines. Any material which is inelastic and of low density, such as ground cork, hairfelt, fiberglass, and rubber compositions, is a good insulator.

Sound waves travel with greater velocity through many solid materials than they do through air. For example, sound waves have a velocity of 11,000 to 16,000 feet per second in wood—14,000 in oak and approximately 16,000 in Norwegian spruce—16,000 in glass and steel, and 17,000 in aluminum. Sound travels through air at a velocity of 1,130 feet per second. Small wonder, then, that street traffic noise can be heard so easily in homes and offices.

According to the *mass law,* the heavier the wall, the more effectively it will dampen noise. But heavy walls are costly; hence the growing use of lightweight materials, which permit more noise to get through. To circumvent the mass law, walls of various materials can be divided into two walls with an air space between them. The need for more weight (density), or more space, or both, makes it difficult to design economical structures that at the same time keep noise out.

The Lead Institute has been investigating the potential use of thin lead sheets as insulating material. Lead's mass and its malleability, even in thin sheets, make it highly resistant to the passage of sound waves. Lead is readily available and is comparatively low-cost.

In July, 1967, the space agency, NASA, took a major step toward the production of quieter jet aircraft engines. In the next few years attempts will be made to produce an engine that will have markedly less roar and whine than today's jets. The "quiet engine project" is part of a national noise abatement program initiated by President Johnson in March, 1966.

The scream of jet engines is due to exhaust nozzles and the stationary-vane inlet assemblies of compressors. The vane assembly noise, initially troublesome only when the engines were throttled back for landing, became the dominant noise when turbo-fan jets were introduced. The principal factors contributing to the noise turned out to be the number and design of stationary and rotating blades, the spacing between the rotor and stator, and the rotational velocity of the rotor. As yet, engineers have been unable to re-design these parts so as to reduce noise levels, without severe loss in power output. It may well require the invention of a completely new engine concept.

Although sonic booms have long been blamed for a variety of ill effects, fatalities were not among them, at least not until quite recently. On August 6, 1967, the *New York Times* carried an account of a group of French farmers in the village of Mauron, in Brittany, who had gathered for lunch and who became the first casualties of a sonic boom. Witnesses heard a "thunderous" sound that shook timbers loose and brought eight tons of barley stored in the loft down on the diners below. Three were killed and another was seriously injured.

According to a study carried out by the President's office of Science and Technology in the summer of 1966, a sonic boom is not the result of breaking the sound barrier, as many mistakenly believe; it is, in fact, an intense pressure wave. This pressure, generated by the nose and tail of planes traveling above 660 miles per hour, strikes the earth and, shortly thereafter, the ear. This series of tests showed that the projected SST (supersonic transport), which could travel at over 1700 miles per hour, will be forced to fly at reduced speeds over land because of the unacceptable thunderous booms it could create all along its flight path. Reduced speeds would be uneconomical, but increasing public and governmental dissatisfaction with current noise levels in urban communities has convinced the airlines that they must reduce aircraft noise, even if it entails economic sacrifices.

During the Detroit meeting of the American Public Health Association, one of the speakers at a session devoted to exploring the consequences of the "population explosion" stated that the

SST was progress, and that progress was good, and that in the name of progress the sonic booms would have to be tolerated. I don't agree. I didn't agree when I heard it, and I don't agree now that I've had time to reflect on the idea. I can't believe that trimming the flying time between New York and San Francisco by approximately an hour is the kind of progress we hold so dear that any of a dozen needs of the inner cities must go begging for lack of funds. I cannot believe that the expenditure of astronomical amounts of hard-to-come-by tax dollars and the discomfort, if not harm, to millions of people beneath the proposed flight paths of the SST have a higher position on some master plan of national priorities than, say, housing, rapid transit, noise, solid waste disposal, or water pollution. I can't believe that flying faster than the speed of sound is progress, in any sense—certainly not when it is achieved at the expense of the needs of people.

Len Deighton's book *The Ipcress File* presented examples of the use of noise for torture to break a man's will. His examples were not creations of a wild imagination, but were solidly based on what psychologists have learned about noise and human behavior. The Chinese have known some of this for thousands of years. They learned rather early that to a man in quiet isolation the sound of slowly but steadily dripping water rapidly assumed the proportions of a loudly beaten drum. Such noise could drive a man mad or break his will. Complete silence or even excessively quiet conditions for an extended period can be terribly disturbing to many people. But sound is one thing; noise is another.

Recently the New York State Supreme Court ruled that one of the inescapable hazards of living in a modern community is the sound of gunfire. It seems that the city of Cortland, New York, had tried to prevent a sportsmen's club from firing high-powered rifles because the noise disturbed many of the residents. The judge, in deciding the case, held that persons living in an organized community must suffer some damage, annoyance, and inconvenience from each other. He went on to say that for these inconveniences they are compensated by the advantages of a civilized society! Perhaps if the judge lived closer to the steady whine and clamor he would not have been able to write so detached an opinion.

Unwittingly, he may have opened a Pandora's box of new problems. If people are unable to obtain the periods of relative quiet they apparently require after a day of work as a means of refreshing themselves before the next day's onslaught, they may well find themselves becoming increasingly irritable, annoyed, and unable to function efficiently. Although this is difficult to establish, there are growing indications that accidents at work, inefficiency, and decreased productivity are related to noise irritation.

Speaking at a meeting of the Citizens for a Quieter City, Inc., Dr. Samuel Rosen asked, "Is the average city person exposed to dangerously high noise levels?" He answered: "Many city noise levels exceed damage-risk criteria suggested for factories. We do not know how much exposure to these intense city noises will cause hearing loss. Nevertheless, the danger is there."

chapter 13

OCCUPATIONAL HEALTH

"Of what trade are you?" Yes, "of what trade are you?" In order to understand and treat the many diseases and ailments that afflict people, and because we spend most of each day at some occupation, physicians have long asked their patients, "of what trade are you?" "Where do you work?" "What do you do?"

Although the association between occupation and ill health and disease was first recorded by Pliny the Elder, who advocated the use of protective masks for workers in mining and grinding operations in the first century A.D., it is Bernardino Ramazzini who is considered the father of occupational health and hygiene. In his book *De Morbis Artificium Diatriba—The Diseases of Workmen,* published in 1700, he described the occupational diseases of his day and suggested preventive measures. It was Ramazzini who first asked, "Of what trade are you?" That was 268 years ago, but the question is still being asked. It is still being asked not because we have not progressed, but because new industries, new chemicals, and new stresses continually confront each new generation of workers, and, as will be seen, old diseases reappear in new industries.

Optokinetic nystagmus is a disease of the twentieth century. Also called "conveyor belt sickness," it was first described in 1966, when a number of women in a potato chip factory in Michigan became strangely ill. The symptoms were giddiness, fainting, nausea, and general mental confusion. When samples of air in the factory were shown to be free of toxic gases capable of producing this set of symptoms, a study of the physical conditions in the factory was undertaken. Because all of the women involved worked on conveyor belt lines, a study of these belts was made, and it was not long before the answer was apparent. When conveyor belts move at speeds up to thirty-two feet per minute, little or no vertigo is experienced by workers inspecting food products or other items carried along on the belt. When, however, the belts fly along at speeds above thirty-two feet per minute, workers trying to focus their eyes on the items experience dizziness, nausea, and mental confusion. Optokinetic nystagmus results from the inability of the eye to respond rapidly enough to keep pace with the units passing by on the speeding belt. As the eye follows individual objects carried along a moving belt, it constantly establishes new focusing points. The eye picks out one object, follows it for a distance, leaves it, picks out another object, follows it, and repeats the process. When the belt speed increases beyond thirty-two feet per minute, the number of focusing points per minute must also increase. Thus, when objects on a belt fly by more rapidly than the eye can focus upon them, involuntary contractions of the eye muscles occur. These contractions cause the eyeballs to move back and forth like pendulums, which triggers the giddiness, fainting, nausea, and general mental confusion.

Trichlorethylene (an organic solvent) is a potential hazard for workers in the modern office. In order for banks or other commercial organizations to process thousands of checks automatically, magnetic ink is used for imprinting. In case of error, trichlorethylene is used to erase the original impression. As a consequence, dangerous concentrations of TCE can occur in the immediate environment, causing irritation to the skin, eyes, and mucous membranes.

Carbon monoxide generated in trace amounts by normal metabolic activity is usually of no consequence. In the sealed microenvironment of a space vehicle, however, it can attain toxic levels if uncontrolled.

These are but three random examples of the stresses imposed by the new technologies of a highly industrialized society in which people are being exposed to new techniques, new materials, and new stresses.

Although these three examples of occupational hazards were unknown to Ramazzini, they have a heritage extending back to two hundred years ago, when the factory system was established in England. The series of inventions and discoveries, both purposeful and accidental, that occurred in the seventy years between 1760 and 1830 and culminated in many of the environmental problems we have today is generally referred to as the Industrial Revolution.

In the years before 1760, production of textiles was limited by the speed of the individual spinners; a good weaver could use up the production of a half-dozen home "spinsters" rather quickly. In fact, he would often have to delay weaving until he could accumulate a supply of thread. In 1768, James Hargreaves, a poor wool-spinner, upset his spinning wheel. While lying on its side the wheel continued to spin and wind the wool. Hargreaves wondered why a half-dozen or more spindles could not be kept in motion by a single wheel. This idea led to the construction of the spinning jenny, in which eight spindles were kept turning by a single wheel. With the introduction of this machine, the industrial revolution was initiated. With sufficient driving power any number of spindles could be kept spinning. Two years later, in 1770, this power was supplied by Richard Arkwright's water frame. It accomplished two things: the spun thread was passed through two pairs of rollers, and because the second pair revolved faster than the first, it stretched out the thread, making it a good deal finer; and driving power was supplied by a water wheel.

In 1779, Samuel Crompton combined the water frame and

the spinning jenny into one unit called the spinning mule, which provided stronger and still finer thread. The next problem was how to weave the thread faster. Crompton's mule had reversed the original limiting factor, and the weaver was now too slow to keep pace with the amount of spun thread that could be produced. In 1783 a clergyman, Edmund Cartwright, working with a local blacksmith, constructed a power loom that was to be the death-blow to domestic work and the beginning of the factory system. Cartwright's power loom used the energy of two strong men, but soon they were replaced by water power, which was superseded by steam power. The use of coal and the steam engine had been developing almost simultaneously with the profound changes in the textile industry. The industrial revolution wrought changes with enormous consequences. It altered the whole character of work. The use of power looms led to the construction of large factories to accommodate hundreds or thousands of workers and the machines they would use. Because the factories needed sources of energy and ore they were built close to the coal- and iron-producing areas. Thousands upon thousands of people migrated from their homes in rural areas to these new locations, with the result that new, densely populated areas developed rapidly. It was in these new industrial centers in both England and the U. S. that many of our present-day problems developed. The mush-rooming of cities proclaimed the changing character of our nation. Foundries, factories, and mills created a new industrial metropolis, whose towering smokestacks belching dark effluents marked the approach of a new age.

When Abraham Lincoln was inaugurated in 1861, fewer than one-sixth of the people lived in cities with populations of ten thousand or more. By 1900, more than one-third of the population lived in cities of this size. And, as the country surged forward, ever-increasing production became the goal. Workers spent long hours in the dirt and wastes generated by the industrial processes. Few factories or foundries provided washrooms, and the worker brought home these wastes on his skin, hair, and clothing. Dust, grime, and toxic fumes were regarded as the necessary byproducts of an industrialized society. Little was known, and few were concerned, about the effect of this industrial environment on human life; employers were not legally responsible for the safety or health of their work force. In addition, extreme heat or cold, dampness, noise, poor lighting and ventilation, and overcrowding were the rule. Children outnumbered adults in some factories. They worked under the same conditions and spent twelve to fourteen hours, seven days a week, on the job. It is small wonder that occupational illness emerged as a major consequence of industrialization.

The workers were not unaware of the health hazards of their jobs. Such terms as "miner's asthma," "brass-founder's ague," "hatter's shakes," "filecutter's paralysis," "baker's itch," and "mulespinner's cancer" were part of their language and bitter experience. Many felt that to change jobs would be simply to exchange one set of hazards for another. Although employers realized that their workers suffered bad health and often early death, they preferred to attribute it to poor conditions at home.

With the advent of the labor movement, there was a drive for better working conditions, and public awareness combined with enlightened industrial leadership began to bring improvements. By the early 1940's our country was on the threshold of the technological age. New industries, new products, new chemicals brought new hazards to the workers, and old hazards appeared in new industries. Lead was used in the manufacture of storage batteries and rubber tires. Thus lead poisoning, a problem in ancient Rome, became a problem once again. The development of x-ray tubes and fluorescent lamps, for example, introduced new materials into industry. Their toxic properties were not known, and workers became ill before suspicion fell on these products. Skin lesions and ulcers were common among workers in the chromate industry, and the cancer rate among electroplaters was higher than among workers in other industries. With the development of the giant petroleum industry, a multitude of byproducts—insecticides, solvents, greases, and drugs—brought new and unfamiliar hazards to workers. Naphtha, benzene, carbon tetrachloride, and acetone were used in thousands of new industrial processes. But the same volatile properties that make solvents so useful as cleaners, thinners, and dryers also made them potentially hazardous when used without proper protection or ventilation.

Today, more Americans are at work than ever before, and although hazardous materials are widely used, knowledge and experience gained over the years have made possible more healthful working conditions. However, the danger of occupational illness has not vanished. New processes, new sources of energy, and the stresses of contemporary life continue to bring new hazards to health.

In 1860, there were only 1.5 million industrial workers. By 1900, there were some 5.5 million, and but still little was done to make the working day pleasant or healthful. By 1960, however, the labor force had risen to 80 million; it was now a powerful action group. The nation's work force of 80 million represents 40 percent of the population and pays 60 percent of the taxes. Despite this substantial contribution to the economy, 80 percent of these workers are employed in places where little, if any, health service is provided. The remaining 20 percent receive excellent to minimal protection. About $320 million is spent yearly by industry to provide in-plant health services for about 15 million workers. The steadily increasing volume of workmen's compensation expenditures for medical care and cash payments to workers and their dependents is a good barometer of the existing occupational health problem. In 1963, for example, $1.6 billion was paid to workers for occupationally induced illness and disease.

Of the common occupational hazards, accidents exact the largest toll, killing about fifteen thousand workers each year and causing over two million non-fatal injuries. As might be expected, the risk of accidental death or injury is highest in building wreckers, electric light and power linemen, handlers of explosives, and window cleaners. Table 16 shows the incidence of nonfatal diseases among a specialized segment of the labor force. Since reliable statistics on the true incidence of occupational diseases for the general labor force are unavailable (it is extremely difficult to obtain such information), the data for federal employees suggest that the national problem is at least several orders of magnitude higher. This supposition is buttressed by the data from

TABLE 16.

Incidence of alleged or suspected occupational diseases as reported in twenty-eight states and for federal employees during a year.

	Total
ALL DISEASES	43,307
1. Systemic effects due to chemical agents	2,252

ammonia, 24; anilin, 23; arsenic, 16; benzol or its derivatives, 16; beryllium, 9; carbon bisulfide, 6; carbon monoxide or dioxide, 233; carbon tetrachloride, 32; chlorine, 29; chrome, 154; cyanide, 15; halogenated hydrocarbons, 14; insecticides, 323; lead, 491; mercury, 14; petroleum products, 23; phosphorus, 5; sulfur dioxide, 14; zinc, brass, 84; gases not specified, 202; paint solvents, 33; miscellaneous and not known, 492.

2. Dust diseases of the lungs	1,999

asbestos, 21; anthracosilicosis, 233; silicosis *, 1,615; pneumoconiosis, other and not specified, 130.

3. Respiratory disorders	667

bronchitis, influenza, pneumonia, 79; respiratory irritations and not specified, 588.

4. Disorders due to physical conditions	4,127

pressure abnormalities, 58; effects of repeated motion, pressure, or shock, 3,748; effects of heat and cold, 304; all other **, 17.

5. Infective and parasitic diseases	1,148

anthrax, 69; brucellosis, 50; tuberculosis, 811; communicable and not specified, 218.

6. Diseases of the skin	23,502

7. Miscellaneous conditions	9,612

allergies (other than skin), 211; cancer, 7; conjunctivitis, 2,034; blisters, abrasions, 567; effects of bites, stings, 1,635; heart disease, 10; neuritis, arthritis, 144; all other, indefinite not specified, 5,004.

* Includes 134 cases reported as silicotuberculosis.
** Includes 14 cases of loss of hearing, 3 due to radiation.

TABLE 17.

Occupational diseases in California, 1961 *

Adapted from the State of California Department of Public Health,
Bureau of Occupational Diseases, Berkeley, 1963, by permission.

AGENCY OF DISEASE	NO. CASES	DISEASE OR SYSTEM AFFECTED	NO. CASES	NO. DEATHS **
Total	*18,495*	*Total*	*18,495*	*369*
Dusts	677	Infective and parasitic	283	7
Gases	432	Ear	316	
Agricultural chemicals	911	Respiratory tract	1,179	116
Metals	398	Digestive system	143	
Solvents	904	Skin	14,006	
Other chemicals	4,923	Effects of toxic materials	1,004	13
Plant and animal products, chiefly poison oak	4,211	Environmental conditions, chiefly heat	795	12
Food products	1,152	Circulatory	243	214
Infectious agents	662	Nervous system	26	
Environmental conditions	1,703	Mental, etc.	41	
Miscellaneous	86	Other allergic	118	
Not stated	2,436	Neoplasms	9	5
		Other	332	2

* Based on "Doctor's First Report of Work Injury."
** Deaths from pneumoconiosis taken from death certificates;
other deaths reported by California Department of Industrial Relations.

California alone. Table 17 shows the occupational diseases reported to the California State Department of Health in 1961. Both surveys show that dermatitis is the leading occupational illness. In fact, it is estimated that 1 percent of the total labor force is affected by occupational dermatoses each year. Although only one chemical injury appears to occur for every ten cases of dermatitis, chemical injury is usually far more severe.

Each year hundreds of new substances are synthesized and brought into use in many industrial processes; many of them are inherently dangerous. The introduction of a large number of volatile solvents has precipitously increased the list of potential poisons. In addition to the obvious hazards of chemicals, dusts, and fumes, many jobs involve potentially harmful conditions: excessive heat, continual dampness, sudden variations in temperature, poor lighting, and continuous vibration, for example. The highest death rates are found in occupations that combine a high probability of accidents with exposure to dust, particularly silicon dioxide. These conditions are present in lead, zinc, hard-rock, and gold mining. On the other hand, clerical workers and professionals, such as physicians, university professors, and clergymen, especially Anglican clergymen, have the lowest death rates of all occupational groups.

A major problem for investigators stydying occupational exposure problems is determining of the concentration of chemicals, dusts or fumes to which a worker may be exposed during his working day, five days a week, fifty weeks a year, without injury. This is particularly difficult to ascertain because the spectrum of workers in any industrial plant includes both men and women from seventeen to sixty-five, of all sizes, shapes, and genetic constitutions, and varying in degree of general health from day to day. To develop a value suitable for all these variables would be impossible. But information of this type is important in evaluating health hazards and establishing controls.

All chemicals vary in their degree of toxicity simply on the basis of the quantity consumed. This variation in degree of response to an amount of chemical—the so-called spectrum of toxicity—is described in Table 18.

TABLE 18.

Spectrum of toxicity*

	LD_{50} **	*Lethal dose*
Extremely toxic	<1 mg.†	taste
Highly toxic	<50 mg.	teaspoon
Toxic	50–500 mg.	an ounce
Moderately toxic	0.5–5.0 gm.	a pint
Slightly toxic	5–15 gm.	a quart
Non-toxic	>15 gm.	More than a quart

* Bear in mind that 1000 milligrams (mg.) equal 1 gram (gm.) and that 30 gm. are just about an ounce.

** LD_{50} is the notation used by biological scientists to express that dose in milligrams per kilogram of body weight that kills 50 percent of the test animals.

† The notation < means "less than," and > means "more than."

Thus, it can be seen that quite a wide range, (an increase of more than fifteen thousand times between <1 mg. to >15 gm.) exists in degree of toxicity. To be harmful to health, some chemicals must be consumed in large doses, while others need be taken only in small amounts. This is why there is such difficulty in determining and establishing levels of chemicals that workmen can be exposed to without harm.

The American Conference of Governmental Industrial Hygienists (ACGIH) each year publishes lists of standards it has set for allowable occupational exposure to chemicals based on an eight-hour working day and a five-day week. These standards are called Threshold Limit Values, or TLV's. Although TLV's exist for hundreds of chemicals, they do not exist for hundreds of others. These values are based on information gathered from industrial experience and experimental studies with animals and human subjects. Thus, it will require many years and much research to gather data on all industrial chemicals. It is important to note that they are only guidelines, not absolute values. As new data becomes available, a value published one year can be reduced or its threshold increased the following year. These standards are pegged to allow the concentration of airborne substances to fluctuate a "reasonable" amount above and below the listed TLV, with the understanding that the average value for the eight-hour day does not exceed the standard.

In remarking on the difficulty of determining these values, I noted the age differences found among workers in a factory, as well as the differences in body type and genetic constitutions. These will all have an effect on the individual's reaction to a specific concentration of chemical. However, the TLV's are based on the reasonably healthy adult; they are not applicable to continuous exposure of the very young and very old, the indisposed, or the diseased.

The American Standards Association (ASA) has also studied the problem of occupational exposures and has set standards called Maximum Allowable Concentrations, or MAC's. These are issued with the proviso that they are only guides in the control of health hazards and are not to be regarded as fine lines between safe and dangerous levels. Rather, they represent a ceiling above which concentration should not be allowed to rise at any time during the working day. Below these MAC's, only the most susceptible or sensitive individual should show ill effects.

It is the unusual industrial environment that has only a single chemical circulating in its environment. It is much more likely that several chemicals are present at the same time. How then is an estimation of a safe or hazardous condition to be determined?

Experience and experimentation have shown that certain combinations of chemicals have an additive effect. That is, their combined effect, rather than the effect of either individually, must be evaluated. To express this, an equation relating observed atmospheric concentration (C) to the TLV of that specific chemical (T) can be set up. For example,

$$\frac{C_1}{T_1} + \frac{C_2}{T_2} + \frac{C_3}{T_3} + \ldots \ldots \frac{C_n}{T_n} = 1$$

This expression says that when the ratios of each of the chemicals are added together their value can be equal to unity, one. If their value is less than unity, the TLV is not exceeded; if it is one, the condition is borderline; and if it is more than one, the TLV is exceeded and the chemicals can be assumed to be potentially hazardous.

If experience indicates that the effects of each chemical are in fact independent of those of the other, the ratio $\frac{C}{T} = 1$ must be ascertained for each substance independently, and the TLV is exceeded only when at least one constituent has a value exceeding one.

Inhalation is one of the most important portals of entry into the body for toxic materials. However, of the various means of exposure, skin contact, as shown in Tables 16 and 17, accounts for more illness and lost time than any other mechanism.

In contact with the skin, a chemical can induce injury in one of three ways: it can react with the skin surface and produce a localized irritation; it can penetrate the skin to combine with tissue proteins, producing a more diffused sensitization; or it can penetrate through a hair follicle, enter the bloodstream, and thereby act as a systemic poison. In this case, any tissue or organ can be affected if it comes in contact with the circulating blood.

Trichlorethylene, a widely used solvent, can dissolve lipids from the skin, causing chapped or cracked skin. Corrosive acids and alkalis attack the skin directly, causing burns and tissue destruction. Aniline and tetraethyl lead can be absorbed through the skin. Aniline has a great affinity for hemoglobin, the pigment of red blood cells. When it combines with hemoglobin, it produces an oxygen deficiency in tissue by preventing the normal transport of oxygen by hemoglobin, thereby giving a cyanotic tint to the skin, tongue, and mucous membranes. Tetraethyl lead, on the other hand, has an affinity for the central nervous system. Severely exposed individuals suffer from convulsive seizures, tremors, and periods of manic behavior, accompanied by auditory and visual hallucinations. Nightmares are not uncommon. The large majority of occupational intoxications that affect the internal integrity of the body results from breathing airborne substances. Chemicals inhaled into the lungs can produce damage there or pass to other organs by way of the pulmonary blood system. However, the type and severity of the action of the potentially toxic agent depends on such factors as the chemical structure of the substance, the amount inhaled, the rate of absorption, and the individual's susceptibility and rate of physical activity. An individual inhaling one ounce of alcohol as vapor would feel the effects much faster than if he drank the same quantity. Most solvent vapors and gases, when inhaled, produce their effects in a relatively short time.

Chronic occupational poisoning can also occur via the alimentary canal. Illness or injury by ingestion and swallowing occurs when contaminated hands, food, or cigarettes are placed in the mouth, or when a worker licks a brush containing a harmful material. Lead, mercury, radium, and arsenic have produced illness in this way.

Physical conditions, such as abnormally high or low air pressure, sudden changes in temperature, excessive vibration, and noise, can also cause injury. In the unique case of ionizing radiation and ultraviolet radiation, internal and external tissue injury, respectively, can be induced. The human being, a hardy creature, apparently can tolerate a wide range of physical stresses, but in many instances, industrial processes may exceed this tolerance. The noise in can manufacturing plants and in foundries can cause both temporary and permanent hearing loss. The severe cold in food-freezing plants can induce frostbite and tissue death, while excessive heat often produces heat exhaustion, heatstroke, and muscular cramping. Operators of pneumatic drills, tampers, and pounders can develop injuries of the bones, joints, tendons, ligaments, and blood vessels. "White fingers" is a condition seen in men who constantly grip tightly the handles of their tools, thereby inducing circulatory changes. The most dangerous of these vibratory tools are those with frequencies or blows of two thousand to three thousand per minute.

With every breath we take, we inhale some dust. As a rule, most dusts are harmless. Certain dusts, however, can produce pathological changes in lung tissue, converting healthy spongy tissue into useless fibrous or scar tissue. Dusts consist of solid particles suspended in air. They are usually considered to range from 0.5 to 150 microns in diameter. Street dusts, plant pollens, and sand, for example, are so large that they either settle out rapidly or are trapped in the nose and upper respiratory passages and thus rarely reach the alveoli. On the other hand, industrial dusts resulting from grinding, drilling, sawing, and the like are about 5 microns or less in diameter and can penetrate to the depths of the lung. The greater the energy used in grinding and the harder the material being ground or broken up, the finer and, therefore, the more dangerous to human health, are the resulting particles (see Chapter 10, p. 188). It is the particles from 1.0 to 0.1 microns that remain suspended in inhaled air and are the most dangerous. In lung specimens of men who have died of dust-induced diseases, the particles most often found measure 1 micron in diameter.

Some twenty pulmonary diseases due to industrial dusts have been described and are classified as pneumoconioses. This word literally means "dust retained in the lungs." Of these twenty diseases, six are considered the major pneumoconioses—the most common and the best understood. These are silicosis, asbestosis, talcosis, shaver's disease, diatomite pneumoconiosis, and coal worker's pheumoconiosis.

Silicosis, the most important of the six, has been well known for centuries. Ramazzini called it miner's asthma; others called it rock tuberculosis and grinder's consumption.

Silicosis can occur in workers exposed to mineral dusts containing free silica, such as sandstone, flint, quartz, chert, or agate. The disease occurs most often in workers who manufacture and pack abrasive soap powders, in sandblasters* working in enclosed tanks, and in drillers working in tunnels. The most detailed descriptions of silicosis were obtained from studies of of South African gold miners who inhaled large amounts of silica when mechanical drills were introduced in the 1880's and 1890's. However, the

---

* Sandblasters are well aware of the hazards of their trade; one of their grim jokes is, "Join the Navy and see the world—become a sandblaster and see the next."

typical chronic pulmonary condition is produced after ten to fifteen years of exposure to dust by potters, foundrymen, stonecutters, tile and clay producers, and glassmakers.

When crystalline silica particles are in contact with lung tissue over a period of years, characteristic fibrous nodules develop. These increase in size until round, hard, discrete nodules of from two to four millimeters in diameter are studded throughout the lung. As a result of this loss of spongy tissue to nodule formation, shortness of breath, difficulty in breathing, chest pains, and a racking cough are experienced by the silicotic individual. The most important consequence is tuberculosis; the more advanced the lung damage, the greater the likelihood of infection by the tubercle bacillus.

Raw asbestos is found in many countries. The largest mines are in Canada, South Africa, and the Soviet Union. It is a unique material in that it will not burn and thus has many uses, such as in protective clothing for firefighters, pads for ironing boards, brake linings, and boiler and pipe insulation. Chemically, asbestos is a hydrated magnesium silicate found in such minerals as serpentine and chrysotile, but it is a fibrous material and its dust is composed of tiny fibers. It has been well demonstrated that the fibers measuring twenty to fifty microns in length are the most active in the initiation of asbestosis. These fibers must be less than one micron in diameter if they are to reach the terminal bronchioles on repeated inhalation. It is during the mining and processing stages of asbestos production that these characteristic fibers are produced.

Although asbestos has been known and used for some two thousand years, it was only in 1927 that asbestosis was described as a clinical entity. In this instance, the lung lesion is not the discrete nodule seen in silicosis but rather is seen as a diffuse fibrous infiltration with thickening of the pleural wall. Within the fibrous material are dumbbell-shaped nodules that have formed around asbestos fibers.

After many years of inhaling asbestos fibers, coughing, expectoration, loss of appetite, and consequent loss of weight occur, followed by progressively increased shortness of breath. In some cases clubbing of the fingers has been reported. During the past five years evidence linking asbestos with lung cancer has been accumulating.

Whereas disease and illness from asbestos, silica, and other dusts has been known for centuries, the toxic nature of beryllium has been recognized only since 1933. As a result of the need for radioactive material before and during World War II, beryllium, a lightweight grayish-black metal obtained from the ore, beryl, was used in substantial quantities in atomic reactors. When colored green by traces of chromium, beryllium is the precious stone emerald. When beryllium dust is inhaled as it is by workers engaged in the manufacture of x-ray apparatus, neon tubes, fluorescent lamps, and non-sparking tools, both acute and chronic systemic effects, as well as contact dermatitis, can occur. The acute form occurs in response to high concentrations inhaled during a brief exposure, and resembles bronchitis and pneumonia. Symptoms can appear as early as seventy-two hours after exposure. They usually subside after hospitalization for thirty to ninety days and do not recur unless the individual is again exposed to beryllium dust. The chronic disease can occur from a month to twenty years after exposure. A striking feature of the chronic case is that even people who live in the vicinity of plants generating beryllium dust have become victims. Chronic cough and shortness of breath are typical symptoms. On x-ray examination of the lungs, fine nodules dispersed throughout the tissue are seen. Unlike silicosis and asbestosis, beryllosis can be treated, and often dramatic improvements are possible. The use of steroid compounds such as cortisone and ACTH can arrest the disease, and in some cases has even reversed the degeneration of the lungs which occurs. Beryllium is the only non-radioactive element which has produced cancer of the bronchi in laboratory animals, but evidence linking it with human lung cancer is not strong.

Control or prevention of exposure to dusts, metals, organic solvents, vibration, or temperature extremes, can be accomplished by personal protective devices; isolation or redesign of a process; substitution of a less toxic or non-toxic material, if one is available;

and regular medical supervision.

The evaluation of occupational hazards, a necessary first step for establishing controls, requires that a well-directed plant survey be undertaken. The survey would delineate which operations or physical aspects of the contained environment constitute a potential danger to those in the area. This must not be a superficial study by semi- or non-professionals. Industrial hygiene engineers or others trained in environmental or public health should be involved in the planning, direction, and actual surveying. It is simply too difficult to evaluate a sample, condition, or process without having firsthand knowledge of the individual plant in operation.

Surveys of the frequency and types of occupational injuries (I avoid using the word *accident,* since many of the injuries incurred in industry may not be chance occurrences; see Chapter 11) have revealed that 25 percent of all disabling industrial injuries occur to the hand. Thus, protection of the hands should be a major concern of both employer and employee.

Perhaps the most effective way to insure a safe environment is to eliminate hazardous chemicals, devices, and practices. Practically, this may not be possible or even necessary. Safety does not mean the complete eradication of all potentially harmful agents. It only means that such materials are used judiciously. The TLV's and MAC's imply that certain chemicals are dangerous when they exceed certain concentrations; they do not imply that the very presence of these chemicals is to be disallowed.

Accordingly, the first step in creating a safe environment is to ascertain the amount and type of contamination in the work areas. It may be that simple dilution of contaminated air by ventilation with uncontaminated air will solve the problem. If an operation is inherently dangerous, such as the use of tetraethyl lead, the entire operation can be isolated from the general work area and the individuals performing the operation can be fitted with protective clothing, such as self-contained half-masks and full-face respirators, or supplied with air hoods and helmets. Personal, self-contained air conditioning units with self-regulating temperature controls are now available for workers who must be totally en-

FIGURE 48. Typical full-face respirator, providing an unobstructed field of vision

FIGURE 49. Protective breathing apparatus for individuals whose larynx has been removed

closed in protective suits.

Hard hats, shin guards, and toe and foot guards are also available. There are protective aprons of many kinds, including the "kickback" type to prevent abdominal injury to sawyers as lumber is ejected by power-driven saws. Gloves, goggles, ear guards, and protective creams can further reduce injuries.

While walking through the lobby of a large hotel in New York City recently, I saw a procedure that seemed guaranteed to produce injury to the men using it. Two men were attempting to stretch and straighten a large wall-to-wall rug. Each was on his hands and knees moving sideways across the rug. As he moved, each moved a rug-stretcher held in his right hand firmly down and forward. The metal prongs on the bottom grasped the rug and held it as each man brought up his left knee and imparted a resounding whack to the padded knob of the stretcher; this stretched the rug considerably, but it took at least eighteen such knee-kicks by each man to finish the job properly. Although I didn't inquire, I'm ready to wager that shooting pains in the leg and even occasional limping has occurred more than once to these men.

New tools such as the rug-stretcher and new processes often engender new occupational hazards. Surely, a less troublesome way of stretching rugs, for example, could be devised.

A great deal of protection can be afforded workers by general good housekeeping practices. Regular removal of waste materials prevents hazardous substances from building up on floors and ledges. Materials that are spilled on floors and tables should be cleaned up immediately. Where feasible, a special team or individual could be trained to handle this.

One of the most important preventive measures is regular examination of employees by competent medical personnel trained to evaluate occupational problems. Examinations at three- or six-month intervals could pick up early signs of illness, spot susceptible individuals, and determine whether an illness is in fact the result of some in-plant exposure.

Medical records can help pinpoint particularly hazardous operations in the plant. Spot maps, like those used to study diseases of epidemic proportions, can signal the process or area in a plant where numerous cases of some illness have occurred. Once these areas are located, conditions can be modified.

Personal hygiene is also important in any program of prevention. Copious use of soap and water can markedly reduce the incidence of skin diseases. This simple expedient is often neglected by many people who come in contact with potentially toxic materials. In-plant washing facilities should include shower rooms.

The working environment need not be a cause of illness or injury. Although final control of occupational hazards is the responsibility of plant owners and managers, individual employees can do a great deal to protect themselves and their families.

CHAPTER 14

IONIZING RADIATION

Unquestionably, the most important scientific discovery of this century was the demonstration that the energy of atoms could be released and controlled. Success on December 2, 1942, proved the feasibility of splitting the atom and harnessing astounding amounts of energy. However, some sixty years ago it was learned that there are traces of radioactivity all around us, that we are subject to natural radiation throughout our existence. It wasn't, of course, until the explosion of a nuclear device that the public health problem assumed importance.

Before we discuss the effects, uses, and problems of relatively large quantities of man-made radiation, some facts about low-level natural background radiation may be helpful.

The natural radiation to which each of us is exposed may be from external sources: granite floors or walls containing traces of radium that emit gamma radiation; the soil upon which we build our homes; or cosmic rays. Internal natural irradiation is emitted by potassium-40, an essential constituent of living tissue. We take natural radioactive materials into our bodies with every breath we take, with the water we drink, and with the food we eat.

Recently, we have begun to be irradiated by man-made radioactive materials such as cesium-137, a gamma emitter produced during atomic explosions and deposited by rain in a thin layer on the surface of the earth. In this form, it can be an external source of irradiation; the same element may be ingested in milk and meat obtained from animals pastured on grasslands on which the fallout was deposited. This type of man-made or artificial external and internal irradiation is not part of the natural background. Table 19 shows the sources of natural low-level irradiation.

The predominent natural alpha radioactivity of our environment comes from the very long-lived isotopes of uranium and

---

TABLE 19.

Sources of natural background irradiation

Sources of Irradiation	Dose rate (millirems per year)		
	Gonad	Bone Marrow	Haversion Canal
External irradiation			
Cosmic rays * (including neutrons)	50	50	50
Terrestrial (including air)	50	50	50
Internal Irradiation			
Potassium-40	20	15	15
Radium-226 (and decay products)	0.5	5.4	0.6
Radium-228 (and decay products)	0.8	8.6	1.0
Lead-210	0.3	3.6	0.4
Carbon-14	0.7	1.6	1.6
Radon-222 (absorbed in bloodstream)	3	3	3
	125	137	122

* The radioactive activity of cosmic rays increases with altitude; thus, Denver, the "mile-high city," is exposed to stronger radiation than New York City, which is at sea level.

thorium. Both of these elements have half lives comparable with the age of the earth. Most soils (soil is, of course, produced by the weathering of rocks) contain traces of radium which were derived from uranium and thorium.

The background of gamma radiation at any given location on the earth is roughly proportionate to the concentration of radioactive material, and thus varies with the soil type. For example, over igneous rock (rock of volcanic origin) radiation may be as high as one hundred to two hundred millirems per year; over chalk deposits, it may be as low as twenty-five millirems per year. Table 20 indicates the range of natural backgrounds.

TABLE 20.

Dose of irradiation to gonads and bones
from natural external sources, including cosmic rays

Region	Dose (millirem/year)
New York City	75
Granitic regions of France	190
Espirito Santo, Brazil	320
Kerala, India	900

The unusually high natural backgrounds in Kerala, India, and Espirito Santo, Brazil, have been cause for cautious concern. Studies are under way in both cities in an attempt to uncover possible hazards to health from long-term residence in this environment. It is still too early to tell whether decreased life expectancy, congenital malformations, metabolic errors, and cancer are more common in these areas than in cities with far lower natural radiation levels.

Radiation, in its broadest sense, means the transfer of electromagnetic waves through space. Radiation is energy in motion, and it produces an effect only if energy is transferred to matter. Accordingly, a major effect of radiation on matter is to increase its energy content. In addition, chemical bonds are broken, permitting ions and chemical radicals to re-form in unique ways. Radiation creates new chemical species.

The radiations or rays emitted by radioactive elements are called alpha (α) rays, beta (β) rays, gamma (γ) rays, and x-rays. All of these taken together are referred to as *ionizing radiations*. They are called ionizing because when they strike atoms of the material through which they pass, they knock out an electron. This removal of an electron confers great reactivity on the atom, which is now positively charged, or ionized. This is simply another way of describing the increase in energy content. Ionization is the mechanism by which radiation causes physical, chemical, or biological changes.

Now, although these rays are highly energized, they are not equally dangerous. By dangerous, I mean capable of penetrating matter. Figure 50 illustrates this concept.

Alpha particles are the least penetrating. They can be stopped by a thin sheet of paper, a thin film of water, or the outer layer of skin. (Alpha particles can be dangerous if they are inhaled or ingested, because of their ability to penetrate into soft tissue.) Beta particles are stopped by the thickness of a cinder block. They can penetrate at least half an inch into skin or tissue. Gamma particles are the most dangerous because of their extremely great ability to penetrate matter.* They penetrate organs, tissues, and bone; thus it is the gamma ray that shielding must protect against. Our clothing is sufficient to protect against both alpha and beta radiations, but not against gamma.

Radiation is measured in terms of the amount of ionization it produces. The unit of measurement is the roentgen (r) or the milliroentgen, which is one thousandth of a roentgen. Since the roentgen ** is a measure of the number of ions produced in a cubic centimeter of air, the total damage done to a tissue or an organ is

---

* This is directly related to the neutral charge.

** A roentgen is the unit of measurement of x-ray exposure. For example, the amount received by the skin during a chest x-ray is about .02.

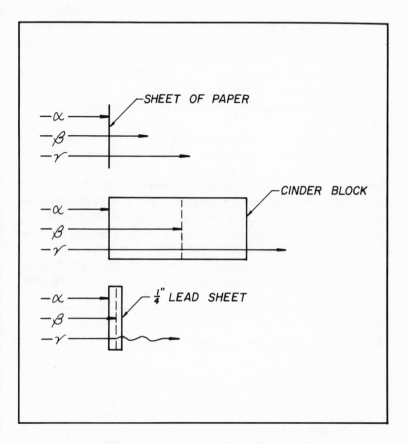

FIGURE 50. Penetration capabilities of three types of particles

dependent upon the area over which the radiation is applied. Accordingly, a dose of 1000 r confined to someone's earlobe would harm only the earlobe; however, the same 1000 r applied over the whole surface of the body would doubtless be lethal.

The word *rem,** short for "*r*oentgen *e*quivalent *m*an," designates a dose unit. It refers to that dose of any type of radiation which produces a biological effect equivalent to the absorption of one roentgen of x-radiation. The rem has largely replaced the roentgen because it offers a way of putting dose measurements on a comparative basis from the standpoint of probability of biological damage.

One of the problems of radioactivity is the persistence of radiation, resulting in continuous ionization. The relative persistence of radiation is determined by the length of time it takes for half the atoms of some radioactive substance to disintegrate: This is the half life of the specific substance, and it is as characteristic of the substance as fingerprints are of a person. Half lives vary from fractions of seconds to millions of years. Table 21 gives the half life of seven representative radioactive elements.

At the end of one period the element has lost half of its activity; at the end of the second period, half of the remaining activ-

TABLE 21.

Half lives of radioactive elements

Element	Half Life
Nitrogen-16	8 seconds
Bromine-85	3 minutes
Sodium-24	14.8 hours
Iodine-131	8 days
Cesium-137	33 years
Radium-226	1,600 years
Carbon-14	5,600 years
Thorium-232	10 billion years

* A millirem is 1/1000 of a rem.

ity has been lost, leaving a quarter of the original activity. At the end of the third period half of that quarter is lost, and so on until none remains. Thus, the shorter the half life the less dangerous the element is, while the longer the half life the longer the period the element is able to emit radiation, which causes ionization and, thereby, injury. In biological terms this means that an element with a relatively long half life, such as strontium-90 from fallout debris (which has a half life of twenty-eight years) can remain sufficiently long in tissue to become carcinogenic. On the other hand, certain radioactive agents with half lives of ten hours to ten days are used to treat disease; this is sufficient to deliver the required dose, but not long enough to cause injury.

The power of a nuclear weapon is due to the almost instantaneous transformation of atomic mass into energy. According to Einstein's formula $E = mc^2$ (energy equals mass multiplied by the square of the velocity of light) the fission of a single atom of uranium-235 will yield roughly two hundred million electron volts. Thus weapons having thousands of times the destructive force of TNT can be constructed.

The energy in a typical air burst produced by a thermonuclear device has been found to be distributed as follows: blast and shock, 50 percent; thermal radiation, 35 percent; initial nuclear radiation, 5 percent; and residual nuclear radiation, 10 percent. The immediate effects of this set of responses would be mechanical injuries, injuries due to heat and those due to radiation.

The mechanical injuries would be caused directly by the blast's shock wave and secondarily by flying debris and collapsing buildings. Tests with dummy figures at the Nevada test site indicate that a man, standing or walking in the vicinity of the blast, could be picked up and hurled twenty feet. The injuries caused by heat or by thermal radiation result from direct exposure to extremely high temperatures. Temperatures within the fireball of a one-megaton device range up to one million degrees Fahrenheit; this is comparable to the temperature in the center of the sun. Accordingly, anything within three thousand feet of the fireball would be vaporized. Varying degrees of flame burns from spreading fires would also occur.

The injuries which we are most concerned with are those resulting from intense, acute doses of gamma radiation received in less than a minute, and those from the delayed effects of fallout. Since a great deal has been written on the effect of radiation on various body tissues, on the carcinogenic effects and even the genetic effects to be expected, I want to focus on the factors that affect survival.

The lethal dose of radiation is generally designated as the LD_{50-30}: that is, the dose of radiation that would be expected to kill 50 percent of a population within thirty days. For obvious reasons, this has never been determined experimentally for humans. Thus, animal studies and the data from Hiroshima and Nagasaki must be used to predict the expected LD_{50-30}.

It has been suggested that 450 roentgens of radiation is the human lethal dose. However, this value has been obtained from animals given no supportive or protective treatment. Consequently, estimates of the lethal dose obtained in a single day have been scaled upwards of 600 to 700 r. Furthermore, if the dose were divided, that is, if it were given over several days or weeks, probably a great deal more could be sustained with survival. Thus, a dose of 1400 r is currently being suggested as the upper limit at which survival is possible. Evidence for this comes from experience with overall body irradiation of patients with incurable cancer.

On March 1, 1954, a thermonuclear device was detonated from a barge in the Marshall Islands. At that time, twenty-eight American airmen were gathering weather data on the island of Rongerik, 160 miles from Bikini, the point of detonation. As a consequence of the blast, radioactive debris fell in such abundance that the monitoring detectors were completely disrupted. In addition to the airmen on Rongerik, a number of people lived on the nearby islands of Rongelap, Utirik, and Alinginae. Several days after the detonation, it was learned that a Japanese fishing vessel, the Fukuru Maru, had been inside the fallout area.

Although the fallout was so great as to be visible, neither the sixty-four residents of the islands nor the twenty-three fishermen took any precautions to reduce their exposure. As a consequence, all of these people lived in intimate contact with the most radioactive environment ever known to have existed. The Japanese fishermen described the fallout dust as being as heavy as a snowfall. It covered the hair and come into direct contact with skin and eyes. Food and water was heavily contaminated. More than two days after the blast, the islanders were taken to a military hospital on the island of Kwajalein for medical examinations. The fishermen had been in contact with this severe fallout for thirteen days before they reached their home port, and only then did they learn why they were ill. All twenty-three of them were hospitalized. Itching and burning of the skin were felt by most of those who had been exposed; ulceration of the skin and severe loss of hair usually followed. It was found that the severity of the ulceration and hair loss of both the fishermen and the islanders was directly related to the amount of clothing they had been wearing. The most severe burns occurred among the fishermen who did not wear hats. Effects on the blood were related to the degree of the whole-body gamma irradiation dose received by the whole body.

Since both groups had been so totally blanketed with fallout the amount of radiation ingested and inhaled was undoubtedly at a maximum. The islanders had drunk water from exposed sources and eaten food that was completely exposed to the atmosphere. Because the Japanese ate fish that had come in contact with the contaminated deck of their ship, they ingested a large internal dose. Chemical analysis of urine specimens indicated that the natives had received from 100 to 150 r to the thyroid in addition to a whole-body dose of 175 r.

Six months after leaving the hospital, one of the fishermen died of a diseased liver. The amount of radionuclides in his tissue was so low that death from radiation due to isotopes with long half lives was ruled out.

In 1960, the islanders were examined again. Both those who had been exposed and those who had not were in generally good health. There was no evidence of disease that could be related to the effects of fallout. It must be noted that the inhabitants of Rongelap returned to their still heavily contaminated island 3½ years after this examination.

In May, 1966, five natives from Rongelap were brought to New England Deaconess Hospital in Boston, because they had developed thyroid gland nodules as a result of ingesting radioactive substances. These growths were removed, and examination showed them to be non-cancerous.

Thirteen of the original eighty-seven islanders and fishermen died as a result of the fallout. According to Dr. Robert Conard, Physician-in-Charge at Brookhaven National Laboratories, the survivors have recovered completely from the ill effects of radioactive fallout.

From repeated examinations of the exposed islanders, fishermen, and airmen, several conclusions emerge: inhalation and ingestion of radioactive substances appear to be very much less of a problem than originally believed, and burns due to fallout can be minimized or completely avoided by using proper clothing, washing exposed parts quickly, or remaining indoors.

In 1954, following a long series of atomic and hydrogen weapons tests, scientists drew public attention to the fact that the atmosphere, the oceans, and the land surfaces of our planet were being contaminated by radioactive fallout. Atmospheric testing of nuclear devices is known to produce in its fallout such isotopes as Iodine-131, a short-lived species; Strontium-90 and Cesium-137, which decay within a human lifetime, and Carbon-14, whose half life is approximately fifty-six hundred years. The scientists revealed that great quantities of radioactive substances ejected into the air by each detonation were caught up by air currents, carried across the globe, and deposited on land and sea. These radioactive elements were then rapidly absorbed by edible food crops and ingested by man. As a consequence of the significant rise in environmental radioactivity, the scientists warned of the potential dangers to humanity and asked for a cessation of all nuclear weapons testings. To objectively assess the problem, the United Nations in 1955 convened a committee of leading scientists from fifteen countries. After three years of deliberations, the committee submitted its report, which stated that if atomic weapons tests continued, hundreds of thousands of people would die or become ill due to altered hereditary mechanisms and leukemia and other forms of cancer.* Subsequently, an international test-ban treaty was proposed.**

During the past ten years, the subject of the genetic effects of radiation has been discussed at such length that it hardly seems possible that anything remains to be said. Nevertheless, I want to present several findings that cannot be ignored in evaluating the potential or actual hazards of man-made radiation.

Without doubt, the outstanding opportunity to study and analyze the possible mutagenic effects of radiation in man arose as a consequence of the atomic bombing of the Japanese cities of Hiroshima and Nagasaki on August 6 and 9, 1945. But it is often said that today, more than twenty years later, scientists know little more about the effects of ionizing radiations on people than they did in July, 1945. Is this so? What has been gleaned from twenty years of studying the Japanese population?

Recognizing the importance of a careful appraisal of ill effects to the survivors of the bombing, the National Academy of Sciences-National Research Council established the Atomic Bomb Casualty Commission (ABCC) and charged it with responsibility for investigating the effects of the bombing. In 1947, the Commission entered the devastated cities. The immediate genetic interest in Hiroshima and Nagasaki stemmed from the demonstration in 1927 by Nobel laureate H. J. Muller that x-rays could produce mutations in fruitflies. Although the bombing of Hiroshima and Nagasaki offered the most propitious opportunity to study the genetic effects of radiation in man, the doses received by the survivors, surprisingly enough, were low by comparison with those used in laboratory experiments with animals. The ABCC designed a population study of approximately one hundred thousand people—probably the largest of its kind ever attempted—in which it proposed to obtain evidence of potential and actual genetic damage.

* These predictions were based primarily on mathematical calculations rather than studies of irradiated population.
** This became a political hot potato. Candidates in the 1964 presidential election took opposing sides on what became an important public issue.

To accomplish such a monumental task, two major requirements had to be satisfied: one was an unexposed control population which would be comparable in age, sex, weight, height, diet, occupation, etc., to the exposed population; the second was a set of criteria or indicators by which to assess damage. The question posed by the ABCC was not, "Is there damage?," but rather, "Can the damage be detected?" This concept recognized that genetic damage need not manifest itself in gross or dramatic aberrations. Thus, the indicators of genetic damage around which the population study was designed were: increase in stillbirths* and neonatal deaths**; increase in deaths during the first months of life; increase in congenital malformations; decrease in birthweight; altered sex ratio; and impaired physical development at nine months. The relative broadness of these indicators created the need for an adequate control population.

Today, more than twenty years after the bombings, analysis of the data for all of the indicators chosen indicates no clearly discernible trends.[1] There were no clear relationships between the radiation dose experienced by the parents and the frequency of stillbirths and neonatal deaths, birthweight, and congenital malformations. In a 1953 summary of the data an equivocal relationship with sex ratio appeared. When, however, thousands of additional cases were studied, the combined total annulled that relationship. Additionally, there were no differences in the frequency of deaths during the first nine months of life, a particularly sensitive criterion of infant viability, among infants born to exposed and non-exposed parents.

The ABCC calculated that, allowing for shielding, the population of Hiroshima and Nagasaki had received about 100 to 175 rads † of gamma irradiation. This is just about equal to the dose received by the exposed islanders and fishermen after the 1954 detonation in the Marshall Islands.

* A stillbirth is a fetal death which occurs after twenty-eight weeks of gestation.

** A neonatal death is one occurring before the twenty-eighth day of life.

† The rad is a unit of absorbed dose, differing from the roentgen (r), which is used as a unit of exposure.

How are we to interpret the apparent absence of radiation effects in the offspring of exposed parents? Evidence from laboratory experiments, which can direct larger doses to any organ or tissue than could the bombings, has clearly shown genetic effects in plants and mice; it is difficult to conceive that man is unique in his response to gamma radiation. Consequently, we must turn back to the indicators or criteria chosen to demonstrate mutations* or other genetic effects; rather than conclude that the atomic bombings had no harmful genetic effects, we should, perhaps, more rightly conclude that thus far such effects have not been demonstrated.

Support for this position comes from two independent but parallel studies. Dr. William Beierwalter of the University of Michigan [2] observed chromosomal abnormalities in human subjects following irradiation with iodine-131. He has been unable to relate these abnormalities to actual or potential genetic or somatic defects. A. D. Bloom and his team examined chromosomal material from leucocytes (white blood cells) of survivors of the bombings in Hiroshima and Nagasaki and found no alteration in the number or condition of the chromosomes. Thus, it bears repeating that the amount of radiation a person can receive and survive without lasting effect remains unknown; but the effects of the atomic bombings on the survivors have not been as grim as many had predicted. However, it must be added that twenty years is a relatively short period; it may well be that more time is needed for effects to become apparent.

The problem of evaluating injury to a population becomes progressively more difficult as the potentially harmful agent is steadily reduced. Radiation studies illustrate this point. In the early years, the permissible exposure level was set at 100 milliroentgens per day. When damage was observed in experimental studies on animals, the permissible level was reduced to 300 mr/week. Still more research suggested that further reductions should be made, so that by the early 1960's, 100 mr/week became the permissible exposure for man. These reductions were made despite the fact that studies with human subjects at each of these permis-

* Mutations are inherited changes in genes and chromosomes.

sible levels failed to show evidence of illness or injury. It should be noted that each successive reduction in permissible level required a significant outlay of money and engineering effort and was done to accommodate calculated scientific judgment of possible mutational damage to human genes.

In 1957, Ehrenberg, Ehrenstein, and Hedgran of the University of Stockholm reported [3] that increased number of spontaneous mutations could be expected with increased temperature to the gonads. They suggested that mutations during the past several centuries were due to wearing of trousers by men, which can increase testicular temperatures by three degrees Centigrade. By calculating the increase in mutations and by extrapolating to men aged twenty to forty, as had been done for ionizing radiation, the researchers concluded that the harmful genetic effect of our clothing was one hundred to one thousand times greater than that from all the radiation to which we are now exposed. They suggested that the kilts worn by the Scots were far less conducive to temperature increases. In addition, they noted that regularly taken hot baths raise the gonadal temperature to levels conducive to mutational changes.

Interestingly enough, in April, 1967, Drs. Derek Robinson and John Rock of The Rock Reproductive Clinic in Brookline, Massachusetts, reported [4] that men who wore tight insulating garments for six to eleven weeks had severely depressed sperm production. They noted that even athletic-type undershorts can raise the temperature of the testes and hinder sperm production.

Even more recently, Dr. Johannes Clemmesen of the Copenhagen Cancer Registry [5] (where the world's oldest national cancer registry is maintained) indicated that testis carcinoma, a relatively rare malignancy, appears to be on the increase among middle-aged men. He pointed out that the incidence of the disease has risen from 3.2 to 6.3 per 100,000 in the past twenty years. According to Dr. Clemmensen, this gonadal malignancy may be due to increased use of Jockey shorts, which is believed to raise testicular temperature and thus foster tumor growth.

In attempting to formulate radiation protection standards, the Federal Radiation Council in 1960 wrote that "if beneficial uses were fully exploited without regard to radiation protection, the resulting biological risk might well be considered too great. Reducing the risk to zero would virtually eliminate any radiation use, and result in the loss of all possible benefits. It is, therefore, necessary to strike a balance between maximum use and zero risk. In establishing radiation protection standards, the balancing of risk and benefit is a decision involving medical, social, economic, political and other factors. Such a balance cannot be made on the basis of a precise mathematical formula but must be a matter of informed judgment."

The Atomic Energy Commission has specified levels of radiation it will allow for the general public. For example, 5 millirems per year to the head, trunk, active blood-forming organs, lens of the eye, and gonads is permissible, while 75 mrem/yr is the allowable level to feet and ankles and 30 mrem/yr to skin of the whole body. In addition, a person working with radioactive material may safely receive a dose to the whole body greater than the figures noted, under certain specified conditions.

All of this is often discounted by people who are primarily concerned with damage to the protoplasm of unborn generations. Of course, obtaining direct evidence *now* either to support or discount such fears is impossible. Recently, however, Dr. E. L. Green, director of the Jackson Laboratory at Bar Harbor, Maine, reported that his studies of eighteen generations of mice (equivalent to five hundred to six hundred human years) revealed that accumulated ancestral radiation had very little physical effect.[6] He indicated, too, that population survival may not be endangered by radiation, as had been thought. Perhaps these findings will bring some measure of comfort to those who rail against air pollution but denounce all plans for clean sources of power in the form of nuclear power plants.

Any discussion of the hazards of ionizing radiations would be misleading and unfair if proper emphasis were not given to the many benefits obtained from this relatively new energy source, through new procedures in medicine and public health, agriculture, food preservation, and a host of industrial practices.

For the past twenty years, research studies dealing with the preservation of foods by ionizing radiation have been in progress. The work begun at the Massachusetts Institute of Technology in 1948 has culminated with the acceptance and certification by the Food and Drug Administration, Department of Agriculture, and Department of Defense of half a dozen foods as safe, nutritious, and suitable for sale to the public.

As laboratory experiments yielded new data on the biological effects of radiation, it was learned that a specific dose could inhibit the sprouting of potatoes and onions. It was also found that higher doses could kill insects and worms, that still higher doses could remove bacteria, and that in the process of irradiation the foods so treated remained relatively cool and raw. These observations suggested a new means of food preservation. Table 22 shows the dose range for several food-preservation processes.

TABLE 22.

Irradiation dose range required for various food-preservation processes

Process	Rads
Inhibition of sprouting carrots, onions, and potatoes	4,000–40,000
Inactivation of trichina (tapeworm)	20,000–50,000
Destruction of grain- and cereal-infesting insects	100,000–500,000
Sterilization of foods (removal of all microbes)	2,000,000–5,000,000
Enzyme inactivation	up to 10,000,000

(Note the increasing dose required with each lower form of life.)

Radiation preservation will not replace such conventional methods as canning, freezing, drying, and pickling, but it could in the near future increase the shelf-life of such highly perishable items as shrimp, crabmeat, and oysters.

For many years, food preserved by irradiation was thought to be toxic and, consequently, unfit for human consumption. Recently, the U.S. Army Medical Service completed a ten-year study of twenty-one food items. They found no evidence of harm or hazard; nor is there evidence that irradiated foods can cause cancers or mutations.

In June, 1966, two hundred scientists from twenty-eight countries met in Karlsruhe, West Germany,[7] to review the current status of food preservation by ionizing radiation. They agreed that irradiation did not produce dangerous radioactivity in foods. The participants ate bacon which had been irradiated and kept at room temperature (20 to 38° C) for twenty-one months. The Russian scientists indicated that they hoped to be able to offer irradiated caviar at the next meeting. Thus far, the Soviet Government has released several fruits and vegetables, meats, and meat products for public consumption.

It was expected that some time in 1968 an experimental irradiation unit will be set up at the Honolulu airport for the purpose of disinfecting luggage, fruit, vegetable, and timber consignments. Apparently, 7 percent of all products and luggage passing through the airport had been contaminated with insect pests.

In 1966, the U.S. Food and Drug Administration certified irradiated canned bacon,* white potatoes, wheat, and wheat flour as safe and wholesome for human consumption; oranges, strawberries, ham, and pork will shortly be certified, and corned beef, codfish cakes, and chicken are scheduled for approval and certification shortly thereafter. Irradiated oysters, barbecued beef, and figs are expected to be available in retail stores by 1969.

As exponentially growing populations seek to feed themselves on already inadequate food supplies, the potentials of irradiation preservation should not be overlooked.

Although physicians and dentists have used radiation in the form of x-rays for a generation, the many additional possibilities for aiding and serving man are only now being widely explored.

A property of radiation gaining wide usefulness is its ability to cause the regression and often the complete disappearance of

* In July, 1968, the Food and Drug Administration rescinded its certification of the sale of irradiated bacon. Currently the army maintains that irradiation causes no adverse effects, while the FDA disagrees.

malignant tumors. The use of radium has been a standard therapeutic procedure for years. Sealed in needles or tubes, and implanted in a tumor or placed on the surface of a malignant growth, its alpha and gamma emissions can suppress the uncontrolled proliferation of cancerous cells.

The administration of radioisotopes orally or intravenously is gaining wide acceptance as a therapeutic tool. Radioiodine-131 is the isotope most frequently employed. Its usefulness is dependent upon the ability of the thyroid gland to take up and concentrate the stable isotope. In this way, selected areas receive a large dose of highly localized radiation.

Another more recent innovation is the technique of dilution-analysis. With this method, a known quantity of iodine-131 or chromium-51 is tagged to a protein such as albumin and injected into the bloodstream. After allowing time for the tracer or "tag" to become distributed, a sample of blood is obtained and its radiation measured. In this way an accurate determination of blood volume can be made. A variation of this procedure is used to determine circulation rate, thereby supplying evidence of circulating impediments.

By placing a radioactive "tag" on insects, the flight range and flight patterns of disease-carrying species can be traced. As the tagged specimens are trapped days or weeks later, their place of capture is spotted on a map. Control and prevention programs thus have a greater chance of success.

In agricultural research, the radioactive calcium-45 isotope has been successfully used to study the uptake of the stable isotope by the roots of plants. From this has come increased crop yields. In other experiments, tracer studies showed that nutrients could be applied to the leaves of fruit trees, thereby increasing the yield of fruit.

In 1965, as a result of gamma irradiation of rice seeds, a new variety, Reimes, was introduced into Japan. Induced mutations have produced several varieties of rice which mature forty to fifty days earlier than the parent strain without losing such desirable characteristics as cooking quality and yield.

Through the support of the International Atomic Energy

Agency, seeds of rice, wheat, barley, beans, and tomatoes have been submitted to mutagen treatment, for projects in Asia, Africa, South America, and Europe.

The metabolism of cattle has been studied using tracers that show the pathway of food utilization. Knowledge of this kind is useful for upgrading both milk and beef production. (Chapter 5, Insecticides, presents additional uses of radiation that ultimately benefit man.)

In industry, the uses of radiation appear limitless: leak detection; measuring liquid levels and thickness; monitoring pipeline flow; actuating cutoff valves; and inspecting the integrity of weldings and castings.

The radiation sterilization of such pharmaceutical products as sutures has advanced to the point where these are commercially available. Human blood vessels and bones that have been sterilized by radiation are successfully used for transplants in many hospitals.

Research into ways of improving the performance of automobile, bus, airplane, and tractor engines has attempted to establish the causes of friction, corrosion, and wear. In the Soviet Union, for example, the use of radioactive piston rings in a single-cylinder diesel engine showed that rings were fully broken in after six hours and that the rate of wear dropped sharply thereafter and remained constant. It was also found that the rate of wear on a piston ring was directly related to the size of dust particles: those measuring 10 to 20μ were the most abrasive.

In the U.S.S.R., France, and the U.S., large sums of money have been saved in oil-well drilling operations by using radioisotope tracers to track underground water movement and to locate oil-bearing geological formations.

Particularly useful has been the use in France of radioactive sulfur and phosphorous to discover small fissures in rock. This type of information is useful to civil engineers, who can thus avoid placement of dams in such areas, thereby avoiding dam breaks.

In Japan, radioactive cobalt has been used to study air pollution. Radioactive cobalt sulfate is placed in a smoke-stack emitting polluting gases. The cobalt mixes with the effluent and is carried along with it. By taking air samples at various locations, the diffusion of the stack gases can be plotted. If necessary, each stack in a given community can be tagged with a different radioactive tracer so that the polluter can be determined.

In the United States, several new irradiated products are already being mass produced. For example, the Atlantic Richfield Company is marketing parquet flooring which has been irradiated to produce a stain-resistant surface.

Irradiation of fabrics can increase their resistance to soiling and creasing. Fabrics with these qualities are being produced by the Deering-Milliken Company.

Beer drinkers will be happy to learn that Russian investigators who tagged lactic-acid bacteria found a way to reduce the time needed for fermentation from six days to one day, and improved the quality of the beer in the process.

The future holds still more promise. While we must be cautious with this unique source of energy and continue to evaluate its potential for harm, we must not be so circumspect that we fail to take advantage of the great technological advances it may make possible.

15

BIOLOGICAL AND CHEMICAL WARFARE

At the culmination of its December, 1966, Annual Meeting, the American Association for the Advancement of Science passed the following resolution [1]:

Whereas modern science and technology now give man unprecedented power to alter his environment and affect the ecological balance of this planet; and

Whereas the full impact of the uses of biological and chemical agents to modify the environment, whether for peaceful or military purposes, is not fully known;

Be it resolved that the American Association for the Advancement of Science:

(1) Expresses its concern regarding the long-range consequences of the use of biological and chemical agents which modify the environment; and

(2) Establishes a committee to study such use, includ-

ing the effects of chemical and biological warfare agents, and periodically to report its findings through appropriate channels of the association; and

(3) Volunteers its cooperation with public agencies and offices of government for the task of ascertaining scientifically and objectively the full implications of major programs and activities which modify the environment and affect the ecological balance on a large scale.

The Council, speaking for its 110,000 members, was the first professional scientific organization to broach publicly the subject of biological and chemical warfare (BCW).

On May 3, 1967, The American Society of Microbiology faced this issue. One of the Society's few standing committees is an advisory group for the Army's biological warfare program at Camp Detrick. At the Society's annual meeting a resolution to dissolve this advisory group as immoral and unworthy of the society was soundly defeated by the membership. Apparently, these scientists believed strongly in the need for a defensive capability on the part of the United States.

As a potential source of extensive environmental contamination, BCW has not received the discussion it surely requires. Aside from the moral and political issues attendant on the use of biological and chemical weaponry, it is important to consider the manner in which man tampers with his environment. Does the possibility exist, for example, that, with the loosing of large quantities of biological and chemical agents on a military objective, long-term ecological dislocations inimical to continued life and health may occur? Or are these weapons of no real concern from the standpoint of long-term environmental pollution? Are the answers to these questions available? What do we know about BCW? This discussion will present some criteria and findings of legitimate scientific investigation. The products of such research, in the form of new treatments for cancer, antidotes for poisons, and numerous others advances in health and agriculture become available regularly. Nevertheless, BCW and BCW research are rarely discussed in either lay or scientific circles.

The idea of the use of BCW agents is generally repugnant to Western traditions of civilization. However, the possibility that a potential enemy of the United States might use such weapons requires that the scientific community and the population at large look at them objectively and understand the criteria for choosing suitable agents from among the plethora available.

Since biological and chemical weapons are militarily used under different sets of circumstances, they will be dealt with separately.

Pathogenic microbes, transmitted via dead bodies hurled into walled cities, or contaminated "gifts," were used in warfare even in ancient times.[2] And even without any intentional help from man, disease has been the leading cause of American casualties during the wars in which the United States has participated (table 23).

TABLE 23.

Causes of deaths among American troops

	Deaths	
	Disease	*Battle Wounds*
Civil War	199,720	138,154
Spanish-American War	1,939	369
Philippine Insurrection	4,356	1,061
World War I	56,447	50,570
World War II	15,779	234,874

Disease has been an even greater force in military operations of other countries where sanitary and medical support have been inadequate. As a cause of disabilities among Americans in World War II, disease ranked first among the three major categories of military casualties; in fact, the number of hospital admissions for disease was more than five times as great as the number for battle and non-battle injuries.[3]

Small wonder, then, that the idea of using pure cultures of

TABLE 24.
*Causes of disability
in the U.S. Army, 1942–1945*

	Number of Man-days Lost	% of Total
Disease	285,918,000	68.5
Battle Casualties	72,000,000	17.2
Non-battle Casualties	59,863,000	14.3

pathogenic microbes as weapons of war should have followed as a logical next step. Besides causing disability and death, microbes can have potent psychological effects. In the Samoan Defense Area, during World War II, a particularly high incidence of filariasis occurred among American troops. Swartzwelder [4] states that "intense fear of the disease almost bordering on hysteria constituted an important military problem. Fear of elephantiasis, of sterility, and of transmission of the disease to their families, coupled with the sight of horribly deformed natives, engendered this attitude."

In the U.S., serious consideration of the military capability of biological agents originated with the publication in 1947 of "Bacterial Warfare: A Critical Analysis of the Available Agents, Their Possible Military Applications and Means for Protecting Against Them," by Rosebury, Kabat, and Boldt.* [5] For the most part, their choices have withstood the test of time. In the ensuing twenty years, investigators have been developing practical military and civilian applications of their work. The tenth edition of *Control of Communicable Diseases in Man* [6] lists approximately seventy illnesses considered transmissible and potentially epidemic in nature. However, the stringent requirements to be met by any microbial species suggested for use as a military weapon limit the numbers considerably.

Particularly pertinent is the fact that there has been no mili-

* During the forty years before World War II some thirty publications dealing with bacterial warfare (as it was called for many years) appeared. All but one were of European authorship.

tary experience with biological warfare comparable to the experience with chemical warfare on which to base predictions of the effectiveness of biological agents as military weapons.

BW is the intentional use of pathogenic microbes or their metabolic products to produce death or illness in man and animals and to destroy plants. The ability to cause disease is not the sole criterion for choosing a BW agent. Certain ancillary medical and military requirements must be met. From the medical aspect, an effective agent should:

1. be highly infectious in small quantities
2. be difficult to identify
3. remain viable and potent when stored or dispersed, and have a low decay rate
4. produce illnesses which are
    a. difficult to identify
    b. not preventable by usual sanitary or immunizing practices (a minimum amount of preexisting immunity would be militarily desirable)
    c. not amenable to available drug or antibiotic therapy
5. be producible on a large scale

From the military viewpoint, it should:

1. be difficult to detect in the field (give no warning of its presence)
2. cover a large area without necessitating a great expenditure of shells to convey the organisms
3. be capable of producing varying degrees of morbidity, enabling a field commander to obtain a desired military effect
4. have unique incubation periods, so that casualties result simultaneously with parallel military operations

Table 25, though not an exhaustive list, includes many of the diseases considered appropriate by experts writing during the past fifteen years. (Of course, the identity of those agents actually available as BW agents is classified.) Interestingly enough, however, few, if any, of the potential BW agents meet all the qualifications listed above.

TABLE 25.

Potential BW agents

I. *Agents of Human Infection and Disease*

A. BACTERIAL

Diphtheria	Cholera
Plague (pneumonic	
and bubonic)	Staphylococcal food-poisoning toxin
Melioidosis	Typhoid
Glanders	Tularemia
Shigellosis	Tuberculosis
Anthrax	Brucellosis

C. Botulinum (toxin only)

B. RICKETTSIAL

Q-fever

Rocky Mountain spotted fever

Scrub typhus

Typhus (flea- and louse-borne)

C. VIRAL

Influenza	Encephalitides
Smallpox	EEE, SLE, WEE, VEE, JE
Yellow fever	Russian spring-summer
	encephalitis
Infectious hepatitis	Psittacosis
Dengue	

D. FUNGAL

Coccidioidomycosis

Histoplasmosis

Nocardiosis

Blastomycosis

E. PROTOZOAL

Malaria

Amoebic dysentery

II. *Agents of Animal Infection and Disease*

A. BACTERIAL

Anthrax of cattle, sheep, horses, mules

T A B L E   2 5 (cont.)
Potential BW agents

Glanders (horses and mules)
Brucellosis (cattle, sheep, goats, pigs)
Contagious pleuropneumonia (cattle)

B. RICKETTSIAL
Q-fever (cattle, sheep)
Veldt disease (cattle, sheep, goats)

C. VIRAL
Hog cholera
Fowl plague
African swine fever
Rift Valley fever (cattle, goats, sheep)
Rinderpest (cattle, sheep, goats, oxen, water buffalo)
Vesicular exanthema (pigs)
Vesicular stomatitis (horses, cattle, mules)
Foot and mouth disease (cattle, sheep, pigs)
Bovine viral diarrhea (cattle)
Newcastle disease (chickens, turkeys)
Encephalitides: WEE, EE, and VE (horses)

D. PROTOZOAL
Sleeping sickness (cattle, horses)
Babesiosis (cattle, horses, sheep)

III. *Agents of Plant Infection and Disease*
A. FUNGAL
Wheat rust
Rice blast
Late blight of potatoes
Corn smut
Curly-top disease of sugar beets
Black rot of crucifers (mustard family)

Among the viral diseases, smallpox is mentioned but measles is not. However, if the World Health Organization's worldwide smallpox-eradication project is mounted, very few unvaccinated

people will be left in the world. Measles vaccine will soon be generally disseminated, making the disease unsuitable as a potential
weapon.

Although both pneumonic and bubonic forms of plague are
listed, the pneumonic form may be the most suitable, as bubonic
involves a rather complex ecological chain of events difficult to
satisfy at will. Currently, natural epidemics of mixed bubonic-
pneumonic plague are occurring from Vietnam. This suggests the
possible feasibility of employing both of these forms in a BW attack
on a susceptible population.

Melioidosis is a form of glanders that rarely occurs in humans;
when it does, it follows an acute course. This could also be a highly
suitable BW choice, as recent natural outbreaks in Vietnam testify.

Protozoa are generally difficult to grow and transmit; thus,
their use would be limited. However, malaria and amebic dysentery are considered potential weapons. For example, a single mosquito bite was found adequate to produce dengue fever in human
volunteers.

Anthrax, a disease of both animals and man, is often mentioned as a possible weapon. Relatively few instances of either
the cutaneous or pulmonary forms of anthrax are seen in humans.
For the most part it has been an occupational hazard of workers in
industries using hides, wool, and carcasses. As a disease of cattle,
it could seriously affect the food supply. During World War II, the
British conducted experiments with anthrax spores on an island
off the Scottish coast. Twenty years later the island was found to be
infected, and is likely to remain so for about one hundred years.

Rabbit fever (tularemia), suggested as a useful BW agent, is
highly incapacitating. It is characterized by sudden onset of fever,
nausea, chills, vomiting, and prostration. Usually it is of long duration, three out of ten victims die. Saslow [7] found that an aerosol
dose of twenty-five to fifty *Pasteurella tularensis* organisms was
sufficient to initiate infection. A similar long-term, incapacitating
illness is produced by brucellosis.

Laboratory accidents over the years have yielded clues to
other possible materials. Cases of various encephalides, and of
psittacosis, tularemia, typhus, and q-fever have occurred without

the presence of arthropod or rodent vectors. This fact should have significance in choosing weapons. Agents such as *Clostridium botulinum* toxin, and pneumonic plague and anthrax organisms, may be useful as lethal agents serving one military objective, while others, such as brucellosis and typhoid fever organisms and staphylococcal enterotoxin, may serve to incapacitate a population for a few days to a few weeks. Biological agents offer a wide degree of selectivity to achieve the desired results. For example, it is generally agreed that the toxin produced by the anaerobe *Clostridium botulinum* is the most potent known. It has been estimated that one milligram (there are thirty grams to an ounce) is a fatal dose for thirty million mice. However, most toxins, including snake venoms and tetanus toxin, are harmless if swallowed; they are destroyed by the acidic gastric juice in the stomach. To have lethal effects, they must be injected into the bloodstream. Thus, the use of toxin in warfare would be extremely limited. Since it is not an infectious agent as is a microbe, it cannot spread or multiply beyond the point of delivery.

Furthermore, although the list of possible BW agents is long, there is no single biological agent, or even a combination of microbes, for that matter, capable of destroying all forms of life in any single locality or area. Microbes, whether bacterial, viral, protozoal, or fungal, have limited host ranges; they are not capable of infecting all forms of life. The important consideration is the dose of a specific microbe needed to set up an infection in a susceptible host. Little is presently known about this. Host susceptibility is yet another variable that cannot be overlooked. All people, or all animals and plants, are not equally susceptible to microorganisms. Here again, a BW agent delivered to an area could not be expected to wipe out either by death or illness all the people or animals living there. In fact, many people would go unscathed.

Although viruses are generally unaffected by antibiotic ther-. apy, which makes them possible BW agents, several other factors militate against their selection: they must be grown in tissues of specific host cells; they have little survival ability outside the host cell; they are widely distributed and usually confer a high-grade, lasting immunity. As a consequence, resistant populations are not uncommon, and the likelihood of producing widespread epidemics among civilian or military populations is poor.

These factors point to bacteria as the most suitable BW agents.

Destruction of food supplies has always been a military objective. Sinking a ship loaded with grain or other foodstuffs is as strategic as sinking a transport loaded with tanks. Food supply could well be decisive in a long war. Accordingly, anti-crop and anti-food warfare is as important militarily as human or animal death or illness.

The use of chemicals against crops and foods is also considered biological warfare. Chemical agents used for this purpose are primarily represented by growth-regulating hormones such as 2, 4-dichlorophenoxyacetic acid. They are extremely potent in small amounts and are effective against a wide variety of leafy plants. In Vietnam [8] their activity thus far has been directed against vegetation generally, rather than food crops. From newspaper accounts, these defoliants seem to have done the job expected of them. American technicians exposed hidden trails by defoliating trees and shrubs. Apparently, extreme sensitivity to public opinion has prevented their use on rice crops for fear it would be labeled chemical warfare.*

Plant-disease agents undoubtedly would be the more destructive. We have had sufficient experience with natural large-scale epidemics to know they can disorganize communities and coun-

* Currently a heated controversy is in progress between antagonists and protagonists of the chemical defoliation program in Vietnam. Each side claims that existing evidence does or does not support their respective position of potential (or actual) widespread ecological dislocations. Unfortunately, the charged atmosphere, beclouded by partisan political positions, and the amount and type of existing information preclude any objective evaluation.

The Viet Cong know the value of disease. They employ a nasty form of biological warfare: the Punji. These are camouflaged pits embedded with needle-sharp bamboo stalks, covered with human and animal execreta in hopes of inducing fatal or incapacitating infections. During one action, a South Vietnamese infantry battalion lost one man by poisoned arrow and ten by Punji traps. During two days of fighting no casualties were inflicted by bullet or bayonet.

tries alike. The consequences wrought by late blight of potatoes (*Phytopthera infestans*) in Ireland during 1846 and 1847 are too well known to be detailed here. Blast disease of rice has repeatedly reduced that crop in the Orient. Stem rust of wheat exacted a great toll from Canada south to the Great Plains and on through the Mississippi Valley. Because we have a well-diversified crop system, the host specificity of most infectious agents would not prove as detrimental in the event of a BW attack as it would in countries dependent upon a single crop, as many are.

The natural absence of disease in an area is an excellent criterion for employing biological warfare. The possible results of a BW attack of Asian or South American hemorrhagic fever or of O'nyong-n'yong or Kyasanur forest disease, illnesses almost completely unknown to medical personnel in the United States, stagger the imagination.

Notwithstanding their initial potency, chemical agents are generally limited to small areas. Biological aerosols, on the other hand, can cover thousands of square miles. Within the exposed area BW agents could effectively bring all daily activity to a standstill by incapacitating 10 to 20 percent of the population. The effects would be quite different from those of a natural epidemic, because the incubation period and onset of illness would occur at precisely the same time throughout the entire community or city. Physicians, nurses, and paramedical support, including transportation workers, would be incapacitated at the same time. Thus, in the view of many writers, the greatest potential danger of BW lies in its strategic threat to the non-military population and the general economy via incapacitation of the labor force, destruction of food crops, and extermination of livestock. Five major premises support this view:

1) Although natural airborne dissemination of many human, animal, and plant infections is well established, artificial aerosolization of pathogenic organisms over large areas has not been adequately demonstrated.

2) The military establishment has well-developed immunization programs in which everyone has obtained or can obtain any or all of the available vaccines.

3) Large-scale immunization of the non-military population

against potential BW agents is utterly impossible. The apathy of the public to existing immunization programs is well known.

4) Current annual production of broad-spectrum antibiotics is entirely inadequate to cope with outbreaks of epidemic proportions that would result from intensive BW attacks.

5) The general lack of awareness among physicians of the unique aspects of BW-provoked medical problems could prove disastrous to the national defense. The important point here is that the average medical practitioner has far less generalized experience in the clinical diagnosis of a variety of infectious diseases than physicians of thirty to fifty years ago. This is particularly true for bacterial, rickettsial, and fungal diseases. This is the paradox wrought by the first-rate biomedical advances of the past thirty to fifty years.

Strategically, the dispersion of BW agents in the air over cities is the most advantageous form of BW attack. Stable microbial aerosols with particle sizes of 1 to 5 μ can drift relatively long distances from release points. With such weather conditions as low sunlight, low windspeed, and a cool blanket of air (inversion), microbial aerosols could effectively spread over hundreds of square miles. This was borne out in two field trials recently described by Fothergill.[9] In the first trial, 450 pounds of 2.0-μ particles of zinc cadmium sulfide were released from a boat ten miles offshore along a run of 156 miles parallel to the coast. Sampling with the aid of ultraviolet light detected fluorescing particles up to 450 miles from the point of release. In addition, they had covered over 34,000 square miles. By comparison, a twenty-megaton nuclear bomb would cause severe burns only within 2,800 square miles.

In a second trial, a biological aerosol was used. A spore suspension of the non-pathogenic organism *Bacillus globigii* (*B. subtilus, var. niger*) was aerosolized to a cloud from 130 gallons of original suspension. The organisms were released from the deck of a boat along a two-mile course. The boat remained two miles offshore, at right angles to an onshore breeze, during the entire release period. A network of sampling stations had been established in homes and office buildings within the trial area. Collections showed that spores had travelled twenty-three miles inland and that an area of one hundred square miles was contaminated to the extent that people breathing at a normal rate of fifteen liters of air per minute could inhale one hundred to fifty thousand spores, depending upon their geographical location with respect to the spore cloud.

Few reports concerning the consequences of large-scale, highly-infectious, unnatural contamination of an area are available.[10] Perhaps restricted or top-secret reports do exist, but this is highly unlikely, since it is unthinkable that such an extensive undertaking could be kept from the many interrelated scientific groups needed to develop such data. We must thus consider that we simply do not know and can only speculate upon the consequences of large-scale BW.

For the most part, the great plagues of history—epidemic typhus, bubonic plague, malaria, schistosomiasis, trypanosomiasis, yellow fever, WEE, EEE, SLE, onchocerciasis, filariasis, etc.—have been vector-borne. In every case, man and some vector—arthropod, rodent, reptile, bird, horse—were involved. Biological warfare, with its release of large numbers of highly infectious particles over a considerable area—a wholly unnatural event—could readily infect vast numbers of species of all phyla, many for the first time. Our knowledge of the range of susceptibility is still extremely meager, particularly with respect to the respiratory portal of entry. The sudden exposure of the myriad flora and fauna in hundreds of square miles to a new infectious agent would be a wholly unprecedented phenomenon. Fothergill [11] poses several pertinent questions: What would the consequences be? Would new and unusual zoonotic foci of endemic disease be established? Would post-attack public health and environmental problems that are unique and beyond our present experience be caused? Although definitive answers to these questions are not available, educated opinion does exist.

Prof. A. A. Imshenetsky, director of microbiology of the Academy of Sciences of the U.S.S.R., has said: "The selection of particularly dangerous strains of bacteria developed in the laboratory is quite feasible and one can hardly exaggerate the disastrous implications of this possibility. A number of questions arise in this connection. What will be the course of infection in man contaminated by experimentally obtained and highly virulent strains? Would "lightning" forms of diseases originate in the case? Would preventive inoculation against this type of agent be effective? We cannot ignore these possibilities."

Dr. Martin Kaplan, director of the Division of Veterinary Public Health of the World Health Organization, has observed that

> in addition to the deaths, illnesses and economic destruction resulting from BW, other possible consequences, perhaps more far-reaching in the long run, should not be overlooked. These pertain to disturbance of the fine ecological balances achieved as a result of evolution over eons of time between human, animal and plant life, and between such life and their microorganisms. Sudden disbalances in numbers, or the insertion of new infective elements into evolutionally unprepared animal and plant life could, if done to a sufficient degree, produce for an indefinite period an unrecognizable and perhaps unmanageable world from the standpoint of communicable disease."

Are we ready to take the calculated risk? Is it worth the military cost, at this time? Are other weapons more suitable? These are some of the questions that must be discussed. Lack of discussion and research helps no one. After wide discussion and much-needed research, reasonable action may be hoped for.

The year 1915 was notable in that both chemical and biological agents were directly employed as military weapons for the first time in the modern era. German saboteurs in the United States, using pure cultures of *Actinobacillus mallei,* the agent of glanders, attempted to infect horses and cattle being sent to Europe.

In an attempt to break the encirclement and blockade imposed by the Allied powers, Germany mounted a large-scale gas attack in April, 1915. Late in the afternoon of the twenty-second, chlorine gas was released north of Ypres, Belgium. There were fifteen thousand French casualties; five thousand men were killed, largely because Allied commanders believed the use of chemicals was not possible and made no attempt to defend their forces against them.

In the ensuing twenty-five years, although having sustained a significant defeat, Germany prepared for the next onslaught. Largely unbeknownst to the countries of the world, Germany was experimenting with and perfecting new types of chemical agents for use as military weapons. Fortunately for the Allied troops, the deadly nerve gases were not employed in World War II. After VE Day, advancing Allied troops stumbled upon huge supplies of nerve-gas bombs. Apparently faulty German intelligence was one reason for not using the newly developed gases. Rothschild [12] noted that: "The Germans were convinced that the Allies possessed the nerve gases. Because they had been carefully examining our scientific literature and had found no references to these chemicals, they assumed that we had discovered them but had censored all such references for military reasons. We, of course, simply knew nothing about them." We may not always be so lucky.

Chemical warfare is the intentional use of any solid, liquid, or gas to produce discomfort, disablement, or death in human or animal populations. Destruction of plants, either as crops or land cover, is generally also included in this definition. To achieve the degree of incapacitation desired, a host of chemicals is available. They are classed according to whether they cause choking, vomiting, tearing, blood, nerve, or psychological effects.

All chemical agents militarily useful against human and animal populations are considered as either lethal or incapacitating to some degree. A lethal agent is one in which there is little difference between an incapacitating dose and a fatal one. Incapacitating compounds are those which can render a person militarily useless but from which he can usually recover without treatment and without lasting impairment.

In modern chemical warfare, the agents most likely to be used are the so-called nerve gases, which are lethal in low concentrations. These are a group of highly toxic, colorless, odorless, and tasteless organic esters of phosphoric acid. Nerve gases are excellent examples of the serendipitous by-products of research. In

1936, Gerhard Schroder, an organic chemist with the German firm of I. G. Farben, discovered the first compound that ultimately became a nerve gas, while working on the synthesis of insecticides. Schroder found a particularly toxic one that was brought to the attention of the Ministry of War, who were particularly interested in all ways to obtain military advantage. It was dubbed Tabun.* With the preparation of Sarin * and Soman * shortly thereafter, three anticholinesterase compounds became available.

Tabun's chemical structure

$$CH_3)_2N-\overset{\overset{\textstyle O}{\uparrow}}{\underset{\underset{\textstyle OC_2H_5}{|}}{P}}-CN \qquad \text{(ethyl N-dimethylphosphoramidocyanidate)}$$

as well as Sarin's

$$(CH_3)_2CHO-\overset{\overset{\textstyle O}{\uparrow}}{\underset{\underset{\textstyle CH_3}{|}}{P}}-F \qquad \text{(isopropyl methylphosphonofluridate)}$$

are both structurally similar to that of the parent compound, the insecticide parathion, which Schroder also discovered:

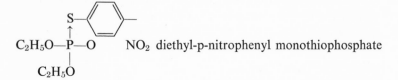

$$C_2H_5O-\overset{\overset{\textstyle S}{\uparrow}}{\underset{\underset{\textstyle C_2H_5O}{|}}{P}}-O \qquad NO_2 \text{ diethyl-p-nitrophenyl monothiophosphate}$$

The anticholinesterase activity of parathion is apparently dependent upon its transformation to the S-ethyl isomer

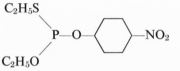

* These compounds are designated GA, GB, and GD in the United States. The less volatile liquid counterparts are coded as V-agents.

Tabun, Sarin, and Soman were stockpiled as bombs to be used against the Allied armies in World War II.

Anticholinesterase chemicals can enter the body as gases via the lungs or as liquids through the skin. Their effects are due largely to their ability to inhibit cholinesterases throughout the body.*

With the transmission of a nerve impulse across the myoneural junction, acetylcholine is released and muscular contraction occurs. An enzyme, cholinesterase, hydrolyzes the acetylcholine as it is formed. Inhibition of this hydrolysis reaction results in the accumulation of acetylcholine. Low concentrations lead to coryza, miosis, and dyspnea; higher concentrations produce nausea, vomiting, abdominal cramps, diarrhea, muscular fibrillation, convulsions, respiratory paralysis, and death. Medical practitioners recognize the signs and symptoms as similar to those resulting from overstimulation of the parasympathetic nervous system.

If newspaper accounts can be relied upon, we apparently have produced sizable quantities of Sarin (GB) at our arsenals in Denver and in Newport, Indiana. Shells and rockets filled with this material are stockpiled at bases around the country for tactical use when needed. Evidently both military and civilian leaders do not intend to be caught by surprise again. It is quite well known, for example, that Tabun has been stockpiled by the Russian government.

Another class of chemicals with potential military usefulness are the hallucinogens, euphemistically called psychochemicals. Because they are capable of rendering a soldier, or a civilian, totally ineffective, or sufficiently disorganized to be unable to offer serious resistance, these pharmacological chemicals may adequately fit specific tactical requirements.

The psychochemicals LSD-25 (lysergic acid diethyl amide), a synthetic compound, and mescaline and psilocin, two products of plant origin, lead to mental derangements such that an individual under their influence is unable to make rational decisions or issue coherent orders. The effects are usually of short duration

---

* 2-pyridine aldoxime methochloride (2-PAM) is currently the most advanced means of reactivating cholinesterase. However, atropine and artificial respiration form the basis of treatment for anticholinesterase poisoning.

and inflict no injury. A unique characteristic of these agents is that individuals incapacitated by them are usually unaware of their altered behavior.

In addition to the three drugs cited above, there are incapacitants which produce effects other than mental disorganization, including transient paralysis, narcosis, blindness, and loss of hearing or balance. Temporary spells of convulsions and persistent diarrhea can be caused by drugs which could also be adapted for military use.

These weapons may be useful where friendly forces are in close contact with enemy troops or when it is necessary to capture enemy personnel for questioning. It has been suggested that incapacitating agents might prove useful when both enemy troops and a neutral population are intermingled in an area that is a military objective. In this event, use of an incapacitating agent could allow capture without inflicting death or injury. Ian Fleming[13] presented a hilarious but perhaps portentous demonstration of this in *Goldfinger,* wherein troops guarding Fort Knox are peacefully but rapidly narcotized via an aerosol released from a plane.

Many of the "old-fashioned" chemicals are kept ready for use. Some have been improved by manipulating their molecular configurations to achieve increased specificity or toxicity. The irritants and vesicants are notable examples.

In World War I, lacrimators and sternutators were effectively employed for the first time on a large scale. Temporary incapacity is the result of tearing, smarting, sneezing, and coughing. Civilian populations are being increasingly subjected to these agents in riot-control operations. Tear gas, 2-chloroacetophenone (CN), developed too late to be used in World War I, has been used extensively against civilian populations in riot control. It has the shortest incapacitating period, approximately three minutes. Adamsite, diphenylamino chlorarsine (DM), a pepper-like compound, causes sneezing, along with copious tears. Grenades containing DM were used in Korea to control prisoner-of-war riots. A new addition to this group is CS, orthochlorobenzalmalonitrile. It is more rapid and more effective than CN. Among its physiological effects are extreme burning in the eyes, chest tightness, and sinus and nasal drip. It is said to leave its victims with an aversion to a second exposure.

No discussion of chemical warfare would be complete without mention of the vesicants: mustard gas, bis-(2-chloroethyl) sulfide (HD), and its tertiary amine derivatives, which have at least two 2-chloroethyl groups. The most important of these are HN1,* HN2,** and HN3 †. They are long-term incapacitating agents.

Although sulfur mustard accounted for approximately 25 percent of all casualties to the American forces in World War I, the new distilled mustards have now been improved to the point where they far surpass their forerunner. In the event of their future use, we should expect even greater casualties. They are suitable for a variety of tactical applications because they enter via the respiratory tract and exposed skin surfaces. This can occur as late as ten days after the initial release because they evaporate slowly but remain thoroughly effective over this period. While moderate exposure causes deep blisters that are often difficult to heal, severe exposure can result in systemic poisoning with shock. Delayed effects can appear as aplasia of bone marrow, destruction of lymphoid tissue, and ulceration of the gastrointestinal tract. Purification of the mustards can yield an odorless product. Lack of odor, combined with the absence of immediate physiological effects, results in prolonged contact, and thus severe exposure.

Interestingly enough, the two agents that initiated large-scale chemical warfare in 1915 and 1916, chlorine and phosgene, can no longer be considered as effective military weapons. Both of these can incite pulmonary edema to the degree that the victims die of oxygen deficiency. However, they have delayed action, low toxicity, and characteristic odors which mark them for retirement.

Chemical warfare is not limited to killing or incapacitating people. Contamination of food supplies would be an effective way of subduing an area. This could be expected to occur in several

* 2, 2′ dichlorotriethylamine
** N-methyl-2, 2′-dichlorodiethylamine
† tris-(2-chloroethylamine)

ways, depending upon whether the agent used is a vapor, a solid chemical, or a fine liquid spray. Gases of the mustard family (the vesicants), being fat-soluble, are readily absorbed and dispersed through foods with a relatively high fat content. These foods are in the minority, however. The bulk of our food is water based and consequently is susceptible to water-soluble agents. Food contaminated by water-soluble chemicals would be extremely difficult to "clean" or decontaminate. (It has been found that peeling apples, oranges, tomatoes, and potatoes renders them edible.[9]) However, after tests have been performed to ascertain the degree of contamination, if such tests can be performed, the food will finally be eaten on the basis of a calculated risk.

It was noted earlier that some 25 percent of all our casualties in World War I were caused by chemicals. However, it must also be noted that recovery in these cases was twelve times that for men injured by bullets and explosives. The incidence of long-term postwar disability was considerably lower among those injured by chemicals than among those injured by high-explosive shells. Despite this fact, chemicals have not been widely used. The noted British historian Sir Basil Liddell-Hart[14] explained it rather candidly: "The chlorine gas originally used was undeniably cruel, but no worse than the frequent effect of shell or bayonet, and when it was succeeded by improved forms of gas both experience and statistics proved it the least inhumane of modern weapons. But it was novel and therefore labelled an atrocity by a world which condones abuses but detests innovations."

Perhaps the employment of the most spectacular of all chemical weapons, the nerve gases, will alter our attitude, they are swift, silent, and sure. And it is certain that within several years the nerve gases will become obsolete. To take their place, such chemicals as the complex aryl carbamates, more than thirty times as potent as Sarin (GB), are already being studied.

My intentions in this chapter will have been fulfilled by signs of mushrooming debate and discussion around the country, in which knowledge is substituted for emotion and the subject stands or falls on its own merits.

THE POLITICS OF POLLUTION

When Herman M. Biggs was appointed State Commissioner of Health for New York in 1914, he coined this motto for his department: "Public health is purchasable. Within natural limitations any community can determine its own death rate."

At the time, communicable disease was rampant and the present concepts of community and public health had hardly been conceived. Although his motto was unduly optimistic for its time, it did reflect a fundamental truth: that a community or nation largely decides its own destiny.

Today, Biggs' motto would not be considered unrealistic: now people even assume that complete health is their right. Medicine and biology are on the threshold of discovering the essence of life. The classical plagues which regularly took the lives of so many are now textbook curiosities. And cost no longer makes control of infectious disease an unreachable goal: funds are generally available for almost any community project, no matter how remotely linked with health. Nevertheless, we must ask, Why haven't urban communities proceeded to attack their many problems more vigorously? I suspect that there are several formidable impediments.

In the introduction to this book I suggested that prosperity and pollution were coincidental. To population and prosperity I should now like to add politicians and prices. Thus, several major factors that appear to be at the heart of our "troubled cities" are population, prosperity, politicians, and prices. In the discussion that follows, I propose to develop this theme and show the contribution each might make to a satisfying urban life, and how each has contributed to our present precarious habitat. To simplify matters further, I will use the term *pollution* to refer to any and all of the environmental problems covered in the previous chapters.

Pastoral America is a thing of the past. As soon as we swallow and digest this unpalatable idea, the better off we will be. Too many of us continue to think, talk, and act as if ours were an agricultural rather than a technological society. We must begin to act on the conviction that life in the urban setting can be a wholesome experience.

Solutions to problems can only be temporary and imperfect, because our communities are continually evolving. Thus, a solution may suffice for five, ten, or fifteen years, by which time new problems will have evolved. For the most part, solving the problems of each time will be hindered by lack of some information that invariably requires additional time to acquire. This should not prevent decisions from being made, but neither should they be arbitrary decisions.

It must be emphasized that we are a healthy people. As a result of improved medical techniques, the result of greater biological knowledge, fewer people die or become ill from infectious disease. More and more of us live on to older age. The "cult of youth" notwithstanding, we are well on the way to becoming a nation of old people.

Although as a nation we are healthier than ever before, we

are also more health conscious.* Health consciousness can mean awareness of the dangers of disease and willingness to protect ourselves against them by, for example, accepting vaccines as they become available, or by visiting a physician routinely. Carried too far, it can also mean an unreasonably morbid fear of the world, rather than comfort in the knowledge that the natural defenses of the body are not easily breached. It is upon these morbid fears that those who would have us believe that our communities are foully polluted and our survival in doubt constantly play. While an aroused public may be useful to "get things done," there is no justification for misleading scares.

The increased health and longevity of the general population mean that more and more of us are living to and beyond that age. And because we are living to advanced years, we are susceptible as never before to the illnesses of old age that manifest themselves in the fifth and sixth decades: lung cancer, emphysema, bronchitis, heart disease, and atherosclerosis. An interesting question is this: As advances in public health and medicine keep more people healthy and sound to older ages, and as these mentally and physically fit people reach mandatory retirement age, what kind of a life can they look forward to? A great deal of leisure time will be available. In what kind of an environment will it be spent?

The ever-increasing population needs things. It needs goods and services whose provision brings with it, for example, increased solid waste, and air pollutants produced by the burning of coal and oil to generate energy. Increased population also means crowded highways and a higher incidence of traffic accidents. Increased population means the need for larger food supplies. Of course, this implies greater and more widespread use of chemical insecticides to protect the crops from insects. The point is that uncontrolled population increases are behind many of our pollution problems. Are we ready to face this fact?

How many of his hard-earned dollars will each taxpayer be

* All too often, people who become educated about the world around them come to fear it. Knowledge of the biological, chemical, and physical processes of nature should be a liberating experience.

prepared to contribute for control and prevention of environmental pollution? The Opinion Research Corporation, Princeton, New Jersey, found that "when the public nationwide is asked what they would be willing to pay per year in added taxes for a substantial improvement in air and water pollution control, about two in three say—nothing."

In the twenty-nine years since 1940, the cost of most items has increased three, four, five, and six times. How is the hot dog, which cost five cents in 1940 and is thirty cents today, related to public apathy concerning environmental pollution? Similar questions can be asked about the penny postcard of 1940, which now costs five cents, or a six-cylinder Chevrolet sedan that in 1940 cost $730 and currently sells for $2,600. I suspect there is a real connection. For the most part, these increases have paralleled wage increases. Shortly after his election to a third term in 1941, President Roosevelt signed a new minimum wage law—thirty cents per hour! When President Johnson signed the latest minimum wage bill in 1967, it had risen five times to $1.50 per hour.

Along with increased wages and costs have come increased taxes which skim off a substantial portion of our higher wages. To appear affluent and achieve the things that are equated with the "good life"—a TV set or two, a refrigerator, a car or two, dishwashers, clothes washers, a home, and travel, for example—women have had to go to work to increase family incomes, and many men have two jobs. This has engendered a distaste for "giving away" hard-earned money for such intangible, impersonal things as sewage-treatment plants, water-pollution control, and the like, when, "after all, I don't pollute the water; I don't pollute the air. Let those that pollute clean up and pay up." These sentiments, heard more and more often, are behind the public apathy concerning control and prevention of community environmental pollution problems.

It is a fact of political and economic life that people do not want to pay taxes. It is another fact that if they must pay, and pay they must, it shall be as little as possible. As a consequence, little enthusiasm can be generated for community improvement. Dr. Lee E. Farr of the University of Texas, speaking at the annual meeting of the American Medical Association in 1967, said "In general, a citizen will support all measures to control atmospheric pollution until it is pointed out that these measures personally affect him [economically]."

Perhaps it is because of this lack of motivation that attempts are made to associate pollution, however tenuously, with dire consequences to health, in the hope that people will be frightened into action.

That the desire for financial security is of greater urgency than vague threats to health was seen in the last election. Overburdened taxpayers in Atlanta and Los Angeles, two dissimilar communities, soundly defeated rapid-transit bond issues. A portent of this may have been signalled some months earlier, when voters in Seattle defeated, by large majorities, bond issues for rapid transit and other civic improvements. It is important to bear in mind that rapid transit and air pollution are intimately related.

Several precedents show that it can be beneficial to impose upon a community what is good for it, rather than wait until they think they are ready for it. Few people were ready for chlorination of water supplies in the early years of the twentieth century. Some of the older public health officials recall being run out of town by irate citizens who didn't want their water "tampered with." Today, chlorination is well established and is responsible for the precipitous reduction in water-borne disease.

Smallpox and poliomyelitis vaccination was also met with much popular resistance. Even at this later date, when these vaccines have proved their value time and again, many people who should know better refuse to be vaccinated.

It seems that each new advance is met by a refractory public. Fluoridation is a case in point. In community after community, more heat than light was generated by overemotional partisans. In another ten years the fury surrounding the issue will have been considered a boon. Similarly, another ten or fifteen years may be needed for taxpayers to grow accustomed to the idea of parting with a portion of their incomes for community problems.

How much loss of "control" will local politicians be willing to sacrifice, for the greater good of the community, to state and federal "interlopers"? I suspect it would be little indeed. How much federal intervention will generally be tolerated? Since the federal government is one of the very few sources of the huge sums needed for carrying out many vital projects, I suspect a good deal of grudging intervention will be permitted.

Perhaps it would be useful to accept as much federal intervention as meets Abraham Lincoln's test: "For the legitimate object of government is to do for a community of people whatever they need to have done, but cannot do at all, or cannot so well do for themselves in their separate and individual capacities." The period in which we live no longer permits the kind of thinking that produced the statement, "That government governs best, that governs least."

If the federal government has moved into the province of state and local government, these sectors have only themselves to blame. Time and again opportunities to restore their own communities have been allowed to slip by, with the result that pollution has steadily increased.

The report, *Alternatives in Water Management,* by the National Academy of Sciences–National Research Council,[1] states that

> planning carried out in concert—if not always in harmony— among federal, state, local and private interests would not only provide a larger input of diverse views but would as well encourage responsibility for decision. The states, had they fully exercised their voices in development decisions and had they not allowed themselves to be bypassed by federal agencies, might have enlarged and upgraded the staffs and programs of their water agencies and improved their performance in regulation. Full participation by local governments, especially if cost-sharing reforms come to pass, might reduce the tendency to look for federal and state "hand-outs." Greater participation by the private sector could result in better planning and more responsible criticism of public projects.

Whereas elite groups within a community, such as business leaders, politicians, ministers, and newspaper editors, try to shape public opinion, it is not until popular impatience reaches a high point that decisions to move on an issue usually will be made. For example, although few studies, if any, correlating the objective fact of air pollution with the subjective evaluation of it have been undertaken, I suspect that the two are far from the same. Current attempts to galvanize community action for an attack on air pollutors is based on the objective fact rather than the subjective perception of it.

Precise measurements of suspended particles or gases mean little to the population at large, particularly when no epidemiological correlations or cause-effect relationships with existing human illness can be shown. An example of the meaninglessness of data on air pollution levels occurred in August, 1967, when the U.S. Public Health Service released its findings on levels of pollutants over some of our major cities. A *New York Times* article of August 4, boldly headlined the "fact" that New York City had the highest pollution level in the U.S. Surely this article would reveal information of great personal import to all city dwellers. Not so. It steadily proceeded to dismantle the initial implication by noting that levels of air pollution had little meaning by themselves, that levels in various cities could not be effectively compared because the type of pollutant varied from place to place. Thus, the fact that New York was listed as number one meant nothing—except possibly to the naive reader. The article appeared pointless and hopelessly confusing to the citizen interested in abating pollution. After reading that New York was first, Philadelphia second, and so on, he found that it was of no consequence; pollution levels had no relation to health. Certainly, no one could say that New York was a less healthy city in which to live than Chicago, Detroit, or Los Angeles. Furthermore, it is interesting to consider that in the past ten years Los Angeles, with photochemically induced smog at least 260 days a year and with one of the country's highest levels of pollution, has the largest population increase of any city in the U.S. Apparently, the existing air pollution is of little concern to the immigrants: people are influenced more by their subjective perception of air pollution than the statistics obtained by precisely measuring pollution levels.

It is also curious that newspaper articles continue to refer to the serious health effects of air pollution as a result of the thermal inversion that blanketed the New York-New Jersey area during the 1966 Thanksgiving Day weekend, when health officials themselves have been unable to adequately interpret the morbidity-mortality data for that month.

While I doubt that anyone cares to live in a dirty community, little meaningful data has been provided to assist the community in improving matters. The fact is that confusion and subjective opinions bordering on personal prejudice have been the daily fare of most city dwellers. If society is to continue to make decisions, decisions serving our best interests, clearer, more reliable dissemination of honest information is essential.

Public health authorities in England have a far longer history of experience in dealing with air pollution than our Department of Health, Education, and Welfare. After twenty years of intensive study of the effects of sulfur dioxide (SO_2) on health, British authorities have concluded, as they testified to our Congress, that adverse effects to health are thus far unprovable. Yet our Public Health Service continues to push for strong anti-pollution legislation which they would be empowered to enforce.

The bill, S.780, now being considered, has set limits on atmospheric SO_2 at 0.1 ppm. To achieve this level requires coal and oil of extremely low sulfur content. In fact, federal buildings in several cities have been ordered to burn coal with sulfur content no higher than 0.2 percent and fuel oil with sulfur content no higher than 0.3 percent. When you consider that the available coal and oil supplies are 4 percent and 2 percent sulfur, respectively, the technical task of effecting a tenfold reduction is formidable indeed, to say nothing of the increased costs that will ultimately be borne by the consumer. If means were presently available to reduce atmospheric sulfur by controlling stack gases, the zeal of the Department of Health, Education, and Welfare in attempting to put this law through might be more understandable. Thus far, however, while several companies are scrambling to design and produce units that might meet the legal standards of the law, none has thus far proved feasible. It seems strange that a government agency attempts to establish limitations—not even guidelines—beyond which reliable evidence of harm does not exist and which existing technical ability cannot achieve.

The New York City Council recently pushed through air-pollution regulations barring the burning of solid waste in incinerators in multi-unit dwellings before alternative means were available for disposing of the waste. The Department of Sanitation could not possibly manage the staggering tonnages diverted to it, having some time before reached its peak capacity. When waste lumber was burned on barges off Staten Island, which is manifestly prohibited by law, the pall of smoke drifting over the city forced the harried mayor to comment weakly that allowances had to be made. Allowances must be made when the commissioners of air pollution and sanitation do not know what the other is up to and when laws are summarily pushed through that can't be enforced or reasonably complied with. While there is a need to regulate and control the amounts of byproducts released into the air, standards should be based on a reasonable ability to comply.

The cry for an instant end to pollution is as unreasonable as it is ill-conceived. As the NAC-NRC report *Alternatives in Water Management* pointed out, to end further pollution and control its magnitude in future will require a great deal of knowledge that is not now available. The report goes on to say that responsible decisions will have to be made about alternative ways to handle a problem. Unilateral political decisions are no longer desirable. Regional preferences based on expediency or leverage or patchwork jobs should be stopped in their tracks by an aroused, indignant, but informed citizenry, who hopefully will be capable of weighing the alternatives. Furthermore, homegrown insularity or the inability to think in terms of regional or overall schemes is to be deplored. But this is not unique with current planners. Shortsighted men have been around for a long time. The report states that "while major steps in land and water policy were clearly tied to economic growth and development, a host of laws and policies dealt with particular resources or with particular places, disregarding pleas by Federal Commissions as early in 1907 for integrated development."

Additionally, an ecological approach to environmental health will be necessary if we are to avoid the patchwork solutions so characteristic of past actions. This implies that fragmentation in response to regional or local pressures will have to be avoided. Thus, air pollution, water pollution, chemicals in foods, radioactive fallout, and a host of other problems must be considered together rather than as separate problems at separate times.

In this regard it may be well to mention the benefits obtained through regional thinking and planning in West Germany, through the combined efforts of municipal, rural, and industrial water users. In the Ruhr Valley, one of the most intensely industrialized areas of Europe, water-resources associations known as *Genossenschaften* (literally, societies or companies) manage the waters of the Ruhr River and several tributaries of the Rhine in such a way that they effectively serve industrial, domestic, and recreational needs.

The *Genossenschaften* are essentially associations of water users—municipal, rural, and private—that control the volume and quality of water resources. They have, in addition, the power to develop and enact regulations needed to establish and maintain this control. Projected regulations to control pollution or water use are brought before the members and given wide discussion; if accepted, they have the force of law.

Basically, users of Ruhr River water are required to return to the river water of the same quality as that originally removed. The overriding value of the *Genossenschaften* lies in their regional and ecological responsibility. Any activity that can pollute the river, directly or indirectly, comes under its jurisdiction. This includes the use of chemicals, such as pesticides, that can be washed from the land into the water. It also includes all sources of effluents that may be discharged into the water.

If our abused environment is to be delivered from further misuse and perhaps irreversible damage, regional organizations patterned after the *Genossenschaften* may be part of the solution. We would do well to study, and perhaps adopt, some of their methods.

A striking example of the need for federal intervention or regional authority to prevent severe water pollution may be developing in sections of Wyoming, Utah, and Colorado that contain extensive outcroppings of Green River shale, where new sources of petroleum are being developed. Because of the high organic content of these sedimentary rocks, up to 65 percent, it is anticipated that large quantities of oil can be extracted from them. Estimates of the available oil resources run as high as two thousand billion barrels—enough for five hundred years, if demand remains at its current level.

To unlock the oil from the shale, heat treatments in the range of 500 to 550° C (932 to 1020° F) will be required. Simultaneously, there will be produced large quantities of alkaline waste, which if dumped into the Colorado, North Platte, or Green Rivers could catastrophically pollute them.

The shale deposits extend over sixteen thousand square miles of public lands. Because the potential oil resources are valued at literally trillions of dollars, private interests, euphemistically called "developers," are scrambling to get control of these lands from the federal government and stake out claims. Local governments are simply unable to deal with problems of this magnitude. The fact is that the federal government or a strong non-political regional authority are the only powers sufficient to prevent pollution of the rivers in this area. Unfortunately, history suggests that new oil resources will be developed and rivers will continue to be polluted. And local politics will have played its usual role, in the name of progress and prosperity.

Another melancholy example in this regard will be the neat maneuvers shaping up between the federal government, the state of Minnesota and rights holders in the Boundary Waters Canoe Area (a million-acre federal wilderness preserve in northwestern Minnesota) as moves are made to exploit the minerals known to be available.

Discovery of minerals of significant value will surely join the issue of whether an economic tour de force will have priority over wilderness preservation. If mining in these woods is to be prevented, it will fall to the one of the governments, either the state of Minnesota or the federal, to buy up the privately held rights. Are recreational and wilderness areas high on any list of priorities?

On September 10, 1969, the state of Alaska sold to the highest bidders (and there were many) 450,850 acres—both on and off shore of what may well prove to be one of the world's richest oil fields.

This 110-mile-wide area, lying between the Brooks Range and the Arctic Ocean, has gained dramatic prominence among oil speculators and the public as the site of a modern-day "black gold" rush.

Never ones to be left at the starting gate, large commercial interests are unabashedly vying for leases that will enable them to tap the five to ten billion or more barrels of oil estimated to lie below the surface.

Although Alaska and Alaskans stand to profit handsomely from the purchase of leases—at least a billion dollars added to the state treasury, one can only wonder at the degree of environmental dislocation almost certain to be wrought on this habitat as a result of the various processes required to gain the "black gold."

I also wonder if in the heady and often frenetic atmosphere of speculation over leases for drilling rights, who at the local, state, or federal levels has thought about the potential and actual effects of water and other types of pollution sure to accrue. Will this be another fatal example of men, money, and machines turning a pristine land to dross? It should be both interesting and instructive to see what attention, if any, is given to the protection of our last outposts.

As we see these "hands played out"—Colorado, Minnesota, Alaska, and others, such as the Everglades—we will learn in no uncertain terms whether the millions of us striving for a satisfying habitat and felicitous environment are simply talking to ourselves.

It will be interesting to watch developments unfold and see whether times have changed sufficiently to prevent the repetition of past indulgences. Several recent community air pollution experiences offer counsel. We can expect to see communities eager for additional revenues invite industrial corporations to set up operations, without any real concern for waste disposal. Only after the waters around the town or the air above become intolerable will grumblings be heard. Committees will be formed and petitions circulated, and the long uphill struggle to control further abuses of local resources will begin. Although the lessons of history are "writ large," few communities read them.

One of the most crucial aspects of pollution and one given little thought generally is the national lack of trained manpower needed to tackle a host of existing problems.

In his masterful book *Living Resources of the Sea,*[2] Lionel Walford concluded that the most important prerequisite to utilization of the ocean's resources was well-trained manpower. Lack of trained manpower may be the shoal upon which prevention and control of pollution could founder.

At the Solid Wastes Conference, held in Chicago in 1963, one of the most trenchant conclusions arrived at after three days of discussing ways and means of solving the solid-waste problem was that there is a need for trained manpower. The President's Science Advisory Committee's Report of the Environmental Pollutional Panel (1965)[3] stated that "in the long run improving both numbers and quality of highly trained manpower engaged in key actions from research to enforcement, will do the most for us and merits the highest priority."

Unfortunately, the national attitude on pollution is sluggish. This sluggishness is manifested by businessmen, politicians, and even scientists.

The problems of waste disposal, whether it be solid or liquid, do not excite the inquisitive, creative mind. Waste-disposal research and development is low in status. Thus, it fails to attract the talented people desperately needed. As a consequence, few innovations are brought into the area. The past fifty years have witnessed little change in waste-disposal practices, which is precisely what is desperately needed. Communities want to spend little, if anything, on their waste, particularly with so many other problems that demand a slice of the tax dollar.

Fortunately (or unfortunately, depending upon your point of view), we humans refuse to part with our money without a clear prospect of gain. Can we really say that the prospect of gain has been made clear to those who must eventually pay the bills?

In September, 1965, the Opinion Research Corporation found that in the mind of the public pollution ranks low as a national problem when compared with other pressing public concerns (See Table 26).

How many families encourage sons or daughters to pursue careers in sanitation, public health, or the environmental sciences?

TABLE 26.

National ranking of air and water pollution with other pressing community concerns

	TOTAL PUBLIC	LARGE CITIES
Juvenile delinquency	40%	55%
Unemployment	37	36
Lack of recreation	30	25
Too much traffic	24	36
Racial difficulties	22	35
Auto junkyards	22	11
Public transportation	20	18
School facilities	19	17
Water pollution	16	15
Air pollution	14	31
Garbage collection	13	10
Highway billboards	8	7
Overhead power lines	6	6
No choice	10	8

SOURCE: Opinion Research Corporation, "Public and Executive Views on Air and Water Pollution," Princeton, N. J., September, 1965.

Few indeed. Yet these are far more immediate community concerns than such luxuries as a billion-volt electron generator.

Certainly, few public-spirited citizens, philanthropists, or private foundations set funds aside or campaign for cleaner water; after all, as Roger Starr pointed out recently in his piece, *On the Side of The Cities,*[4] "Who wants a sewage-treatment plant named for him?"

Joseph Wood Krutch stated the case when he wrote, "Mankind as a whole, so bold in its attack upon problems of achieving more speed, more power and more wealth, is very timid in its attack upon other problems."

Surely professional scientists have not contributed in significant measure either by alerting the community to the potential dangers of a host of polluting sources or by their own lack of concern with the results of their own research. The clear fact is that scientists busy in their laboratories cannot continue to evade their social and civic responsibilities.

Politicians, the community statesmen, believing they have their fingers on the pulse of the community, claim that the meager funds available should be used for housing, welfare, schools, and clinics before they can be used for solid-waste disposal, control of water and air pollution, accident prevention, and noise abatement. These products of industrialization and swelling populations do not appear to have the same urgency as a decent dwelling, three meals a day, and freedom from infectious disease.

It is primarily among the more affluent segments of the community that time and effort can be given to considerations of green, open spaces, pristine brooks, and air free of noxious odors. Unfortunately, all members of an urban community do not see the same problems with equal intensity and do not always recognize "problems" as problems. The ranks of those pressing for cleaner skies and water, less noise, fewer accidents, chemical-free foods, and the like are composed almost exclusively of the affluent.

Priorities are based on urgency. If the land available for waste disposal by New York City runs out by 1974, well, "that's so far away"; who can be bothered now, when so many other concerns demand immediate attention? Who can be seriously concerned with accidents, even though fifty-two thousand people were killed on our highways and streets in 1967 and additional millions permanently maimed or disabled, when there are riots in our cities. Besides, accidents are considered fortuitous events that "no one can do anything about anyway." The fact that this is patently false reasoning has no bearing on the matter. As long as such opinions are widely held, the purse-strings will not be loosened. G. B. Shaw, not usually given to sparing the feelings of those he considered knaves, rogues, or hot-air artists, said, "There is no harder scientific fact in the world than the fact that belief can be produced in practically unlimited quantity and intensity, without observation or reasoning and even in defiance of both." [4]

In its summary, the Task Force on Environmental Health and Related Problems stated that, "As the facts become clear, the public will be shocked at the price it is paying for its affluence." I doubt it; if past experience is any criterion, the bulk of the people will never learn the facts, because there is no mechanism for bringing them to the public, and because too many other concerns are simultaneously demanding attention. And after the steady pounding of the Cold War since World War II, I suspect the public is shockproof.

Politicians who want to remain in public office seem to believe they must go along with public opinion rather than shape it. But just let state or federal officials attempt to remedy existing problems and they will set up a hue and cry.

When in the history of man has the general community ever been in favor of attempts to upgrade the conditions of life? Advances have usually come through the efforts of a few bold men who had to struggle against organized opposition and the inertia of masses of people.

For years, dumping of high-oxygen-demand waste (see Chapters 7 and 8) directly from industrial processing plants into rivers and streams was permitted by city administrators because of the weekly payroll that the plant contributed to the financial well-being of the area. The threat that the plant would move elsewhere hung over the mayor's head as he attempted to balance water pollution against full employment. Full employment, of course, regularly won out. Similar conditions prevailed with respect to air-polluting industries. (This attitude is depicted in Figure 51.) Someday, hopefully, this kind of threat will become a thing of the past. Owing to the efforts of bold men in communities throughout the country, fewer towns and cities will welcome polluting industries. Plants will have to clean up their pollution or be shut down.

Princeton and New Brunswick, New Jersey, for example, reflect opposing points of view as to what the primary needs of a state are.

New Brunswick's largely laboring population of middle-European immigrants and their children, is largely unconcerned with air pollution, water pollution, noise, accidents, and the host of other environmental problems. Their world is the world of immediate necessities; regular employment, fair wages and hours, hous-

FIGURE 51. "You want business in this town or don't you?"
From *The Herblock Gallery* (Simon & Schuster, 1968)

ing, and education for the children.

In Princeton, on the other hand, the bulk of the population consists of professionals: university professors, industrial scientists, business leaders, and others with time for consideration other than their immediate jobs. For them, the beauty and charm of the community is of great importance. Air pollution for most Princetonians means "barn smell" from a nearby dairy farm. While air and water pollution have begun to occupy the minds of the governor and the citizens of Mercer County (Princeton), it is of lesser concern to the citizens of Middlesex, Hudson, and Essex counties (New Brunswick, Jersey City, Newark), where job security is of far greater concern. Princeton can afford to seek only non-polluting types of businesses; New Brunswick, Jersey City, and Newark cannot yet afford that luxury—or so they think. Little thought is given to the long-range health of their communities.

This difference in attitude is not unique to the U.S. Developing countries in Africa, Asia, and Latin America, viewing the extent of pollution in the U.S., England, France, Germany, the U.S.S.R., and Czechoslovakia, are rapidly moving in the same dirty direction, as though there were insufficient examples for them to profit by. Their need to become industrialized apparently permits no concern for the byproducts of progress. The harbors and beaches of several of the new African states are already sewage-laden and oil-covered; many of the major cities are overpopulated and slum-ridden. Their credo appears to be, Let us first build; later there will be time for beauty. But will there?

Addressing the Third International Conference on Water Pollution Research held in Munich in 1966, Dr. August Rucker, former Bavarian minister of education and currently a professor at the Technical University, asked if life in the teeming metropolitan cities of the world would, in the future, be worthwhile. Although Dr. Rucker did not answer his question directly, he discussed the idea of an urban landscape (*stadtlandschaft*), the future shape of the city based on ecological considerations. He predicted that "the aim to let such an ecological consideration emerge out of the chaos of today will be realized during the period under consideration (2000 A.D.) neither in the advanced, highly industrialized countries, nor in the other ones, since there neither exists decisive legislation which would permit the planning to treat the entire area in an unrestricted way, nor is it to be expected that such legislation, while it has to come will still be passed in time." He went on to say that "the idea of the urban landscape is not yet clearly enough established, so as to have sufficiently convincing power for parliaments and governments." Not a terribly encouraging prospect; nor does it compliment political leaders and planners the world over. Creativity and boldness have never been the genius of committees, but creative individuals can in the final analysis only suggest and advocate: action must come from communities.

At this point, some readers may be ready and waiting for grand solutions to the "urban crisis." Surely, after a discourse on the many problems currently afflicting our cities, a panacea should be offered.

I wish I could say that plans have been drawn and are so far along that, by 1975, we will have attractive cities, free of air and water pollution; that solid wastes will be disposed by methods so sophisticated that landfills wil be obsolete; and that life in our central cities will be gratifying. Unfortunately, I cannot say this. There are no instant cures, no ready-made solutions, no panaceas. This does not mean that there is no hope for the future. On the contrary, there is a great deal; but it will take time, and money— lots of money—and a willingness on the part of all the people to see it through. It will also require that members of the community understand the problems they are called upon to consider. This book seeks to serve that need.

One further point concerning the demand on the part of some for great haste in solving problems of major proportions.

In reviewing remarks made by some of the participants in the conference on "Man and His Future" (London, 1962) [6] Professor Peter Medawar noted that "one of the lessons of history is that almost everything one can imagine possible will in fact be done, if it is thought desirable; what we cannot predict is what people are going to think desirable." It is significant to dwell for a moment on the word *people*. In this context *people* means many people, not simply a few vocal types. If pollution of one type or another is not removed, controlled, or prevented fast enough, it may be well to consider what is being done to motivate large numbers of people to attain the desired goal. I suspect that the referenda regularly voted down in communities around the country indicate that most people do not yet consider these measures desirable.

In his closing remarks Professor Medawar said: "One thing we might agree upon is that all heroic solutions of social problems are thoroughly undesirable and that we should proceed in society as we do in science. In science we do not leap from hilltop to hilltop, from triumph to triumph, or from discovery to discovery; we proceed by a process of exploration from which we sometimes learn to do better, and this is what we ought to do in social affairs."

Perhaps this statement will dampen the ardor of those seeking quick and easy solutions; I hope not. We need ardor, but along with it we should require sound knowledge.

In Chapter 10 I mentioned Dr. Goldsmith's critical essay "Air Pollution Epidemiology." Although he wrote specifically about the need for more discriminating air pollution research to bridge the yawning gap between what are actually established facts and relationships and what is merely believed, his message is universal. The type of investigation and reasoning for which he petitions is directly applicable to any of our environmental problems, and more than likely with salubrious results.

The unpalatable fact is that too often more heat than light is generated by the plethora of unsubstantiated data impeding the resolution of our many problems.

A discussion of this kind, which seeks not specific answers but an overview, cannot conclude without some attention to the phrase, "a hazard to health," which so often appears in speeches, discussions, lectures, and diatribes on environmental pollution. As I view it, this phrase is meaningless, for it implies a striving for a germ free, illness-free, danger-free, risk-free world. Such an implication must be an absurdity. It is not necessary to flee from each environmental factor that may be seen as a threat. Our health, so much more precious as life-span and leisure markedly increase, is not so fragile. It becomes absurd, for example, to develop a "salmonella complex," to avoid the mere presence of salmonella bacteria (see Chapter 3) in dog lollies, chickenfeed, candy bars, and a hundred other products. Is sterility * to be our goal?

The presence in food of subclinical levels of microbes may in fact be a blessing. As with other microorganisms in air and water, subclinical levels may well be sufficiently antigenic to elicit antibody production that can protect us against clinical manifestations of disease.

As it is currently used, the word *contamination* is apparently supposed to conjure up visions of appallingly awful conditions. The fact is that the planet on which we have lived since Adam and Eve met in the Garden has never been biologically, chemically, or physically sterile; therefore, by definition it is contaminated. Populations of microbes are present in the surfaces of our skin; the linings of our mouth, ears, eyes, nose, and throat; the air we breathe; all the oceans, rivers, lakes and streams (which were contaminated long before man appeared on the scene), and all the food we eat—raw, canned, frozen, dehydrated, pickled, and smoked. These microbes are harmless and often beneficial. Surely we are not becoming so confused as to believe that bacteria are our mortal enemies. Every college freshman knows that life on earth would be impossible without the many beneficial activities of microbes.

Too many articles on the environment and its potential hazards to health depend for their effect on highly inflammatory words. Writers of such articles purposely avoid defining these terms, so that the reader will project his own psychological needs onto them. Some people are revolted by the words *filth* or *filthy,* others by *unclean,* yet others by *taint, dirty, rancid, moldy, odorous,* and, of course, *polluted* and *contaminated.* Although these words are not all synonyms, they are often used as though they were. As generally used, none of them really has anything to do with health or disease. For the most part they are concerned with

* Sterility is an absolute term. It means the complete absence of life. "Almost sterile" or "partially sterile" is a contradiction in terms.

aesthetics, which is a far different concept. "We live in a dirty world" may be suitable as an advertising slogan aimed at our emotions, it is meaningless as far as health is concerned. Tirades composed of inflammatory words that quicken the emotions serve no useful end. They do not clarify; they do not educate; but they often do confuse and mislead.

The title of this book could have been *Our Habitat*. But after some consideration, I felt the need to insert *precarious* to describe the *potentially hazardous* condition of our environment.

Pollution of some type and degree, like death and taxes, will be with us always. As this verse testifies, it has long been part of our lives:

> Nature's polluted.
> There's a man in every secret corner of her
> Doing damned wicked deeds. Thou art,
> Old World, a hoary, atheistic,
> Murdering star.

Thomas Beddoes composed these lines in the summer of 1824. I suspect another Beddoes will memorialize the pollution of 2024 A.D., whatever type it may be. At that time, our children's children will be still healthier than we were, 145 years after Beddoes penned his verse.

BIBLIOGRAPHY

Chapter 2: Ecology of Health and Disease

LITERATURE CITED

1. Elton, Charles. *Animal Ecology*. New York: Macmillan, 1927.

SUGGESTED ADDITIONAL READING

Dubos, Rene. *The Mirage of Health*. New York: Doubleday Anchor, 1961.

Hanley, Amos. *Human Ecology: A Theory of Community Structure*. New York: Ronald Press, 1950.

Spicer, Edward H., ed. *Human Problems in Technological Change*. New York: Russell Sage Foundation, 1952.

Stamp, L. Dudley. *Some Aspects of Medical Geography*. London: Oxford University Press, 1964.

Top, Franklin H. "Environment in Relation to Infectious Diseases," *Archives of Environmental Health* 9:699, 1964.

World Health Organization. *Report of the Inter-Regional Seminar on the Health Aspects of Industrialization*. Dacca, East Pakistan, Nov. 6–16, 1963.

Chapter 3: Bacterial Food Poisoning

LITERATURE CITED

1. Foster, E. M., et al. "Clostridium Botulinum Food Poisoning," *Journal of Milk and Food Technology* 28:86, 1965.

2. Dack, G. M. *Food Poisoning.* 3rd ed. Chicago: University of Chicago Press, 1956.

SUGGESTED ADDITIONAL READING

Bond, Richard G., and Lee D. Stauffer. "Food Sanitation and/or the Infectious Process," *Journal of the American Dietetic Association* 31:993, 1955.

Bowner, Ernest J. "Salmonella in Food: A Review," *Journal of Milk and Food Technology* 28:74, 1965.

Dewberry, E. B. *Food Poisoning.* 4th ed. London: Leonard Hill, 1959.

Gould, G. W., and A. Hurst, eds. *The Bacterial Spore.* London: Academic Press, 1969.

U. S. Department of Health, Educaton, and Welfare. *Food Service Sanitation Manual.* Public Health Service Publication No. 934, 1962.

CHAPTER 4: Chemicals in Food

LITERATURE CITED

1. Pike, Magnus. "Food Facts and Fallacies," *Journal of the Royal Society of Health* 82:10, 1967.

SUGGESTED ADDITIONAL READING

Food and Agriculture Organization of the United Nations. *Evaluation of the Toxicity of Pesticide Residues in Foods.* Rome, 1965.

Food Protection Committee of the Food and Nutrition Board. *Problems in the Evaluation of the Carcinogenic Hazard from Use of Food Additives.* National Academy of Sciences–National Research Council Publication No. 749, 1959.

——— *The Use of Chemical Additives in Food Processing.* National Academy of Sciences–National Research Council Publication No. 398, 1956.

Meyer, L. H. *Food Chemistry.* New York: Rheinhold, 1960.

CHAPTER 5: Insecticides

LITERATURE CITED

1. President's Science Advisory Committee, Environmental Pollution Panel. *Restoring the Quality of Our Environment.* Washington, D.C., Nov. 1965.

2. Steinkraus, K. H. "Studies on the Milky Disease Organisms, II: Saprophytic Growth of Bacillus Popilliae," *Journal of Bacteriology* 74:625, 1957.

SUGGESTED ADDITIONAL READING

de Bach, Paul, ed. *Biological Control of Insects, Pests and Weeds.* New York: Rheinhold, 1965.

Hoffman, C. H., and L. S. Henderson. "The Fight Against Insects." Chapter 3 in *Protecting Our Food. Yearbook of Agriculture* Washington, D.C.: U. S. Government Printing Office, 1966.

Knipling, E. F. "The Eradication of the Screw-Worm Fly," *Scientific American* 203:54, 1960.

CHAPTER 6: Zoonoses

SUGGESTED ADDITIONAL READING

Kaplan, Martin. "Social Effects of Animal Diseases in Developing Countries," *Bulletin of the Atomic Scientists,* Nov. 1966.

Schaube, Calvin W. *Veterinary Medicine and Human Health.* Baltimore: Williams & Wilkins, 1960.

Steele, James H. *Animal Disease and Human Health.* Basic Food Study No. 3. Rome: Food and Agriculture Organization of the United Nations, 1962.

United States Government. *Animal Diseases. Yearbook of Agriculture.* Washington, D.C.: U. S. Government Printing Office, 1956.

University of Michigan School of Public Health. *Occupational Diseases Acquired from Animals.* Continued Education Series No. 124. Ann Arbor, 1964.

CHAPTER 7: Sanitary Sewage

SUGGESTED ADDITIONAL READING

Bruce, F. E. "Water Supply, Sanitation and Disposal of Waste Matter," in W. Hobson, ed., *Theory and Practice of Public Health.* London: Oxford University Press, 1961.

Ehlers, V. M., and E. W. Steel. *Municipal and Rural Sanitation,* 6th ed. New York: McGraw-Hill, 1965.

McKinney, R. E. *Microbiology for Sanitary Engineers.* New York: McGraw-Hill, 1962.

Parker, W. S. "Sewage Disposal." Chapter 5 in *Public and Community Health.* London: Staples Press, 1964.

CHAPTER 8: Water Pollution and Its Control

LITERATURE CITED

1. Berg, Gerald, ed. *Transmission of Viruses by the Water Route.* New York: Interscience Publishers, 1967.
2. Volkov, Oleg. "Pollution in Lake Baikal," *Literaturnaya Gazeta,* Jan. 29, 1966. Translated in *Current Digest of the Soviet Press,* Feb. 1966, p. 14.

SUGGESTED ADDITIONAL READING

American Public Health Association. *Standard Methods for the Examination of Water and Wastewater.* 12th ed. 1965.

Farooq, M. "Progress in Biharziasis Control: The Situation in Egypt," *WHO Chronicle* 21:175, 1967.

Hynes, H. B. N. *The Biology of Polluted Water.* Liverpool: University Press, 1960.

James, A. "The Bacteriology of Trickling Filters," *Journal of Applied Bacteriology* 27:197, 1964.

Klein, Louis. *Aspects of River Pollutions.* London: Butterworth's Scientific Publications, 1957.

Wisdom, A. S. *The Law on the Pollution of Waters.* London: Shaw, 1956.

CHAPTER 9: Solid-Waste Disposal

LITERATURE CITED

1. First, Melvin W., F. J. Viles, and Samuel Levin. "Control of Toxic and Explosive Hazards in Buildings Erected on Landfills," *Public Health Reports* 81:419, 1966.

SUGGESTED ADDITIONAL READING

American Public Works Association. *Proceedings of the National Conference on Solid Waste Research.* Chicago, Dec. 1963.

Ehlers, V. M., and E. W. Steel. *Municipal and Rural Sanitation.* 6th ed. New York: McGraw-Hill, 1965.

Gotaas, Harold B. Composting: *Sanitary Disposal and Reclamation of Organic Wastes.* WHO Monograph Series No. 31. Geneva, 1956.

Merz, R. C., and R. Stone. *Factors Controlling Utilization of Sanitary Landfill Sites.* Los Angeles: University of Southern California Press, 1963.

University of California. *Proceedings of the National Conference on Solid Wastes Management.* Davis, Calif., 1966.

CHAPTER 10: Air Pollution

LITERATURE CITED

1. Pearson, L., and E. S. Skye. "Air Pollution Affects Patterns of Photosynthesis in *Parmelia sulcata,* a Corticolous Lichen," *Science* 148:1600, 1965.

2. Myrvik, Q. M., and D. G. Evans. "Metabolic and Immunologic Activities of Alveolar Macrophages," *Archives of Environmental Health* 14:92, 1967.

3. Tromp, S. W. "Biometeorology and Asthma in Children." 8th AMA Conference on Air Pollution Los Angeles, March, 1966.

4. Winklestein, W. "Air Pollution Respiratory Function Study." 8th AMA Conference on Air Pollution. Los Angeles, March, 1966.

5. Anderson, D. O., and B. G. Ferris, Jr. "Community Studies of the Health Effects of Air Pollution: A Critique," *Air Pollution Control Association Journal* 15:587, 1965.

6. Amdur, M. O. "Respiratory Absorption Data: SO_2 Dose-Response Curves," *Archives of Environmental Health* 12:729, 1966.

7. Ott, J. N. "A Rational Analysis of Ultraviolet as a Vital Part of the Light Spectrum Influencing Photobiological Responses," *Optometric Weekly,* Sept. 5, 1968.

8. ———— "Some Responses of Plants and Animals to Variations in Wavelength of Light Energy," Annals of the New York Academy of Sciences 117:624 (article 1), 1964.

9. Dixon, J. P., and J. P. Lodge. "Air Conservation Report Reflects National Concern," *Science* 148:1600, 1965.

10. Goldsmith, J. R. "Air Pollution Epidemiology: A Wicked Problem, an Informational Maze and a Professional Responsibility," *Archives of Environmental Health* 18:516, 1969.

11. Princi, F. "Air Pollution: Facts and Fables," *Journal of Occupational Medicine* 5:461, 1963.

SUGGESTED ADDITIONAL READING

"Air Pollution and Its Effect on the Respiratory System," *The Allergic Patient and Respiratory Disease News,* Jan., 1967.

Cleary, G. J., and C. R. B. Blackburn. "Air Pollution in Native Huts in the Highlands of New Guinea," *Archives of Environmental Health* 17:785, 1968.

McDermott, Walsh. "Air Pollution and Public Health," *Scientific American,* Oct., 1961, p. 206.

Meethan, A. R. *Atmospheric Pollution.* 3rd ed. New York: Macmillan, 1964.

New York Academy of Medicine, Department of the Committee on Public Health. "Air Pollution and Health," *Bulletin of the New York Academy of Medicine* 42:588, 1966.

CHAPTER 11: Accidents

LITERATURE CITED

1. Schulzinger, Morris. *The Accident Syndrome.* Springfield, Ill.: Charles C. Thomas, 1956.

2. Rees, Dewi. "Physical and Mental Disabilities of 1,190 Ordinary Motorists," *British Medical Journal* 1:593, 1967.

SUGGESTED ADDITIONAL READING

American Public Health Association. *Accident Control in Environmental Health Programs: A Guide for Public Health Personnel.* New York, 1966.

Chanoit, P. F. "Accidents: Rarely Accidental," *World Health,* Feb. 1969.

"The Epidemiology of Road Accidents," *World Health Organization Chronicle* 20:393, 1966.

Herbert, Evan. "Safety Thinking," *International Science and Technology,* March. 1967, p. 66.

International Labor Office. *Accident Prevention: A Worker's Education Manual.* Geneva, 1961.

"Reducing Highway Slaughter," *Medical World News,* Aug. 29, 1969.

CHAPTER 12: Noise

LITERATURE CITED

1. Kupferman, T. "Noise Pollution," *Congressional Record,* April 12, 1966, p. 8339.

2. Hermann, E. R. "An Epidemiological Study of Noise," *Proceedings XIVth International Congress of Occupational Health.* Madrid, Sept. 1963.

3. Lipscomb, David M. "High-Intensity Sounds in the Recreational Environment," *Clinical Pediatrics* 8:63, 1969.

4. Rosen, S., and P. Olin. "Hearing Loss and Coronary Heart Disease," *Archives of Otolaryngology* 82:236, 1965.

5. Rosen, S., M. Bergman, D. Plester, A. El-Mofty, and M. H. Satti. "Presbycusis Study of Relatively Noise-Free Population in Sudan," *Annals of Otolaryngology, Rhinology and Laryngology* 71:727, 1962.

SUGGESTED ADDITIONAL READING

Bell, A. Noise: *An Occupational Hazard and Public Nuisance.* Public Health Paper No. 30. Geneva: WHO, 1968.

Beranek, Leo. "Noise," *Scientific American* 215:66, 1966.

Callier Hearing and Speech Center, Subcommittee on Conservation of Hearing. *Guide for Conservation of Hearing in Noise.* Dallas, 1964.

Harris, Cyril M., ed. *Handbook of Noise Control.* New York: McGraw-Hill, 1957.

CHAPTER 13: Occupational Health

SUGGESTED ADDITIONAL READING

Enterline, P. E., "Social Causes of Sick Absence," *Archives of Environmental Health* 12:467, 1966.

Gafofer, W. M., ed. *Occupational Diseases: A Guide to Their Recognition.* Public Health Service Publication No. 1097. Washington, D.C., 1964.

Hatch, Theodore. "Conditions of Work and Man's Health: Tomorrow's Problems," *Archives of Environmental Health* 11:302, 1965.

Hunter, Donald. *Health in Industry.* Baltimore: Penguin, 1959.

CHAPTER 14: Ionizing Radiation

LITERATURE CITED

1. Hollingsworth, J. W., G. W. Beebe, M. Ishida, and A. B. Bratt. *Medical Findings and Methodology of Studies by the ABCC on Atomic Bomb Survivors in Hiroshima and Nagasaki, in the Use of Vital and Health Statistics for Genetic and Radiation Studies,* pp. 75, 99. New York: United Nations, 1962.

2. Al-Saadi, Abdul A., and William H. Beierwalter. "Chromosomal Changes in Rat Thyroid Cells During Iodine Depletion and Repletion," *Cancer Research* 26:676, 1966.

3. Ehrenburg, L., G. V. Ehrenstein, and A. Hedgran. "Gonadal Temperature and Spontaneous Mutation Rates in Man," *Nature,* Dec. 21, 1957, p. 1433.

4. Robinson, D., J. Rock, and M. F. Menkin. "Control of Human Spermatogenesis by Induced Changes in Intrascrotal Temperature," *Amer. Med. Asso.* 204:290, 1968.

5. Clemmesen, J., "A Doubling of Morbidity from Testis Carcinoma in Copenhagen, 1943–1962," *Acta Path. et Microbiol. Scand.* 72:348, 1968.

6. Green, E. L. "Genetic Effects of Radiation on Mammalian Populations," *Annals of Rev. Genetics* 2:87, 1968.

7. Food Irradiation: Proceedings of a Symposium. Karlsruhe, June 6, 10, 1966. Vienna: International Atomic Energy Agency, 1966. Publication No. 127.

SUGGESTED ADDITIONAL READING

Blatz, Hanson. *Introduction to Radiological Health.* New York: McGraw-Hill, 1964.

Bloom, A. D., S. Neriishi, N. Kamada, T. Iseki, and R. J. Keehn. *Cytrogenetic Studies in the Exposed Populations of Hiroshima and Nagasaki.* Atomic Bomb Casualty Commission.

Eisenbud, Merrill. *Environmental Radioactivity.* New York: McGraw-Hill, 1963.

Hollingsworth, J. W. "Delayed Radiation Effects in Survivors of the Atomic Bombings: Review of the Findings of the Atomic Bomb Casualty Commission 1947–1959," *New England Journal of Medicine* 263:481, 1960.

Neel, James V. *Atomic Bombs, Inbreeding and Japanese Genes: The Russel Lecture* for 1966. Ann Arbor: University of Michigan Press, 1966.

CHAPTER 15: Biological and Chemical Warfare

LITERATURE CITED

1. American Association for the Advancement of Science. Annual Meeting. Washington, D.C., Dec. 26, 30, 1966.

2. Zinsser, H. *Rats, Lice and History.* New York: Bantam, 1965.

3. *Preventive Medicine in World War II,* Vol. VII *Communicable Diseases,* pp. 12, 14. Washington, D.C.: Office of the Surgeon-General, Department of the Army, 1964.

4. Swartzwelder, J. C. "Filariasis Bancrofti." Chapter 5 in *Preventive Medicine in World War II,* Vol. VII, *Communicable Diseases.* Washington, D.C.: Office of the Surgeon-General, Department of the Army, 1964.

5. Rosebury, T.E., A. Kabat, and M. Boldt. *Journal of Immunology* 56:7, 1947.

6. American Public Health Association. *Communicable Diseases in Man.* 10th ed. New York, 1965.

7. Saslow, S., et al. "Studies on the Evaluation of Tularemia Vaccine in Man." Paper presented to the Central Society for Clinical Research, 1962.

8. Neinast, W. H. "United States Use of Biological Warfare." In *Biological Warfare: Two Views* (symposium). *Military Law Review,* April, 1964. Department of the Army Pamphlet No. 27-100-24.

9. Fothergill, L. D. "Biological Warfare Threat," *Advances in Chemistry* Series 26, *Non-Military Defense: Chemical and Biological Defenses in Perspective.* Washington, D.C.: American Chemistry Society, 1960.

10. Fothergill, L.D. "Some Ecological and Epidemiological Concepts in Antipersonnel Biological Warfare," In *Defense Against Biological Warfare* (symposium). *Military Medicine* 128:132, 1963.

11. Rothschild, J. H. *Tomorrow's Weapons.* New York: McGraw-Hill, 1964.

12. Fleming, Ian. *Goldfinger.* New York: Macmillan, 1959.

13. Liddell-Hart, B. H. *A History of the World War 1914–1918.* Boston: Little, Brown, 1935.

SUGGESTED ADDITIONAL READING

"Biological Warfare: Off Limits to Doctors," *Medical World News,* July 25, 1969.

"Report on Disposal of Chemical Munitions," News Report, NAC-NRC, August–Sept. 1969.

CHAPTER 16: The Politics of Pollution

LITERATURE CITED

1. *Alternatives in Water Management.* National Academy of Sciences–National Research Council Publication 1408. Washington, D.C., 1966.

2. Walford, Lionel A. *Living Resources of the Sea.* New York: Ronald Press, 1958.

3. President's Science Advisory Committee, Environmental Pollution Panel. *Restoring the Quality of Our Environment.* Washington, D.C., Nov. 1965.

4. Starr, Roger. "On the Side of the Cities," *Horizon,* Autumn, 1966.

5. Shaw, G. B. *The Doctor's Dilemma.* In Robert Warnock, ed., *Representative Modern Plays.* Glenview, Ill.: Scott, Foresman, 1964.

6. Medawar, Peter. In Gordon Wolstenholme, ed., *Man and His Future: A Ciba Symposium.* London: Churchill, 1963.

SUGGESTED ADDITIONAL READING

Forbes, R. J. *The Conquest of Nature: Technology and Its Consequences.* New York: Praeger, 1968.

Goldman, Marshall I., ed. *Controlling Pollution: The Economics of a Cleaner America.* Englewood Cliffs: Prentice-Hall, 1967.

National Academy of Sciences–National Research Council. *Research Needs in Environmental Health: A Symposium.* NAS-NRC Publication No. 1419. Washington, D.C., 1966.

———— *Waste Management and Control: A Report to the Federal Council for Science and Technology.* NAS-NRC Publication No. 1400. Washington, D.C., 1966.

Task Force on Environmental Health and Related Problems. *A Strategy for a Livable Environment: A Report to the Secretary of Health, Education and Welfare.* Washington, D.C.: U. S. Government Printing Office, June, 1967.

Walozin, Harold, ed. *The Economics of Air Pollution: A Symposium.* New York: Norton, 1966.

INDEX

Aberdeen, Scotland, typhoid epidemic in, 53
Aberfan, Wales, 152
Abrasions, occupational, 250
Accident syndrome, 204
  reasons for, 205–6
  trigger episode in, 206
Accidents, 197–219
  by age groups, 201, 207, 209
  bodily parts injured in, 208
  carriers of, 208
  causes of, 197–98, 207, 209–10
  community apathy toward, 216–17, 219
  cost of, 199
  environmental change and, 197–98, 202–3
  fatalities from, 197–98, 209, 214, 249
  injuries in, 197, 207, 208, 214, 249
  motor vehicle, *see* Motor vehicle accidents
  physical factors in, 205
  by place, 202, 207, 249
  reasons for, 199–200, 203
  reducing, 210–14
  by seasons, 202
  by sex, 201
  by states, 202
  strategy for analyzing, 200

  war deaths compared with, 218
Acetylcholine, 301
Acoustic nerve, 231, 232
Acoustical instruments, 224–26, 238
Activated sludge aeration tank, 122
Acute toxicity tests, 76–77
Adamsite, 302
Adolescents, hearing profile of, 228
Aeration of sewage, 122
Aerosol dispensers
  of BW agents, 295, 296–97
  of food, 67
Africa, ecology of disease in, 28–29
  See also specific countries
African sleeping sickness, 101
  agriculture limited by, 101
  causes of, 28
  ecological factors in, 28–29
African swine fever, as potential BW agent, 291
Afterburners, 181–82
Agene, 66
Agricultural chemicals, occupational illnesses from, 251
  See also Herbicides; Insecticides
Agriculture
  arable land for, 61
  BW agents for, 294–95, 304
  disease limitations on, 101
  domestic animals in, 103

Lincoln, Abraham, 310
Lindane, 88
Lindsay, John, 138, 142
London, England
air pollution in, *see* London-type
air pollution
early sewage removal in, 116
London-type air pollution
components of, 182
fatalities in, 184
Long Island Sound, 22
Longevity and degenerative disease,
307
Los Angeles, Calif., 309
air pollution in, *see* Los Angeles-
type air pollution
geography of, 177
lung-cancer rate in, 193
population growth in, 311
Los Angeles-type air pollution
automobile as source of, 179–80
photochemical smog in, 178–79
temperature inversions in, 177–79
Lung cancer
from cigarette smoking, 34, 190,
193
longevity of, 307
multiple causation in, 33
Lycopene, 65n
L-lysine, 57, 58
Lysergic acid diethylamide (LSD-
25), as chemical warfare agent,
301–2

Maabans, hearing acuity and health
of, 236–38
McFarland, Ross A., 200
MacQueen, Dr. Ian, 54
Magnetism, 26
Malaria
control by insecticides, 84
fatalities caused by, 83
as potential BW agent, 290, 292
problem of eradicating, 111
Malathion, 88
Malicious additives, 69–70
Manatees, 97
Manganese, toxicity of, 72

Manufacturing plants, measuring
noise levels in, 224
Marshall Islands, thermonuclear ex-
plosion at, 272
Mass Law, 240
Maturing agents, 66
Mauron, France, 241
Maximum Allowable Concentration
(MAC), 254
Measles, 291–92
Meat and meat products
irradiated, 281
perishability of, 42
proper heating of, 58–59
as source of food poisoning, 45,
48, 51, 55, 56
storage life of, 64
as typhoid carriers, 52–54
See also specific meats
Mediterranean fruit fly, sterilization
control of, 95, 99
Meister, Joseph, 110
Melioidosis, as potential BW agent,
290, 292
Mellanby, Sir Edward, 66n
Melnick, Joseph, 142
Men
accidents among, 201
hearing loss by, 222
Mercury
chronic illnesses from, 256
occupational illnesses from, 250
Mescalin, as chemical warfare agent,
301
Metals
occupational illnesses from, 251,
255, 256
See also specific metals
Metamorphosis of insects, 81
Methoxychlor, 87
Methyl eugenol, 93
N-methyl-2, 2′-dichlorodiethylamine,
303n
Meuse Valley, Belgium, air pollution
episode in, 183
Mexico
air pollution in, 184–85
rabies in, 110
Mice, 30